Successful Fundraising

Successful Fundraising

A Complete Handbook for Volunteers and Professionals

JOAN FLANAGAN

CB
CONTEMPORARY
BOOKS
CHICAGO

Library of Congress Cataloging-in-Publication Data

Flanagan, Joan,
    Successful fundraising : a complete handbook for volunteers and
professionals / Joan Flanagan.
      p.   cm.
    Includes bibliographical references and index.
    ISBN 0-8092-4090-4 :
    1. Fund raising—United States.   I. Title.
HG177.5.U6F58   1991
658.15'224—dc20   91-10844
                                          CIP

Acknowledgment of Permissions

Grateful acknowledgment is made to the following for permission to
reprint previously published material.

    The AAFRC Trust for Philanthropy (money pie chart from *Giving USA
        1990*)
    The Bishop Desmond Tutu Southern African Refugee Scholarship
        Fund
    Christ Church Sunday Bulletin
    Cubs Wives for Family Rescue
    Dean and Chapter of Canterbury Cathedral
    The Foundation Center (Cooperating Collections Network list)
    "How *Not* to Ask for Money" reprinted with permission, *Ms.*
        magazine, copyright © 1980.
    Nabisco Foods Company
    The New Yorker Magazine, Inc.
    run, jane, run, inc.

Other Contemporary Books by Joan Flanagan

The Grass Roots Fundraising Book
The Successful Volunteer Organization

Contents

"For everything, there is a season; for
every task, someone is given the
tools."
　　　　　　—Sheila Cassidy
　　　　　　Sharing the Darkness

Acknowledgments

So many tools—kindness, wisdom, laughter, the right answers,
and the right questions—have been given to me by so many
people that I cannot thank them all. I am deeply grateful to all
the great fundraisers who go out every day and show the doubt-
ers what is possible. Every canvasser who rings one more door-
bell, every volunteer who addresses one more envelope, and
every fundraiser who helps one more donor plan a major gift
are weaving the fabric of freedom. Their ideas and arguments
inform and improve my work; their examples inspire me to try
harder.

At Contemporary Books, I am indebted to Associate Publisher Nancy Crossman for intelligent management of the whole
project and to Managing Editor Kathy Willhoite, who introduced me to the computer age. Superior editors Karen Schen-
kenfelder and Craig Bolt improved every page of the manuscript
and saved me several times from becoming the laughingstock
filler at the end of a *New Yorker* column. Production Editor
Cyndy Raucci synthesized all the additions and made the book
look great. Also special thanks to Editorial Production Mana-

ger Mary Eley, whose careful work enables me to update my earlier books and keep them useful for the readers.

My colleagues in Chicago have been invaluable. Information specialists Shelby Pera and Kim Simmons; computer experts Morgan Gale and Arlette Slachmuyler; my mentors Kim Bobo, Heather Booth, and Jackie Kendall; and all the others at the office have inspired me with their values and delighted me with their good humor. The fundraising techniques of the Chicago chapter of NSFRE gave me many wonderful examples of effective, ethical fundraisers. The writers in the Roslyn Group made me believe writing was worth the hard work, discipline, and isolation. Heartfelt thanks go to the superb librarians at the Donors Forum of Chicago, Marty Bowes and Gina James, and all the valiant professionals at the Chicago Public Library who have helped me over the years.

I am also grateful for my continued happy association with the outstanding foundations that supported my first two books: the Partnership for Democracy, in Washington, D.C. and the W. Clement and Jessie V. Stone Foundation in Chicago. Most of all, many thanks to my family and friends for your patience and consideration. I couldn't have done it without you.

Successful Fundraising

"I want you to be first in love. I want
you to be first in moral excellence. I
want you to be first in generosity."
  —*Rev. Martin Luther King, Jr.*
    February 4, 1968, sermon

Chapter 1
Opportunities for
Fundraising

Successful fundraising enables a worthwhile nonprofit organization to create the kind of community its leaders want for
themselves, their families, and their neighbors. In boom times
or hard times, with friendly governments or hostile administra-
tions, for popular movements or controversial causes, the volunteers and professionals who ask for money get both the money
and the quality of life that only self-sufficient organizations can
provide.

The best fundraisers meet the challenge of shrinking government funding by devising more effective ways to raise money
from individuals, corporations, foundations, and other grant
makers. In the 1980s contributions to charities (after adjusting
for inflation) increased by more than 35 percent, five times more
than they did in the 1970s. In constant dollars, annual donations to nonprofits are now $20 billion higher than they were in
1980.

However, it is clear that nonprofits are not on easy street.
From the heartland of rural Kansas to the bright lights of
Broadway, fundraisers are working harder than ever before to
reach their goals. Whether your organization's goal is saving the

old railroad depot or saving the ozone layer, every volunteer and professional fundraiser will need to ask more people more often in more ways for more money.

It is not enough to simply work harder, although that is a good place to start. You also need to work smarter. What are the best fundraising strategies for your organization, your leaders, your cause, and your community? What is going on in the fundraising environment today? What are your opportunities and challenges?

BIG GOALS

Awesome goals are being set and achieved by the largest charities and the boldest fundraisers. Harvard University set a $350 million goal to celebrate its 350th birthday; it exceeded its goal. Not to be outdone, Stanford University announced a $1.1 billion campaign, Columbia University is aiming for $1.15 billion, the United Jewish Appeal–Federation of Jewish Philanthropies of New York City wants $1.2 billion, and Cornell University currently leads the Billion Dollar Club with a $1.25 billion goal. Rumors of $2 billion goals in the near future are on the grapevine.

Rotary clubs around the world have set a goal to eradicate polio by the year 2000. So far they have raised more than $230 million and made grants in one hundred sixty countries to immunize 500 million children. Their long-range goal is to immunize 529 million children.

SPECIAL EVENTS

Special events also are getting bigger and better. Irish rock & roll star Bob Geldof organized concerts for Band Aid in London and Philadelphia in 1985; the global telethon raised $117 million in one day. Hands Across America got 5,602,960 people to hold hands and raised $36 million to help eradicate hunger and homelessness.

There are new opportunities for special events. The American travel industry generates about $350 billion every year, and about $53 billion of that comes in from 38 million foreign visitors.[1] For the first time the United States has more tourists coming to America than Americans going overseas, and what foreign tourists want to see is real Americana. This is perfect for charities. If you want to join the locals and the "leaf-peepers" (as the tourists are known), you have to reserve weeks in advance to get into the boiled dinner in September at the Congregational Church in Peacham, Vermont. The Spring Pilgrimage to see antebellum plantations was launched as a fundraiser by the Garden Club in Natchez, Mississippi, in the 1930s; tourism is now the largest industry in the town.

Smaller communities also are using their fundraising strategically to build business. Fulda, Minnesota, population 1,308, has the dubious claim to fame of being the first town in the Midwest to have its bank fold during the farm crisis in 1985. To raise money to save the wood ducks, support local charities, and promote the town, two Fulda businessmen volunteered to promote the idea of "Wood Duck Days." Furniture store manager Charlie Hopkins wrote stories about "Wadalena the Wood Duck," and Gerald Johnson published them in the *Fulda Free Press*. In the past three years Wood Duck Days has expanded to three days in July and includes food and events that are fundraisers sponsored by the Fulda Area Community Club, the Future Farmers of America, the Boy Scouts, the Lions Club, the Fine Arts Club, and Women of Today. Local merchants profit from increased traffic.

The event has put Fulda back on the map. Human visitors see the town and buy houses. Wood ducks see the new houses made for them and move in, too. Result: today Fulda has a prosperous new bank and credit union, four other new businesses, a full-time director of economic development (Charlie Hopkins), and plans for a motel and a golf course.

FUNDRAISING FASTER AND SLOWER

Successful fundraising in the future will need to be both faster and slower. The money race will be won by both the swift and the persistent. High-tech marketing systems and down-home personal contacts will enable the best fundraisers to reach more prospects and get more big gifts at the same time.

New technologies—user-friendly computers, fax machines, desktop publishing—and a generation of employees raised on computers and television have yielded the means and the need for faster, more high-tech fundraising tools. Consumers raised on television, where every problem can be resolved in thirty minutes (minus six minutes of commercials), want speed. Airplane catalogs offer shoppers the easy envelope order form and the 800 phone number, but if those are too slow, they can also call *from* the airplane on an Airfone.

If nonprofits want to get a larger share of the public's discretionary dollars, they will need to offer the same variety of fast, simple opportunities for making gifts. Popular causes can link their television coverage with their 800 or 900 phone numbers to allow callers to charge donations to their credit card in one minute or their telephone bill in six seconds. Urgent causes can cooperate with consumer product companies in cause-related marketing efforts. Consumers can give to a charity with *no* extra effort. Shoppers simply choose the brand of coffee or dog food or toilet paper that supports the causes they like, and the company makes the donations for them.

On the other hand, cultivating major gifts from individual donors can take two or three years, or even longer now. It took Christopher F. Edley, CEO of the United Negro College Fund, with help from his top staff and volunteers, twelve years to attract a $50 million challenge grant from *TV Guide* publisher Walter H. Annenberg.[2] As the tax and legal choices get more complicated, donors need more help to invest their charity dollars wisely.

For nonprofit and for-profit marketers, making money in direct mail will cost more and take longer than ever before. You can no longer write a great letter and send it to the right list, then sit back and wait for the checks to roll in. Today a new direct-mail campaign will take at least three years to show a profit, and the lead time will get longer in the future.

Even more long term are planned-giving services. Today the most common way of making a planned gift is still a bequest in a will. However, some gifts of property can be structured so that the donor receives the greatest income and pays the lowest possible taxes for the next two generations.

GREATER MIX OF FUNDRAISING STRATEGIES

Every organization needs more dependable ways to raise money, so fundraisers are looking for new strategies that will mix with the old. In the 1980s direct mail was used best by the political right wing; Republican mail solicitations raised thirteen times more money than Democratic mail in the 1980 presidential campaign. By the end of the decade, the Democrats copied what had worked for the other side and cut the margin down to two to one.

On the other hand, the professional door-to-door canvass has been the money machine for progressive causes on the left. It is only a matter of time before the right also uses the door-to-door canvass to cut into the Democrats' majorities at the state and local levels.

DEMOGRAPHICS:
BUZZWORD OF THE NINETIES

What marketing was to the eighties, demographics and psychographics will be to the nineties. Every technique fundraisers use—mail, phones, door-to-door canvassing, parties, personal requests, and planned giving—can be more effective both financially and politically if you understand and use demographic data as shrewdly as your for-profit brothers and sisters.

GLOBAL ECONOMY

Nonprofits work locally, but they are locked into the global economy. Charities may be doing a great job of fundraising in Tampa, La Crosse, or Bakersfield, but they are still at the mercy of the financial markets in Tokyo, London, and Bonn. Many charities had to watch helplessly as their endowments lost 25 percent of their value in the stock market crash of 1987.

Political change also has an impact. West Coast organizations in the United States and Canada (as well as nonprofits in Australia and New Zealand) are seeing an influx into their areas of people with wealth from Hong Kong, getting their money out before Hong Kong goes back to China in 1997. The European economy will be transformed with the end of most European trade barriers in 1992. A similarly unified North America could present different fundraising opportunities for fundraisers in Canada, the United States, and Mexico. The reunification of Germany and *glasnost* raised hopes for a "peace dividend" for more federal funding for special programs, but continuing wars in Central America, Africa, and the Middle East have drained away any peace dividend domestically.

GLOBAL PHILANTHROPY

Like for-profit businesses, American nonprofits are competing on a global scale. American foundations, corporations, and individuals now give money around the world. IBM makes grants in all 132 countries where it sells computers. American Express has managed cause-related marketing campaigns to repair the Statue of Liberty in the United States, to save the puffin, the national bird of Norway, and to study the koala in Australia. Multiple American Express promotions raised money to send national teams to compete at the 1984 Olympics in Los Angeles from Argentina, Australia, Brazil, Ireland, Japan, Mexico, Spain, Sweden, and the United Kingdom. H. J. Heinz company CEO Anthony J. F. O'Reilly honored his Irish heritage with a personal gift of $3 million to Dublin University.

International grant making is not limited to the corporations and major givers. The predominantly African-American Bethel Lutheran Church, in one of Chicago's poorest neighborhoods, raised $600 to help Amextra build houses for the poor in Mexico and gave $1,000 to the Lutheran bishop from Namibia. The University of Illinois at Chicago has the first U.S. chair of Lithuanian studies, courtesy of a worldwide fund drive—organized by Chicago's Lithuanians—that has raised half a million dollars so far.

Foreign companies with plants in the United States are giving more here. Mitsubishi and Toyota have both endowed chairs at MIT for $1.5 million; Hitachi has endowed a chair at Stanford for $1.2 million.[3] The International Visitors Council in Columbus, Ohio, got grants from Honda and the German Sherex Corporation to build its unique international visitors' center in the airport. For multinational corporations, giving to good nonprofits is a way to show they care about the communities in which they have offices and plants.

Not only are foreign corporations giving in America, but foreign charities are systematically raising money here, too. Oxford University has announced a campaign to raise £220,000 through offices in Oxford, London, Toronto, and New York.

MORE DOMESTIC COMPETITION
The Reagan/Bush cutbacks in social spending have meant a big increase in demand for services and hence a need for more

This poster was used in the successful 1975 campaign that surpassed its goal of £3.5 million.

fundraising. More groups are asking more aggressively and getting more money than ever before.

In 1990, 950,000 tax-exempt organizations were registered in the United States, including 450,000 charities with 501(c)(3) tax status. All of these compete for money with tens of thousands of other causes. There are thousands of various organizations too informal to incorporate, such as block clubs, tenant associations, and children's groups. More and more local governmental units also are raising money either directly, such as a park district raising money for a swimming pool, or indirectly through 501(c)(3) auxiliaries, such as the "Friends of the Library" or a foundation created to raise money for a school district.

Fundraisers for nonprofits compete every year with fundraisers for politicians, political parties, and political action committees (PACs). The two major U.S. political parties reported spending more than $182 million during the 1989–90 election cycle, according to the Federal Election Commission. If this is what they *report*, one can assume the real total raised was much higher, since discretionary funds, also known as bags of cash, are still an effective tool for winning elections in many districts.

Thousands more organizations raise money although they operate outside the political system. These include organizations involved in civil disobedience, such as groups giving sanctuary to political refugees, and ACT-UP, which protests insufficient funding for AIDS research. Many groups of immigrants raise money in the United States to send home to another country.

Old fundraising strategies such as direct mail, telemarketing, and door-to-door canvassing are much more competitive. In most big cities it is impossible to find a Saturday night for a gala dance without competition from two or three other great parties. In New York City you cannot find a *week night* without competition. Even the United Way, America's largest grant maker, is faced with competition from women's, minorities', and environmental funds in many of its 2,300 markets.

NEW NEEDS AND OLD STRUGGLES

Dr. Cicely Saunders began the first modern hospice, called St. Christopher's, in London in 1962. This better form of caring for the dying and their caregivers was first copied in North America in the 1970s at the Palliative Care Service of the Royal Victoria Hospital in Montreal, the Hospice of Marin in northern California, and the Connecticut Hospice in New Haven. By 1978 there were 78 hospices in the U.S., caring almost exclusively for cancer patients. Today there are nearly 400 hospices in Canada[4] and 1,700 in the United States that treat a growing number of patients with AIDS, Alzheimer's disease, and ALS (Lou Gehrig's disease).

Many new needs demand successful fundraising. Among these are solutions for homelessness and hunger, both at home and abroad, and community-based economic development. Changing patterns of immigration have challenged school systems to accommodate those who speak the languages and hospitals to study the diseases of countries such as Ethiopia, Haiti, and Cambodia. Ongoing struggles, such as the work to stop racism and sexism, to find a cure for cancer, to teach people to read, and to present the best performing artists, need more money. Family problems, once considered private, are now recognized as social problems that will require expensive social solutions; these problems include drunk driving, incest, child abuse, and domestic violence.

Local issues are still the most popular and the easiest to raise money for. However, creative fundraisers are making it possible for even small-town Americans to support the rain forest in the Amazon or to oppose apartheid in South Africa.

TECHNOLOGY

On the positive side, new technologies give fundraisers the chance to reach more people more effectively than ever before. Computers, fax machines, and car phones are standard equipment in organizations that only a few years ago were storing their receipts in shoe boxes and sorting their data with a hole punch and a knitting needle. New strategies that incorporate 900 telephone numbers, electronic funds transfers, and cause-related marketing are making money now; fiber optics and new uses of two-way television communication will provide new opportunities before the century is over. If people can buy imitation diamond rings and oil paintings of Elvis Presley via television, you know the same technology will be used to raise money for good causes.

New software makes it easier to research and analyze demographic data bases to find the people who may support your organization. The Foundation Center data bases can enable fundraisers to retrieve data on forty-five thousand grants made every year. In minutes, computers can project the most profitable planned-giving trust or annuity for a donor.

Although the specific technologies may be new, the use of state-of-the-art technologies by fundraisers is not new. Clara Barton used the then-new technology of the telegraph, and the fledgling Associated Press to lobby the United States to sign the Geneva Convention in 1882. Then she learned to use direct mail, mass-marketed memberships, and an endowment campaign to launch a national fundraising drive for the new American Red Cross. She was sixty-one years old at the time.

COOPERATIVE PROGRAMS

As competition for money gets hotter, nonprofits are getting better at working with each other and their allies in business and government. For example, when hard times hit Pittsburgh, Pennsylvania, five organizations led a massive project to provide fresh produce for the area's food bank. The Western Conservancy gave the land, H. J. Heinz Company gave the tomato plants, the Allegheny Parks Department gave the agricultural expertise, and the Mellon Bank gave funding. Volunteers from the Army Reserves, National Guard, Boy Scouts, Girl Scouts, and churches harvested more than eighty tons of tomatoes and other fresh produce for the Greater Pittsburgh Community Food Bank. Every volunteer got a T-shirt with a big red tomato and the slogan "I know how to pick 'em!" As a final cooperative effort, volunteers contributed recipes for *The Great Tomato Cookbook*, which was tested, edited, and underwritten by H. J.

Heinz Company. More than twenty-three thousand copies have been sold by the food bank.

On a much larger scale, the Carrier Alert program helps elderly and disabled citizens, especially in rural areas, maintain independent lives. Each participant gets a sticker to put on his or her mailbox. If the mail carrier sees too much mail has accumulated, he or she notifies the local Red Cross. This program is a joint effort of the Association of Letter Carriers (AFL-CIO), the U.S. Postal Service, the American Red Cross, the U.S. Administration on Aging, and the United Way.

RESULTS

Fundraising is a success because volunteer organizations get results. Mothers Against Drunk Driving (MADD) has seen its income go up by as much as 44 percent in recent years; it has cut the number of deaths in America due to drunk driving by 20 percent since its founding in 1980. In Canada deaths from heart disease in people under sixty-five have been reduced by 36 percent since the Canadian Heart and Stroke Foundation began funding research in 1955. Rotary Clubs, working with the World Health Organization (WHO) and UNICEF, have made great progress in eradicating polio worldwide. In Turkey alone, reported cases of polio dropped 90 percent in the first five years of the PolioPlus program, because of a strong partnership between the fifty-nine local clubs and Rotary International.[5]

HOPE

Against the 1980s' backdrop of greed and corruption, nonprofits give hope for the 1990s. Fundraisers have the courage to raise the money to fuel good groups. These people are as noted as Mother Teresa, revered around the world, and they are as anonymous as the tens of thousands of "points of light" volunteering on Main Street. They include the volunteer who gives a cup of soup and a peanut butter sandwich to a hungry person, as well as the organizer who works to change the policies that made that person homeless in the first place.

The world needs the famous and the unsung heroes. We need the service givers and the system changers. And most of all we need the fundraisers.

"Being a worker and a man of
concrete work, I must tell you that the
supply of words on the world market
is plentiful, but the demand is falling.
Let deeds follow words now."
—Lech Walesa, President of Poland[1]

Chapter 2

Strategies for Success

A diversity of fundraising strategies can be the Declaration of
Independence for your organization. If your money comes from
several *different* income sources, you know you will always have
the money you need for your core budget, especially for salaries.
No organization needs to use every strategy, but successful
fundraisers can find several techniques that work well. Choose
a mix of ideas to make the most money in ways that are conso-
nant with your values.

GOVERNMENT FUNDING

Despite eight years of the "return to self-reliance" touted by the
Reagan administration, 26 percent of funding for nonprofits
was from all levels of government in 1987, barely changed from
27 percent in 1977.[2] Thus, government money still accounts for
more than one-fourth of all nonprofit revenue. Of course, this
percentage is much higher in some fields, such as health care,
and much lower in others, such as community organizing.

Government money is not a free ride; it will always cost
your organization in terms of bookkeeping hardware, software,
personnel, and aggravation. It can also cost more for time lags,

12

services not covered, and vouchers not accepted. As long as your organization's leaders can project the real costs, and if they commit to raising the extra money to cover them, government funding is a very large source of money for you to consider.

If your organization wants to pursue funding from your village, city, county, state, or federal sources, ask for advice from other nonprofits in the same jurisdiction. Find out what you need to do in order to apply, what the time lag on payments is, and how much money you will need to raise from other sources to cover the time between your spending the money and the government's paying it.

PRIVATE MONEY

If public funds pay 26 percent of the bills of nonprofits, then private funds must pay the other 74 percent. In its annual publication *Giving USA*, the American Association of Fundraising Counsel has kept track of private philanthropy since 1955. In 1989 Americans gave away $114.7 *billion* to good nonprofits. This is more than the total national budgets of most of the countries in the world.

WHERE U.S. CONTRIBUTIONS COME FROM (1989)

Source	Amount (in Billions)	Percent of Total	Increase from 1988
Individuals	$ 96	84%	+12%
Bequests	7	6	+ 0
Foundations	7	6	+ 9
Corporations	5	4	+ 4
Total giving	$115	100%	+10%

INDIVIDUALS

As the table of U.S. contributions shows, individuals gave 90 percent of the charity dollars in America in 1989. Living individuals, who drive the growth in philanthropy, gave 84 percent of donations. Bequests—gifts specified in the wills of deceased donors—accounted for another 6 percent. Experts predict that money from bequests will triple in the next ten years.

FOUNDATIONS AND CORPORATIONS

The remaining 10 percent of American donations in 1989 came from foundations and corporations. About a nickel out of every dollar came from foundations; about another nickel came from corporations. These percentages have remained constant within one or two percentage points for decades.

Foundations give a little more when their investments do better, a little less when the market is doing poorly. Most foundation grants support human services, education, and health care. Five percent of grants go to organizations serving women and girls. Less than 5 percent go to African Americans, Hispanics, Native Americans, and Asians and Pacific Islanders. Two percent of foundation grants go to religious congregations.

Corporate giving leveled off at the end of the eighties. For the past four years, corporate giving has grown at less than the rate of inflation and much less than the rate of individual gifts. Nonprofits got spoiled in the go-go years of 1976 to 1986, when corporate contributions grew by an average of 15 percent annually. Those days are over.

Most corporate contributions support the groups that help companies recruit executives (the symphony, the opera, and other fine arts organizations), hire a competent work force (elementary and secondary schools and literacy programs), improve their public image (recycling), or deliver services (United Ways).

Foundation grants can make great venture capital to start new ventures, and corporations can be terrific partners for good programs in their communities. But in every year, in every community, for every cause, the *big* money comes from gifts and bequests of individuals.

WHERE THE MONEY GOES

Regardless of your cause, giving is going up. The amounts change slightly from year to year, but most of the percentages are pretty constant. The table of "where the money goes" gives a breakdown by sector for 1989.

WHERE THE MONEY GOES (1989)[3]

Sector	Amount (in Billions)	Percent of Total
Religion	$ 54.3	47%
Human services (includes $3 billion to the United Ways)	11.4	10
Education	10.7	9
Health	10.0	9
Arts and culture	7.5	7
Social action (includes civil rights and the environment)	3.6	3
Other (includes international)	17.2	15
Total	$114.7	100%

RELIGION

Note that most money, by far—about 47 percent of the total every year—is given to religion and religious causes. There are five reasons for this—four reasons that your group can apply and one that is beyond your use.

One reason religious congregations make the most money is that they offer the best premium, a premium you cannot offer: you give them money, and they give you eternal life. This is hard to match with a bumper sticker or even the best cookbook in Carson City.

On the other hand, think about the ways that congregations ask for money, and use your imagination to apply these to your own cause.

Regular Requests

Congregations ask for money at least fifty-two times a year, every week on the Sabbath. If you count extra requests for the missionaries, the seminaries, the building fund, the Spring Fling, the Fall Fair, and on high holidays, they probably ask sixty to seventy times a year.

How many times do you ask your donors? Twice a year? Four times? Ask more often, and you will get more money and more committed donors.

Especially if you want to raise money from low-income people, it is vital that you give them the opportunity to donate small amounts of money many times a year. Rich people buy what they want with one payment. Poor people buy what they want by making a down payment, stretching out the financing as long as possible, then paying a small amount every week or month. If they can buy a car this way, why not let them buy the great work your group does in the same way? Ask often.

Broad Base of Support

Congregations ask everybody: the oldest member of the congregation and the stranger who just walked in, the millionaire who paid for the new organ and the bag lady. Do you ask everyone? Or do you make choices for other people, eliminating your wealthiest prospects because "we can't bother them" and your low-income prospects because "we know they can't give." Practice what you preach; allow each person to make an individual choice and to control his or her own giving. Ask everyone.

Options for Giving

Congregations give their members many different ways to give. People might make a weekly or monthly pledge; donate extra amounts at high holidays; contribute for special flowers or music; give memorials in memory of departed members; buy merchandise such as cookbooks from the women's organization, devotional readings from the library team, recordings from the choir, or T-shirts from the youth group; purchase tickets to special events; make a major gift for the buildings or important causes; and remember the church, temple, mosque, or synagogue in their will. How many *different* ways do you ask your donors to give?

Volunteering

Congregations provide many ways to volunteer. Volunteers give more than twice as much money as nonvolunteers. Volunteers can teach, sing, read, care for babies, clean up, make refreshments, drive the seniors and disabled members, usher, count the money, prepare the programs, greet newcomers, sign up members, sell merchandise, offer tours, and serve in the worship. How many *different* ways do you ask people to volunteer?

WHO GIVES?

Individuals give 84 percent of the money in America. To make it easier to ask, you need to know which individuals give and how you can find the people who will give to your particular organization.

The Independent Sector, a coalition of leading nonprofits and grant makers, has commissioned several professional surveys on volunteers and giving in America. These surveys provide interesting data on who gives:

- Forty-eight percent of the money comes from households with incomes under $30,000. Do not think you need millionaires and movie stars to do good fundraising. Even if you are working in a low- or middle-income community, you can raise the money you want.
- Seventy-five percent of Americans reported they gave money to charities last year. This means that if you ask ten people, at least seven can say yes.
- Thirty-eight percent of Americans say they wish they had given *more* money. This means out of every ten people who gave to you last year, four *want* you to ask them more often or to ask for a larger amount of money.
- Fourteen percent of Americans revealed they would have given money, but nobody asked them. Think of it! This means that if you ask ten people, one of them is a charity virgin. That person is not giving to any other cause. If he or she likes your cause, you can get *all* of this person's charity dollars.

How much does the average person give? Although many synagogues and churches urge people to tithe—that is, give 10 percent of their income—in reality the average American gives between 1 and 2 percent of his or her income. Figuring most conservatively, if you can estimate someone's income, project that 1 percent of it will go to charities. So if Harry makes $20,000, he donates at least $200 each year; if Sally makes $100,000, she gives at least $1,000 a year. If you are asking for only $10, you are asking for too little.

If you want to find the people who give at the high end (the 2 percent givers), here are the indicators discovered by Independent Sector about donors who give 2 percent or more of their income to charities:

- These people belong to a church, synagogue, mosque, or temple. Eighty percent of Americans active in religious organizations made gifts, compared to only 55 percent of people not active in religious organizations. People who regularly attend religious services made 70 percent of all contributions to charity and gave more to nonsectarian causes than those who did not worship.

- They have some discretionary income. Remember, this is what the *donor* decides is extra money.

- They have no worries about money. For your planning, look for the people who are in control of their lives and their money, so they can confidently make a donation to you. The other prospects in this category are the people who are so rich they never need to be concerned about paying the bills and the people who live with a "don't worry, be happy" attitude. Giving money to a good cause makes the donor feel *good*, so the people who give the most, worry the least.

- They volunteer. According to the 1990 Independent Sector survey, American households with a volunteer contributed an average of $1,192; households without a volunteer gave an average of $601.[4] More than ninety-eight million Americans volunteer, and the number is growing.

The most common mistake fundraisers make is to exclude their own volunteers. Volunteers are your *best* prospects. Who knows better how wonderful your group is? Who sees the results? Who knows the real people who benefit? The volunteers!

INDIVIDUAL GIFTS

Since 90 percent of the money in America comes from individuals, focus 90 percent of your efforts on getting individual gifts and bequests.

Of course, the temptation here is to say, "Great. We can get money from individuals. Let's get J. Beresford Tipton to give us a million dollars. Then we'll never need to ask again!"

This strategy has an elegant simplicity, but it probably will not succeed unless the person proposing it is Mrs. Tipton. Even if it *did* succeed, the organization would become totally dependent on one person's money, which makes it very fragile (he can change his mind at any time) and very weak (the group has no political power.)

At the other extreme, someone will want to say, "We're poor and everyone I know is poor. Let's sell one million raffles at one dollar each. Everyone can buy one."

This is true, but it is not the truth. Everyone *can* buy a one-dollar raffle chance. But will your volunteers burn out before they have completed one million sales? (Or before one hundred sales?) Even worse, at the end of one million transactions, you will have identified everyone who wants to win a television. You will not know who wants to support the mission of your organization.

Your fundraisers can devise a strategy that will balance getting the most money per transaction with the real skills and enthusiasm of your leaders and volunteers. You can continue all the fundraising techniques you already know and like. Plus you can add on new sources of dependable income for today and the future.

THE FUNDRAISING PYRAMID

The pyramid on page 20 is a planning tool to help your fundraisers. The fundraising pyramid can help them visualize their overall strategy for raising money from individuals. What is the best strategy for your group for each step?

The bottom layer represents the most people. They will give the least amount of money, have the least commitment to the organization, and take the least time to cultivate. The top of the pyramid has the fewest people, who give the most money, are the most committed to the mission of the group, and need the most time to cultivate. There is a direct relationship between time and money: the more money, the more time it takes to get. So start now.

Build the base of small gifts first. Eighty to 90 percent of planned gifts and major gifts come from people who have been members or annual donors for three to five years.

As the size of the gift increases, so does the time required to get the gift. Special events, merchandise, and memberships can be sold in minutes. Major gifts take much longer. The average $100,000 gift to a university requires at least seven personal visits over eighteen months. The United Negro College Fund needed twelve years to negotiate a $50 million challenge grant from Ambassador Walter H. Annenberg, retired CEO of Triangle Publications, Inc., publisher of *Seventeen, TV Guide,* and the *Daily Racing Form.*

Let's look at each level of this pyramid. As we do, make notes on what steps your organization has already mastered and which pieces need more work.

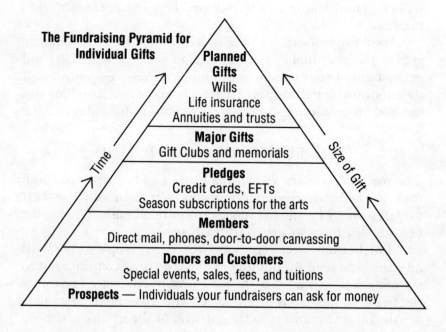

The Fundraising Pyramid for Individual Gifts

Planned Gifts
Wills
Life insurance
Annuities and trusts

Major Gifts
Gift Clubs and memorials

Pledges
Credit cards, EFTs
Season subscriptions for the arts

Members
Direct mail, phones, door-to-door canvassing

Donors and Customers
Special events, sales, fees, and tuitions

Prospects — Individuals your fundraisers can ask for money

Time

Size of Gift

HOW TO START

The very bottom represents all the people who could donate. I wish I could tell you that everyone in your community will donate to your group. (Of course they *should*.) But no matter how wonderful your organization is, you will never get 100 percent of the possible donors to give to you. However, you can always get more than you have now.

FIRST DONATIONS

The first donations to your organization may come from sales, special events, or fees for service. These are the easiest transactions, because the donors get something tangible in return. You are asking for the smallest amounts of money, and this takes the least time. Usually there is a high volume of transactions involving many fundraisers.

ANNUAL CAMPAIGNS

Once you begin asking for money for the mission of the organization, you have moved beyond selling to fundraising. Instead of looking for customers to buy cookies or come to the carnival, you are looking for people who share your values and vision. You want them to give money to get the results of your work. The most efficient way to find your supporters is a well-organized annual campaign.

Membership dues are the ideal form for annual fundraising, because they are the most democratic, dependable, and renewable form of fundraising. The members pay a set amount of money for one year. Some publicly funded institutions do not have members directly, but create membership organizations such as Friends of the Library to get unrestricted money.

For smaller organizations, your current members can sell memberships in person. If your cause has a broader appeal, especially if it is very popular or very controversial, you can hire professional fundraisers to mass-market memberships through direct mail, telemarketing, or a door-to-door canvass.

PLEDGES

The next step up in terms of commitment and money consists of people who pay a pledge. This is the system most religious congregations use, and it triples the amount of money given. A pledge is just a promise to give a certain amount more often than once a year, usually every week or month. The most common forms of pledges are the weekly pledge to a congregation, a bimonthly pledge through payroll deduction, or a monthly pledge through a bank credit card. Season subscriptions are a form of pledges for performing arts groups.

CLUBS

The next step up the pyramid is clubs, which are a strategy used to get people to increase their annual gift. You simply create the Silver Buckeye Club for $500 donors, the Golden Buckeye Club for $1,000 donors, and the Platinum Buckeye Club for $5,000 donors, and then urge generous people in Ohio to give at the higher amount. Clubs work very well because they make it easier for the fundraisers to ask for a larger dollar amount, and they give donors an ego reward.

MEMORIALS AND HONORARY GIFTS

Some of your donors will want to make a gift in memory of a loved one or in honor of someone they admire. More and more obituaries now include requests that gifts go to the local hospital, hospice, association for a specific disease, or the favorite cause of the deceased rather than for flowers. Honorary gifts to a worthwhile nonprofit may be preferred as a retirement gift, gifts for a second or third wedding, or in lieu of presents for certain anniversaries. Many smaller gifts can result in a significant total for your organization.

MAJOR GIFTS

Major gifts are the largest contributions your organization gets. You get them by asking the people who have contributed to your organization for the past three to five years. Major gifts take much more time and person-to-person visits. The payoff for you is more money and a more committed donor.

College fundraisers used to say it would take eighteen months and seven personal visits with a donor to get a gift of $100,000. Today the cultivation period has lengthened to two to three years, with obviously more visits. The payoff can be just as large, or larger.

PLANNED GIFTS—WILLS AND LIFE INSURANCE

Planned gifts used to be called "deferred gifts," but fundraisers changed the name because the temptation is to defer forever. The most common planned gift is a bequest that will go to the organization at the time of the donor's death. Bequests are the most volatile form of fundraising, since there is no accurate way to predict when specific people will die. In the past ten years, bequests have accounted for 5 to 13 percent of total giving.

The typical American donates to eleven to fourteen charities every year. Americans with a will remember two to five charities with bequests. So two to five charities that get annual gifts from a donor also get a gift in his or her will, and nine are left out. Usually the charities that get bequests are the ones that asked for bequests.

The second most common planned gift is the proceeds from a life insurance policy. This is especially popular with younger donors. In its simplest form, the donor buys a life insurance policy and makes the annual payments, which are deductible from his or her taxable income. The organization is the beneficiary, so it will receive a large amount of money at the time of the donor's death.

Planned gifts also can include appreciated stocks, bonds, or other financial instruments, works of art, and real estate. In a well-planned program, donating appreciated property to a charity can mean that the donor saves money on income and estate taxes, may receive a higher annual income, can provide better for his or her children and grandchildren, and supports a good organization, all at the same time.

Whom do you ask for major gifts or planned gifts? The people who have given you money every year in your annual campaign. Research shows that from 80 to 90 percent of large gifts and bequests come from donors who have given the organization donations for the past three to five years. So it is vital that you begin your strategy with a plan to build a broad base of regular contributors, and then build relationships to move them up to making larger gifts and putting the organization in their estate plans.

PLANNING CHART

There is a worksheet at the end of this chapter to help you plan your fundraising strategy for the next year. First, discuss what your own group already does well. Continue that and increase it if you can.

Second, ruthlessly evaluate your fundraisers that are not producing what you want from them. If they can be fixed, fix them. For example, perhaps your thrift shop is not doing as well as it used to because you are having trouble finding daytime volunteers. If so, open it in the evening when you can get more volunteers and more shoppers.

If something cannot be fixed, prune it out of your plan. For example, many groups do fundraising dinners because they have always done dinners. Today it is very difficult to make money on a dinner unless you can get corporate underwriting. If it is too much work for too little money, take it out of the plan and replace it with another strategy that can make more money with less work.

Then add on new strategies you want to test this year. Not every group will want to use every strategy, but every group can ask for major contributions face to face and ask for bequests.

Talk to other local groups that shine at fundraising, and ask your national organization for ideas on what is working best for similar groups. Then make your long-range plan to intentionally recruit a big base of small donors. Finally, systematically ask them for larger gifts and bequests.

FUNDRAISING STRATEGY

Source of Funds	$ Now	Goal for Next Year	Goal in Five Years

Product Sales

Fees

Tuitions

Business Ventures or Earned Income

Special Events

Mail

Phones

Door-to-Door Canvassing

Membership Dues

Pledges

Season Subscriptions (Performing Arts Groups)

Workplace Giving
1. United Way
2. Combined Federal Campaign
3. Other

Clubs

Memorials/Honorary Gifts

Planned Gifts

Bequests

Life Insurance

Real Estate

Art

Stocks/Bonds

Grants

Foundations

Corporations

Religious Congregations

Civic Organizations

Cause-Related Marketing

Other Strategies Good for Your Organization
1.
2.
3.

"Always take your job, but not yourself, seriously."
  —*Dwight D. Eisenhower*

Chapter 3

The Fundraising Team

Ruth Andrea Seeler, M.D., is an ex-president of the Illinois Hemophilia Association, founder of a summer camp for boys with hemophilia, and a no-nonsense type from New York. When I told her I was writing a new book on fundraising, she growled, "Fundraising! Ask for money—send thank-you notes. What else is there?"

Actually, she's right. Successful fundraising could be condensed into one sentence: ask for money and send thank-you notes. If you, your staff, and your volunteers did those two things every day, you would have all the money you need.

What if there is only "you" and not "your staff" or "your volunteers" yet? Fundraising is a team sport and you need a team of caring people to make it fun and profitable. Both paid professionals and volunteers have an important role to play in successful fundraising. If your daily mantra is "I could do this easier myself . . . ," read, mark, and inwardly digest every bit of this chapter.

27

WHY USE VOLUNTEERS?

You're right—it *is* easier to do it yourself. Especially if you are a good proposal writer and foundation charmer, you may be able to get along for quite some time without having to find, train, and motivate volunteers. So why all this work?

It is the American Way. In every community, our society runs better because the people who live there care enough to give their time to the library, the hospital, and the civic groups.

Volunteers enable your agency to tell its story to many different networks: workplaces, congregations, schools, unions, clubs, and neighborhoods.

Today's volunteers are tomorrow's leaders. Whether we want our own people to go on to become the chair of the festival or governor of the state, we need to begin testing them today with small challenges so they will have the skills tomorrow for the bigger challenges.

It is only easier for the first year. If you do not take the time now to recruit and train good volunteers, you will have to do all the work *every* year. On the other hand, if you develop good volunteers, the first year is a lot of work, the second year is a little supervision, and the third year you put on your hat and go to the party. Many wonderful organizations operate entirely with volunteer labor and they do just fine. Your own organization will also benefit if you practice what you preach and literally let the people run their own lives and their own organization.

WHERE DO I GET GOOD FUNDRAISING VOLUNTEERS?

You ask for them. According to the latest Gallup survey on volunteering, the most common reason Americans gave for becoming involved as a volunteer was that someone asked them. Who did the asking? Most common responses were a friend (52 percent), someone at their church or synagogue (25 percent), and someone at work (11 percent). What is your organization doing to make it easy for your active members to ask the people with whom they play, work, and worship?

The same poll asked Americans why they first volunteered with a nonprofit organization. By far the most important motivators were the desire "to do something useful" (63 percent) and something the volunteer "thought I would enjoy" (34 percent).[1] Do your volunteers feel useful and have fun?

Most people will join the organization because they care heart and soul about the cause. In addition to the true believers, you may want to recruit specific kinds of people who will make successful fundraisers.

NEWCOMERS

The days when workers commonly received ten- or twenty-five-year pins for faithful service to the same company are over. Today, the average American worker has held eight jobs by the age of forty, and often this requires several moves. For people who want to get involved in their new community, fundraising gives them the chance to meet good people quickly. New people can offer tested ideas that worked elsewhere to complement your own fundraising plans.

SENIOR CITIZENS

In some parts of the world it is *normal* for people to live to be more than a hundred years old. When scientists studied these people they found several reasons for long lives: little pollution, no smoking, no guns, and a good diet. But the *most* important predictor for long lives is not retiring: the farmers farm, the shoemakers make shoes, the homemakers make happy homes forever.

Although more Americans are choosing to retire earlier, their life expectancy is increasing. In the armed forces and some unionized jobs you can retire after twenty years—so you could be retired at forty-two and live to be a hundred. What do you do with the other fifty-eight years? Ideally, you volunteer.

When your organization recruits retirees and gives them responsible work to do, you not only get decades of education and experience (and a fat address book) but you literally keep people alive. More and more of the best people are looking at volunteering, especially fundraising, as a second career.

According to the U.S. Census Bureau and the Social Security Administration, there were 31.7 million Americans over sixty-five years old in 1990. On a per capita basis this group has the highest discretionary income, $5,219, of any age group, and the financial assets of household members aged 65 to 75 average $65,000.[2] Surveys show volunteers give twice as much as nonvolunteers, so senior volunteers are also great prospects for both current and planned gifts.

DAYTIME VOLUNTEERS

The daytime volunteer of yesteryear was a housewife in a shirt-waist dress at home all day. Yesterday's Lucy Ricardos and June Cleavers are today's Roseanne Conners and Clair Huxtables, dressed for success and working at the mall or a law office. Only one job in five in the United States pays enough to support a family of four, so both parents work for salaries as well as raise the family. So where can we find good volunteers for daytime fundraising?

There are still people available to volunteer during the day. These include retired people, people with night jobs (18 percent of all American jobs), people with inherited wealth or a successful spouse, and people in retail. Any salesperson on commission wants to work on the weekend and get weekdays off. They can volunteer with you in the daytime.

MOVERS AND SHAKERS

Every committee will say, "If we could only get George Washington. He's the kind of person we need." But they surely will not recruit George if nobody will volunteer to ask George.

You get what you ask for. If you want the best people in your community to help with your fundraising, aim high and ask them. You have nothing to lose by asking and a great deal to gain, so ask.

WOMEN

Remember when your mother used to tell you to wear clean underwear in case you were hit by a truck? Today, writer Letty Cottin Pogrebin asks, "Suppose you get hit by a truck and someone finds your checkbook? What would the check stubs reveal about your giving habits? How recently did you make your last contribution, and how generous was it relative to your means?"[3]

She suggests the acid test for giving is, "Will this money empower women and children or will it just reinforce dependence? I want to fund change, not charity. I want to enable, not just help." These questions can also be a good test for recruiting women volunteers. To get the best women today, offer the challenge of changing the world.

LOW-INCOME VOLUNTEERS

If you want low-income people to respect your organization, ask them to give and to raise funds. Poor people, better than anyone else, know that if you want something, you have to pay for it. Writer Nicholas von Hoffman was a community organizer on Chicago's South Side in the 1960s. His team of organizers and leaders filled forty-six buses with poor people from The Woodlawn Organization (TWO) to register to vote at City Hall. There was no free ride. As von Hoffman said, "We had these endless fundraisers for buses. One apartment house after another . . . TWO never put up any money for [this] because you knew that you'd never fill a bus unless the people who are going to ride in the bus pay for it."[4]

In 1985 the Salvation Army raised $110,000 in San Francisco's Chinatown for the victims of the earthquake in Mexico City. Their study showed that most of the money came not from the wealthy merchants but from ordinary residents, including boat people.[5] The 1985 Band Aid concerts and worldwide telethon raised $117 million; the people of Ireland, the poorest country in the European Community, donated £7 million or £2 for every person in the country. That would be the equivalent of U.S. citizens donating a total of $500 million.[6]

Low-income households in America are proportionately more generous than wealthier households. In 1989, households earning between $50,000 and $75,000 a year gave an average of 1.5 percent of their income, while households that made less than $10,000 donated 2.5 percent of their income.[7] Especially if you give them a chance to pledge, low-income households can make generous contributions to the causes they care about. For example, even in households with incomes of less than $12,000,

12 percent of black families and 15 percent of white families gave more than $500 a year.[8]

YUPPIES

At the other extreme are the young urban professionals, or yuppies, generally stereotyped by nonyuppies as having more money than sense.

Actually, this group is pretty easy to work with. By definition you know they are young (mostly healthy), urban (easy to find), and employed (have a good paycheck). The only thing standing in your way is a negative stereotype.

The secret to success is choosing the right leadership. If yuppies organize your campaign, this group will participate actively and give generously. (The same applies to other high-income clusters that are hard to reach, such as doctors, dentists, and lawyers.)

What do they want? A challenge. Belonging. Meeting nice people of the opposite sex.

Once when I was leading a workshop for a group of hospital auxiliaries, a fifty-five-year-old woman complained that her twenty-five-year-old successful single daughter would not get involved in the hospital auxiliary. The mother described her group as all women in their fifties, sixties, and seventies who met monthly to plan the one annual event that netted about $5,000. The best part of their meetings was the desserts.

Now can you see anything here to attract someone who is single, ambitious, and on a diet? The daughter routinely handles million-dollar amounts on her job. Will she get excited about twelve meetings to make $5,000?

On the other hand, the Children's Memorial Hospital, located in the middle of a yuppie neighborhood in Chicago, wanted to recruit yuppie leadership to improve community relations and to raise money. Their plan has been very successful and could be copied by other urban groups.

The hospital interviewed the leaders from their boards and asked which of their sons and daughters might like to get involved. This yielded the perfect set of leadership prospects. All had parents who had volunteered for the hospital for decades. Many had been patients at the hospital or had siblings who had been patients. All were single and wanted to meet other singles with family values. Best of all, they all were committed to the mission of the hospital.

The hospital formed a new coed auxiliary of yuppies and gave them the biggest and most controversial goal: raise $100,000 for the pediatric AIDS patients. The group accepted. Although the older auxiliaries always meet at the hospital, the yuppies sometimes meet at a nearby pub. They have organized a variety of events, including the Snow Ball in January, an informal beer bash in a parking lot, a party for the kids at the hospital on St. Patrick's Day (a high holiday in Chicago regardless of your ethnic background), and more. They made their goal of $100,000.

Children's Memorial Hospital's formula for success is one that your organization can copy:

- Make the group coed.
- Give a challenging dollar goal.
- Connect the dollar goal to an urgent need not funded by any other source.
- Recruit bold leadership and assign trained staff.
- Allow the committee to run itself.
- Connect it to the mission of the hospital.

Although yuppies are numerically a small group—probably only 3 to 4 percent of the total U.S. population—they will be the leaders of the future in urban areas. If your organization can recruit them in their twenties and thirties, you can take your pick of the best for leadership roles later.

RURAL VOLUNTEERS
Finding and keeping good rural volunteers is the most difficult challenge for fundraising recruiters. There are fewer people, so the same handful of leaders are asked to do everything; there are fewer prospects so fundraisers feel as though they are asking the same people again and again; and there are fewer organizations, so there are fewer places to test the youngest and newest volunteers.

To get good rural volunteers, first ask the landed gentry who have owned a farm or a ranch for generations. Someone from that family will have the best access to local people. Second, look for someone who has a self-interest in being accepted in the community. Who needs to build good will to do his or her job? This may be a member of the clergy, the editor of the paper, or the owner of the largest store. These people need to be known in the community and to help the community grow. Third, who has access to and knowledge of the latest technology? If volunteers are burnt out on meetings because they need to drive an hour each way, could some of the meetings be eliminated through computers, teleconferencing, or faxing? Is there someone at the library, high school, or local utility who could help save time and money through technology? Then the people who do get involved can focus on raising money and getting results.

CORPORATIONS

Corporations can give you more than money. They can also offer valuable goods, special services, and a terrific source of volunteers. For example, at the Mellon Bank in Pittsburgh, management trainer Dennis McCarthy first learned American Sign Language in order to give a fair and legal job interview to a deaf woman. Then he started a voluntary lunchtime class that has taught more than three hundred Mellon employees to sign, for their own use and to serve deaf customers. With three alumni of the Mellon class he formed "The Signing Friends" to raise awareness of the deaf at hospitals and schools. At Christmas time, Dennis volunteered as the "Signing Santa" so deaf kids could tell Santa what they wanted. He learned sign language to do his job better; now he uses it in many ways to make his community better. There are hundreds of employees in the businesses in your town with special skills. They can help your group, too, if you ask them.

PROBLEMS?

Cesar Chavez, founder of the United Farm Workers Union, once said, "We found out that the harder a guy is to convince, the better leader or member he becomes. When you exert yourself to convince him you have his confidence, and he has good motivation. A lot of people who say OK right away wind up hanging around the office, taking up the workers' time."[9]

Some volunteers will simply take more work to persuade, so do more work if needed. You may find your best leaders that way.

No matter how hard you try, there will always be a few people who will never end up working on the fundraising committee or serving on the board of directors. Most people can learn to overcome their fears of fundraising if they care enough about your cause. But other people may never be able to ask for money, no matter how much they love your organization.

In some cases you can pair timid volunteers with more assertive fundraisers. Someone with a personal experience with your cause can simply tell his or her own story, and then the good fundraiser can actually close the sale. Or you can find a different job that will use his or her talents better. People used to giggle at Thomas Jefferson when he gave speeches in Virginia's House of Burgesses because he had a high squeaky voice and a stammer. So the American patriots did not ask him to make speeches; they asked him to write the Declaration of Independence. Do the best you can to involve all volunteers in fundraising in a meaningful way. If they are not asking for money, what *else* can they do to help the organization achieve its goals?

HOW TO GET GREAT
FUNDRAISING LEADERSHIP

Every successful organization wants to find volunteer fundraisers who will

1. Give money
2. Ask for money
3. Keep asking for money
4. Ask other people to ask

You get great leaders the same way you get big gifts—you know what you want and you say what you want. So the first step in recruiting outstanding fundraising leadership is to describe the qualities you want for your organization.

At your next fundraising meeting, ask the volunteers and staff to talk about the individual leaders they admire. Think of the great leaders from history, such as Jane Addams, Susan B. Anthony, or Harriet Tubman; leaders of the international democracy movements, such as Lech Walesa, Vàclav Havel, or Nelson Mandela; leaders of American causes, such as Barbara Bush, Jimmy Carter, or Cesar Chavez; and leaders of your own local community. Then make a list of the qualities these people exhibit. A partial list could include

1. Integrity
2. Humility
3. Ability to think on the spot
4. Willingness to listen and learn
5. Willingness to grow and stretch
6. Trust the group process
7. Ability to develop new people
8. A goal-oriented nature
9. A sense of humor

Ask the committee to add other qualities and think about this list until your next meeting. At that meeting, ask the group for names of local individuals both outside and inside the organization who embody these qualities. Those are the people you want for your organization's fundraising leadership.

DEVELOPING NEW LEADERS

There are two ways to get great volunteer fundraisers. You can intentionally recruit great talent from the outside or you can develop your own leaders from the inside.

RECRUIT TALENT FROM THE OUTSIDE

If you are asking for leadership from the outside, build a team with the "Four Ws":

• Work   • Wealth   • Weight   • Wisdom

In this system, the nominating committee intentionally works to recruit leaders who can give your board a balance of *work*—people willing to ask for money, organize events, and do other fundraising work; *wealth*—people willing and able to give big money; *weight*—people with power in the community whose names can open doors, such as the mayor, the manager of the largest workplace, or the most famous local celebrity; and *wisdom*—people who are experts in your field.

Asking for all four kinds of skills on the same board works best when the group is new. Then you get the most diversity and everyone learns new skills. Also, frankly, unless the founder is a celebrity a new group is limited to the people who are willing to gamble on a new idea. Once the organization has achieved some results, it will be able to attract more prestigious people and bigger donors.

Honorary Board

Some organizations prefer to take the volunteers from the *weight* category and put them on a separate honorary board. Although these people have great prestige they probably will not actually ask for money for your organization. Most honorary board members simply lend their names to the organization, which is fine—the mere name of a celebrity will open doors. Honorary board members may send a check once a year or attend an occasional special event; unless the cause really matters to them they may never attend a meeting. There is no reason an honorary board needs to meet as a group—what you want is their endorsement.

Your honorary board is a great place to put celebrities, sports idols, and politicians. Some of the sparkle of celebrities will rub off on your group and make it easier to recruit workers and givers. The most dazzling stars can give you their own money and use their fame to raise money for their favorite cause.

If the celebrity is important enough, even their pets can make money for you. For example, First Dog Millie Bush dictated her memoir to the First Lady and produced a best-seller on life at the White House. All of the profits from *Millie's Book* go to The Barbara Bush Foundation for Family Literacy.[10] The Purina Company wanted to use a photo of former President Jimmy Carter's cat, Misty Malarky, on its 1986 calendar. The

Carters agreed on condition that a gift of $5,000 be made to their favorite charity, the Habitat for Humanity that helps low-income people build affordable housing.[11]

Advisory Board

An advisory board is just that—a board of people who give advice. Some organizations have more than one advisory board. For example, Horizon Hospice has a medical advisory board, a financial advisory board, and an advisory board of volunteers with assorted skills—an architect, a funeral director, a lawyer, and a social worker.

Look at your current board members and then consider the skills that your organization will need to meet its fundraising goals for the next three years. For example, if you intend to begin or expand your campaign to ask for planned gifts, you will need people who know the most about current tax laws and investment opportunities. If you do not already have these kinds of people in your leadership, recruit a lawyer, a banker, and a CPA for your advisory board. Almost any organization can benefit from someone who specializes in computers and the newest telemarketing technologies. Historic properties could benefit from people with expertise in fine and decorative arts, genealogy, and real estate.

Especially if you set measurable goals, hold your volunteers accountable, and keep good records, after a few years it will be apparent which people are asking for money in the community and which people are just talking at meetings. An advisory board gives your organization a good place to put the volunteers who only want to talk. An advisory board may meet if it wants, or the members may just be available when their expertise is needed.

If your organization chooses to set up an honorary board for people with prestige and an advisory board for people who want to give advice, then the real board of directors can be limited to the two sets of people you want most: the *work* people and the *wealth* people. The more the workers, givers, and askers see similar people on a board, the more they will work, give, and ask.

OTHER FUNDRAISING COMMITTEES

In addition to the board of directors, an honorary board, and one or more advisory boards, your organization may want to create other volunteer groups with a specific fundraising goal. These may be called committees, guilds, auxiliaries, or another board.

For example, some organizations working in low-income communities limit the board of directors to people who live and work in the community. This requirement functionally eliminates the possibility of business leaders serving on the board. So a low-income group can create a "corporate fundraising committee" made up of business and professional leaders who give management advice and raise money from the business community for the organization.

Performing arts groups that attract audiences from beyond their own community may set up guilds of fans to raise money and build audiences for them. For example, the Santa Fe Opera has fundraising committees in California, Colorado, and New York. The Stratford Festival in Ontario has an active group of Shakespeare fans raising money in Chicago.

Communities with a large number of people who own second homes can double their fundraising forces. For example, Manhattanites who spend summers in the Catskills can work on the summer concert series for the arts association in July, then ask for major gifts in Manhattan in the winter. Many organizations in Florida, Arizona, and Texas schedule their events to use the talents of the "snowbirds" who move in from Thanksgiving to Spring.

Some hospitals have as many as twenty auxiliaries, focused on special fundraisers such as running the gift shop or the thrift shop, on a special need such as raising money for cancer patients or pediatrics, or founded in memory of a specific patient. Churches may have separate committees to run the bingo, carnival, and product sales. Art museums and symphonies have created "junior boards" to test the best young talent and provide volunteers for special events.

Put It in Writing

Be explicit about what you want from your volunteers and leaders. Many groups find it helpful to write out the benefits and responsibilities of serving on the board, including the specific dollar amount they want board members to give and to get. This allows people who do not want to donate or ask for money to remove themselves from the process before they are nominated. You will need to ask more people this way, but the people you get will be enthusiastic givers and askers.

DEVELOPING TALENT FROM INSIDE

If your organization has a large number of volunteers, develop a system of upward mobility so the people who produce the most are rewarded. For example, the volunteer who recruits the most members this year can chair the membership committee next year and serve on the board the year after that. This way everyone sees that hard work is rewarded and that it is the doers, not the talkers, who get promoted.

This system is especially good for organizations that want a diverse membership and leadership because it is a good way to overcome prejudice. In big cities prejudice may be manifested in ethnic or racial terms; in small towns it may be focused on who did or did not graduate from the local high school. In either case, one of the beauties of fundraising is every campaign has a measurable goal and measurable results, so you can quantify each volunteer's contribution to the organization.

If members are promoted because of what they *do* rather than who they *are,* everyone gets the same chance at leadership. So if someone says, "I don't want any short Irish people on the board—let's not nominate Joan," it is easy to reply, "She sold twice as many platinum memberships as anyone else on the committee. She has the commitment and the energy we want. She deserves to be nominated."

To make upward mobility work, there must be terms of office for the board of directors. After one or two terms of office, *every* member of the board has to rotate off the board and make room for new people. The best leaders can move up to serve at a state, national, or international level of your own organization or go on to use their skills in electoral politics.

PROFESSIONAL STAFF

Professional fundraisers are the unsung heroes of democracy. Money is power. Professionals who teach community leaders how to raise money are also empowering citizens to control their own destinies.

Fundraising staff need to be great trainers to give volunteers the skills and confidence they need to ask for money. Then they need to be great organizers to encourage the first successful leaders to find and train the next bigger and better set of leaders.

Ralph Waldo Emerson said, "The chief want in life is somebody who shall make us do the best we can." Your leaders *know* they should be building relationships with prospects, setting higher goals, and asking for larger gifts and bequests. But they always want to do it next week. It takes skilled staff to force volunteers to think big and be bold—now.

HOW TO HIRE A FUNDRAISER

Although the CEO and board members need to keep asking for money, if you want full-time, in-house professional help doing this work, hire a director of development. Ask similar charities for advice to write up a job description. Agree on your dollar goals before you advertise the job. Any stooge can help you raise "some money" or "more money," but a good professional can help you run an annual campaign for $300,000 or a capital campaign for $3,000,000.

As for any job, the best recruits come through the grapevine. Tell all your volunteers, employees, allies, funders, and friends that you are hiring a full-time fundraiser. Then advertise through the local chapter of the professional associations and their national journals (see the list at the end of this chapter), the fundraising trade press (see Chapter 14), your network's press, and the local newspapers. Be explicit about what you want and do not want, and budget enough money to hire a skilled person.

Your local chapter of the National Society of Fund-Raising Executives (NSFRE) or your United Way may have current salary and benefit data for local professional fundraisers. Ask the Chamber of Commerce for what the local for-profits pay sales and marketing staff.

If you are looking for a good professional fundraiser, the best people want more than money. In a recent NSFRE survey, only 6 percent of the fundraisers surveyed said they would change jobs for more money; almost 41 percent said they would change jobs because they want more challenge. So do not despair if you have a controversial organization or work in a tough neighborhood and need to hire a professional fundraiser. There may be people out there who think this job is just the challenge they want.

Unfortunately, at this time there are more good jobs than there are good professional fundraisers. If you cannot hire an experienced fundraiser, look at your current employees for talented people who would like the job. They already know the organization; now they can learn fundraising skills, too. If someone on the staff has impeccable integrity, a positive attitude, and good verbal and math skills, he or she could become a full-time fundraiser. New fundraisers can learn the ropes through membership in a professional association; being adopted by a mentor; cross-training with a similar organization; attending fundraising workshops and conventions; and reading fundraising, sales, and marketing books and magazines.

If you cannot hire a professional fundraiser or promote a current employee, consider putting an experienced volunteer on the payroll. Many volunteers do almost everything a professional fundraiser does, and they already have a network of contacts in your community. If the organization puts a volunteer on the payroll, that volunteer must resign any elected or appointed offices, including membership on the board of directors.

The last possibility for hiring a fundraiser is hiring someone with sales, marketing, or organizing experience and then retraining him or her to do fundraising. Most of the skills are transferrable, and all the fundraising skills can be learned.

CONSULTANTS

Your organization may also want to hire a consultant to work on a special assignment, such as direct mail, telemarketing, or a capital campaign. For more information on hiring a consultant, see Chapter 7.

VOLUNTEER/PROFESSIONAL DIVISION OF LABOR

Mother Teresa, founder of the Missionaries of Charity, met Bob Geldof, founder of Band Aid, in an airport in Ethiopia in 1985. She told him as she left, "Remember this. I can do something you can't do and you can do something I can't do. But we both have to do it."[12]

This could be your motto for dividing the fundraising work between the professionals and the volunteers. Work together to emphasize what each member of the team does best to guarantee fundraising success. Here are a few advantages and disadvantages of professionals and volunteers asking for money.

ADVANTAGES OF PROFESSIONALS ASKING FOR MONEY

- The biggest advantage is that professionals know a lot about the group and the programs. They are on duty at least forty hours a week. Most have terrific anecdotes to enliven your work.

- The professionals will have more know-how about fundraising itself. If your volunteers are bus drivers, doctors, cooks, or homemakers, they may be committed to the cause but naive about asking for money.

- It is in their own self-interest. The money will pay their salaries, so they will be motivated.

DISADVANTAGES OF PROFESSIONALS ASKING FOR MONEY

- Professional fundraisers will have more fundraising expertise, but they may lack first-hand knowledge of the programs, issues, or constituents.

- Nonprofit CEOs who need to raise money will have other demands on their time. If CEOs have to handle other program work or calamities during the day, they may not find time from nine to five to meet with corporate leaders in their offices or wealthy prospects in their homes.

- They may feel uncomfortable around rich people.
- They may feel uncomfortable asking the low-income clients.
- They may be reluctant to ask for their own salaries.
- There is a cost—their salaries. If paid employees ask for money, you can only count the net.
- If the professionals leave for any reason, some of the organization's contacts may leave, too.
- Control.

ADVANTAGES OF VOLUNTEERS ASKING FOR MONEY
- Volunteers are free. It is a labor of love.
- There can be more of them. Your volunteers can come from diverse backgrounds to allow the organization to reach many different economic, professional, geographic, racial, ethnic, religious, social, political, and civic networks.
- They can work for the largest employers in your community, with hundreds or thousands of co-workers.
- Some volunteers may have more time during the day.
- Volunteers can be more aggressive about asking for money for the staff's salaries and benefits.
- If volunteers raise the budget, the professionals become literally accountable to the elected leadership and constituents.
- Asking for money is the acid test of leadership. If volunteers do the fundraising you get an accurate measure of who cares the most about the organization.

DISADVANTAGES OF VOLUNTEERS ASKING FOR MONEY
- Fear and loathing about fundraising: they may hate doing it.
- Volunteers may lack fundraising know-how.
- They may lack expertise about your issues.
- Volunteers may not be dependable.
- Control.

HOW TO GET THE BEST FROM BOTH PROFESSIONALS AND VOLUNTEERS

Adjust these lists to fit your organization. Then talk about how you can maximize strengths and minimize weaknesses. For example, if the professionals have more fundraising know-how than the volunteers, could they offer some training for the volunteers? Or take a volunteer every time they go fundraising until the volunteer is ready to go alone? On the other hand, if the volunteers know community and business leaders with power and money, can they introduce them to the professionals? Or bring the prospects out to the next event so they can see the organization?

Note that one problem on two of the lists is control. Professionals and volunteers both need to face this problem and find a fair way to handle it. Otherwise, the professionals may want to write grant proposals rather than ask individuals for money and end up with programs the grant makers want rather than what your people want. Or the volunteers may not be willing to share the names of their best prospects, so the donors' allegiance is to a friend rather than to the organization.

A team of the senior staff and volunteer leaders can work together to set measurable goals and create a fundraising plan that uses everyone's strengths. Plan the teamwork so both professionals and volunteers give the best they can and help the other team members to improve their skills and contacts.

CALENDAR

The fundraising calendar is the best tool to guarantee a harmonious relationship between the volunteers and the professionals. If you plan your calendar a year in advance, everyone will get more results and feel better about the work, too.

If your organization is predominantly families with school-age children, plan the calendar in September when your members know the dates for school holidays and vacations. If your organization is active only part of the year, like the snowmobile club in the winter or Little League in the summer, plan the calendar two months before the busy season. For other organizations, plan the calendar the week after you elect new officers, so each leader has a say in the plan, or else in October for the next calendar year.

First, review the fundraising strategies you chose on the chart at the end of Chapter 2. Put the names of specific staff or volunteers by each part of your strategy. For example, let us say that your group plans to make $100,000 next year using these techniques and supervised by these people:

GOAL: $100,000

Source of Funds	Amount	Person Responsible
Dues	$30,000	Betty
Four mailings	15,000	Juanita
Corporate gifts	10,000	Tom
Foundation grants	10,000	Carlos
Major gifts	10,000	Hassan
Spring event	10,000	Jane
Fall event	10,000	Patrick
Local congregations	3,000	Frank
Sales	2,000	Viola

ONE JOB, ONE PERSON

In every case, one person has to be accountable for making the goal amount. "We" may all agree on the strategy, but one person makes each piece happen. Some things, like proposal writing, may be done easier by the professionals. Others, like special events, may be done better by the volunteers. As long as each volunteer and professional knows his or her goal, the plan can move forward.

Remember, real life goes on while you are making your plans, so the leaders will need to revise the plans based on what happens to their people. For example, in November Jane agreed to chair next year's spring event. Then her daughter got engaged at Christmas to be married in June, so Jane wants to spend next spring making dresses and resigns as the spring event chair.

Now the planners have several choices. They may

1. Find a new spring event chair and leave the plan as it is with a new person accountable for the goal.
2. Discover no one will volunteer to chair the spring event, but three people say they could work on the fall event. Cancel the spring event and double the goal for the fall event to $20,000.
3. Discover no one wants to lead the spring event, but two people want to start a new chapter in the next county. Cancel the spring event and raise the goal for dues to $40,000.
4. Discover no one wants to lead the spring event, and every other person is already stretching to make his or her projected goals. Take $10,000 out of the plan and meet with the officers and CEO to discuss which programs will need to be cut.

A fundraising plan never exists in a vacuum. Unless you can name a person responsible for each dollar amount, you do not have a plan. The CEO and the director of development cannot (and should not) raise the entire amount in the budget. It is their job to be sure that each person is clear on his or her goal and deadlines and that each person succeeds.

MAKING YOUR CALENDAR

This is where the actual calendar comes in. Get a copy of next year's calendar. They go on sale in office supply stores and catalogs in August for the next calendar year. Hand them out at a fundraising meeting and ask each leader and fundraising professional to think about what he or she wants to do next year. Discuss personal goals and ask them to discuss next year's calendar with their families. At the following meeting ask for commitments from volunteers and professionals. This way no one will feel pressured into taking a job and people can clear their assignments with their families. If Patrick discovers that his son will be the starting quarterback for the football team next year, he will not volunteer to chair the fall event. If the son is going out for track in the spring, fall will be a good time for Patrick.

This is also a good time to ask the leaders to commit to a gift. How much are they going to give and in what form— weekly cash gifts, a monthly pledge, or one check? Ask the leaders what kind of help each one wants from the professionals and *exactly* when that will be needed. This will save the paid staff from those nightmare days when twelve board members call with an emergency that needs to be handled first.

Schedule vacations. Time off is mandatory for stressful jobs, and asking for money every day is stressful. Depending on your organization, try to take off at least one month with no fundraising meetings at all. August is ideal for most groups since the corporate and foundation people are unreachable, volunteers are on vacation and getting the kids ready for school, and the professionals want a vacation, too. In December schedule a holiday party but skip meetings except for important major donor visits to get year-end gifts.

PLAN AHEAD

The calendar can make your life easier by giving you the lead time you need. For example, Margaret Lauderback is the event director for the Galveston Historical Foundation's festival "Dickens on the Strand" that grosses half a million dollars for the foundation and produces a total of $12 million for the county. The event is always the first weekend in December; Lauderback says 75 percent of the decisions are made by July. All of the cooperating groups and financial sponsors sign on in July. This enables the foundation staff to write the brouchure in August and have it ready in September.

Margaret Lauderback says her goal is to have everything completed two weeks before the event, so the last two weeks can be spent "putting out fires." Anyone who has organized major events knows you spend most of the last week fixing things you thought were already taken care of. By planning ahead and enforcing deadlines, you get a more professional and successful event, and you give yourself the time to do everything well.

The Galveston event requires about six thousand volunteers. You can get that scale of participation only if everyone knows *you* know what you are doing. Planning months in advance allows the undependable people to be weeded out of the process, too. I was in Calgary in May 1987, before the city hosted the 1988 Winter Olympics. The daughter of the workshop coordinator was fussing because she had to go to a costume fitting for one of the opening pageants and could not understand why she had to try on clothes in May for an event in February. Her mother patiently explained that if the daughter missed this fitting she would not get to be in the show. No wonder all the volunteer pageants looked so terrific at the Calgary Olympics. All the unreliable people had opted out of the process eight months before the event. By the time they got to the dress rehearsals, only the most dependable people were left. If you hate pruning out deadwood from your volunteers, use your calendar and enforce volunteer deadlines so the lazy people will eliminate themselves early.

THE CEO

Money is the oxygen that keeps the organization alive. Money must be the top-priority item in any work plan and at every staff meeting. Every nonprofit CEO must commit at least one half of his or her time to fundraising. More is better but probably not realistic. If the boss is not spending at least 20 hours a week on fundraising, you should reassign work, hire more program staff, recruit committed volunteers, or reduce the programs.

To make sure that the CEO focuses on fundraising first, ask him or her to fundraise every day from 9:00 A.M. until noon. Is this realistic? Yes—if you choose to make fundraising your priority.

Fundraiser John Pruehs tells about when he was working for the Rockford, Illinois, YMCA. Every time he came in the morning to see CEO George Brening, Brening was out—with a prospect. He used breakfast, lunch, and special events to tell the key people in town about the Y and its plans. Of course Brening did not ask for money at every meeting. But the end result was that when the Y needed money for a special campaign, the right people were not strangers to the Y and its plans. At a time that the Rockford economy was in trouble, Brening built up the Y to be one of the largest YMCA facilities in the country; in a town with a population of 100,000, some 25,000 people were members.

As John Pruehs says, "Brening was a genius at time management. He was always out of the building by 4:30 P.M. and virtually never had to work nights or weekends. Because he focused on fundraising and cultivation the first thing every day, he had the funds he needed to get the best staff, facilities, and programs."

If you are the CEO and you are tired of cranking out proposals by the light of the moon, discipline yourself to put fundraising first every day. Put it first on every agenda. Include money, or at least what the money will buy, somewhere in every conversation with the key players in your community.

NEVER WORK ALONE

Although it is vital that the top staff person commit to asking for money, he or she should never have a monopoly on asking. It is always tempting to say, "George is really good at fundraising: he knows all the right people, he says the right things. Let's get George to do it all."

A single fundraiser makes for a dangerously fragile organization. If the boss leaves by fate, force, or choice, all the fundraising contacts leave, too. We can all name tragic examples of good organizations that collapsed when the Lone Fundraiser left. One example was the National Welfare Rights Organization (NWRO), an aggressive outfit that fought for economic justice for welfare recipients. Almost all of NWRO's money was raised by the charismatic founder, George Wiley. From 1966 to 1972 he raised more than $3 million from a variety of foundations, churches, and wealthy individuals. Wiley drowned in 1972; the organization was virtually out of business in eighteen months.[13]

THE FUNDRAISING TEAM

Volunteering or working for a worthwhile nonprofit organization will give you many tangible rewards. One reason people *like* to do fundraising is that you can see measurable results quickly. In addition, you and everyone on the team will know that your hard work asking for money is what makes everything else possible.

But even more than the money raised, or all the good things the money can buy, is the reward of working with fine people who care deeply about their community. The qualities you seek in your fundraising volunteers and professionals— integrity, sincerity, leading by example, courage, and persistence—are the qualities that make the fundraisers such a pleasure to work with. Beyond the cold hard cash is the warm feeling of doing good work with people who can see beyond the bottom line.

PROFESSIONAL ASSOCIATIONS

Every professional fundraiser can join the national professional organizations listed at the end of this chapter. Become active on a committee in your local chapter and ask for a mentor. If there is no chapter in your community, join the state group or the national organization to receive its publications and job notices. Or ask the nearest chapter and the national membership office to help you organize a chapter in your town.

Membership in your local professional association will force you to expand your thinking about money. I work with some groups where $50 is a big gift and $1,000 is a cause for champagne at the board meeting. So it really helps me to attend my local NSFRE meetings, where I have heard a Stanford University professional fundraiser whose full-time job is asking for gifts of $5 million or more, a consultant whose client persuaded one woman to give $4.3 million for an alcohol treatment center, and a University of Chicago volunteer who said that it was "fun" getting a million-dollar gift from another alum over lunch. If you work in a low-income community, the chances of getting a million-dollar gift may seem like flying to the moon. However, if you hear these stories every month, you will soon realize that your cause is just as worthwhile as theirs is, and you can ask for bigger gifts just as they can. At the very least you will stop saying that no one ever gives more than ten bucks.

PROFESSIONAL ASSOCIATIONS FOR FUNDRAISERS

All of these offer a written code of ethics, a membership directory, excellent publications, training, local and international conferences, mentor programs, research on giving trends and salaries, and employment services. Call the national office to locate your local chapter.

For Every Professional Fundraiser: NSFRE

National Society of Fund Raising Executives (NSFRE), 1101 King St., Suite 3000, Alexandria, VA 22314; 703/684-0410. Dues: $150 a year for national and $25 to $75 for local chapters. Open to all professional fundraisers, NSFRE offers local networking, continuing education programs, an international conference, and job notices.

ASSOCIATIONS ORGANIZED BY EMPLOYER

For Education Fundraisers: CASE

Council for Advancement and Support of Education (CASE), Suite 400, 11 Dupont Circle, Washington, DC 20036; 202/328-5973 (membership department). Voting membership is by school rather than individual; dues are based on number of students. If you work for an American or Canadian nonprofit elementary or secondary school, college, or university, your institution's membership in CASE gives you support specialized for the work you do. CASE also runs the National Clearinghouse for Corporate Matching Gift Information.

For Hospital and Health Care Fundraisers: AHP

Association for Healthcare Philanthropy (AHP), 313 Park Ave., Suite 400, Falls Church, VA 22046; 703/532-6243. Dues: $350 a year for active members. (Formerly called the National Association for Hospital Development, NAHD.) Helpful development advice; as regional director Eileen Kennedy says, "We don't plagiarize—we share."

For Large Fundraising Firms: AAFRC

American Association of Fund-Raising Counsel, Inc. (AAFRC), 25 W. 43rd St., Suite 1519, New York, NY 10036; 212/354-5799.

Dues: 1.2 percent of annual billings. Has published *Giving U.S.A.* every year since 1955 to track philanthropy from individuals, bequests, corporations, and foundations.

ASSOCIATIONS ORGANIZED BY PROFESSIONAL SPECIALTY

For Direct-Mail/Marketing Professionals

Association of Direct Response Fundraising Counsel (ADFRC), 1501 Broadway, Suite 610, New York, NY 10036; 212/354-7150. Annual dues range from $200 to $3,000 based on the number of employees in the member firm. Association of direct-mail businesses, vendors, and consultants; no nonprofit members. Publishes a list of direct-mail firms that follow its code of ethics and a free brochure to introduce direct mail.

For Planned-Giving Professionals

The National Committee on Planned Giving (NCPG), 550 W. North St., Suite 304, Indianapolis, IN 46202; 317/684-8918. Dues: $15 per capita per council. Planned-giving professionals in forty-three U.S. cities have formed local councils for support and professional growth. In 1987 these councils and two national groups, the Council of Jewish Federation Endowment Professionals and the United Way Planned-Giving Council, formed a national organization, the NCPG, to assist fundraisers who specialize in planned giving and other professionals such as lawyers, accountants, and financial planners.

For Prospect Researchers

American Prospect Research Association (APRA), Membership Director, 1600 Wilson Blvd., Suite 905, Arlington, VA 22209. Annual Dues: $50.00. Begun in 1988 to promote professional prospect researchers in the U.S. and Canada, APRA members work to oppose government censorship, maintain confidentiality of private information, and improve standard reference sources.

"Dream, diversify, and never miss an angle."

—*Walt Disney, 1958*[1]

Special Events

Special events, also known as benefits or galas, are among the most popular fundraising strategies. The organization sells tickets to a party, concert, dinner, dance, or other event and adds on a margin of profit. Unlike asking for donations to support the mission of your organization, selling benefit tickets requires only that you sell the event itself.

Events have been the backbone of successful fundraising for centuries. The premier performance of G. F. Handel's great oratorio *Messiah* was a benefit in Dublin in 1742 for "relief of the prisoners in several gaols, and for the support of Mercer's Hospital in Stephen's Street, and for the Charitable Infirmary on the Inn's Quay."[2] Demand for tickets was so high that sponsors tried to make more space by asking ladies to attend without hoops under their skirts and gentlemen to attend without their swords. Altogether seven hundred people heard this performance of the *Messiah*, which raised £400 for the charities. It was fitting that this money paid for the release of 142 debtors from prison, since the Messiah came to free the prisoners.

Although it was Handel's most popular work, during his lifetime he never made money from the *Messiah*; it was always performed as a benefit. The next year in London, it was per-

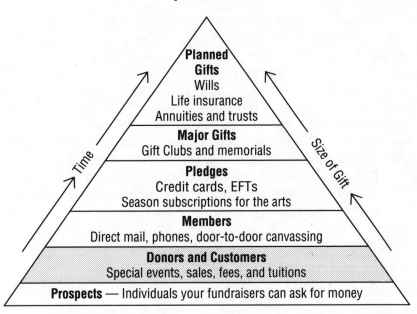

formed at Westminster Abbey. Some historians say that King George II was so swept away by the "Hallelujah Chorus" that he stood up and caused everyone else to stand up too. This created a tradition that lives on today in the thousands of *Messiah* benefit concerts and sing-alongs that raise money every December in English-speaking countries around the world.

Special events are a great fundraising strategy for beginners because your own people already know how to stage them. Many Americans have masterminded special events since they were teenagers. Anybody who organized the Junior Prom, the family reunion, or the office Christmas party can organize a special event for you. Especially if your organization is new, without a track record, it often seems easier to sell tickets to a party than to ask for donations.

In the same way, selling products or services allows your volunteers to use skills they already have to make money for your organization. Almost anyone can sell T-shirts, crafts, or cookbooks. Customers get a tangible product and volunteers get easy sales. Any group can start small and work up to bigger profits.

Special events and sales are positioned at the bottom of the fundraising pyramid. They are a good way to introduce new people to your organization, the transactions are quick, and the amount of money changing hands is relatively small. Since some people want to do events and sales anyway, ask your committee to be intentional about your plans. How can you make money and advance your program at the same time? How can you make this the *first* contact with each person, so you can work systematically to turn customers into donors?

This chapter will discuss special events. For more information on selling products and fees for service, see Chapter 12, "Business Partners and Business Ventures."

CONNECT TO YOUR MISSION

What makes a special event special? Many things: the people, the place, the theme, or the price. But what makes a special event truly special—different from a normal party—is the cause.

The best special events link the mission of the organization to the way they raise money. It is not enough to have a novel or swanky party. It must also harmonize with the mission of the organization. If your community organization is concerned about neighborhood safety, sponsor a Halloween party in a safe place with good supervision. If you want to promote your ethnic heritage, throw a Cinco de Mayo fiesta or a Chinese New Year's Day parade. The Audubon Society sells birdseed and celebrates the bird feeder season at their party called the "Suet Ball."

In 1988 a group of young teens in the Cabrini-Green public housing project in Chicago decided they wanted to go to Disney World in Florida. Some kids said Disney World was "only for rich people," but led by Rochelle Satchell, coordinator of group activities for the Near North Health Services Corporation, thirty-three kids decided they could go, too. So they washed cars every Saturday for two months, held a carnival and bake sale, and sold raffle tickets. They held a "grade-a-thon" collecting pledges for every A or B grade they earned; in June they collected $1,000. Altogether they raised $8,200 in one of the poorest neighborhoods in America.

The purpose of the Health Services program is to help the younger siblings of pregnant teenagers avoid pregnancy, drugs, and gangs. Coordinator Satchell used the fundraising and the trip to build up good work habits, good attitudes, and high hopes in the teenagers. They learned they could set a high goal and achieve it.

On the trip home, Satchell planted in their brains the seed of an even bigger goal. They stopped to visit Morehouse College, a predominantly black school in Atlanta, where they could see students arriving for the first day of college. She wanted them to imagine doing the same thing themselves. In 1991, three of her group will enter college.

ADVANTAGES OF SPECIAL EVENTS

Special events are fun. This plus should not be underestimated. Especially if your organization is controversial, special events help produce the glue that holds the group together during the rocky times.

FUN

Remember, fun is in the eye of the beholders. The Vermont Food Bank received $1,000 in 1988 from the receipts of a food fight organized at Taste of Vermont. For an entry fee of $25, teams of four wore bull's-eye targets and threw lard at each other. The winning team got to face off with the actors who played Larry, Darryl, and Darryl on the popular TV show "Newhart." Most of the teams were sponsored by corporations; they had a wonderful time and made the front page of the biggest newspaper in Vermont.

Special events are not meetings. Any volunteer knows the Seven Last Words could be "we have to get through the agenda." Special events give you a chance to discuss all the things that are *not* on the agenda: families, friends, sports, fashion, hobbies. Those who attend get to meet new people as well as the families of colleagues. I've seen a lot of romances bloom and babies grow up year to year at the great special events in town.

PUBLICITY

They are also an opportunity for good press. The biggest special event of all time, the 1985 Band Aid concert from London and Philadelphia, received a worldwide audience for sixteen hours and raised $117 million.

You can use an event strategically to counter a criticism of your agency. For example, a health counseling center for teenagers wanted to raise money and raise the community's awareness of the need for its services. Despite the county's soaring teenage pregnancy rate, the most frequent criticism of the program was that the counselors discussed sex and contraceptives with the teenagers. Their critics said that only families should tell their own children about safe sex; no outsider should interfere.

So the organization decided to turn a negative into a positive. It used this criticism as the basis for its annual walkathon and designed an event called "Walking and Talking." As in any walkathon, the money was raised from pledges per mile walked. The special twist was that the walkers were mother/daughter or father/son teams, who could discuss the problems of dating, peer pressures, and safe sex at the same time they raised money for the counseling service.

HELPING THE ORGANIZATION MANAGE ITSELF
Special events give the organization many ways to test the leadership. Sales can be traced, so you know who is really selling, as opposed to just talking. Special events also are good for morale.

REACHING OUT
Benefits allow you to reach beyond your own people for support. Especially in low- and middle-income communities, there are only so many times you can ask your own people to give. Benefits allow the general public to support the cause.

They meet a social need. Especially in rural communities, the nonprofit groups may provide the best dances, art shows, movies, lectures, sports events, and parties.

Multiple events can reach multiple constituencies. For example, most of the supporters of the United Negro College Fund's Lou Rawls' "Parade of Stars" telethon are black women. So UNCF has organized a series of celebrity sports events to reach men—such as the Magic Johnson "Midsummer Night's Magic" black-tie dinner for the middle-income, middle-management crowd, and the Michael Jordan and Bryant Gumbel golf tournaments to reach white, affluent corporate men. The 1989 results: Magic's party netted $800,000; Jordan's tournament, $117,000; Gumbel's $53,000.[3]

BRINGING PEOPLE OUT

Good events serve as an antidote to "cocooning," the term sociologists use for the growing trend of Americans to spend more time at home. Nonprofits can use benefits to meet the needs of lonely people. Events can get them away from staring at videotapes and into meeting real people.

More importantly, some experts such as Curtis Gans say cocooning helps explain why people do not even bother to vote. "We're becoming spectators, consumers. People are not being invited into communities." Special events are one effective way literally to invite people into your community. In a *Rolling Stone* poll that asked what it would take to get them involved in public affairs, eighteen- to forty-four-year-olds listed local personal events, not general issues. One-third said they could be mobilized to battle drunk drivers, and another third said they would join a neighborhood crime watch.

In the same poll of eighteen- to forty-four-year-olds, only one-half of this group said they vote regularly, and only one-third said they follow the news. Since these are the people you need to be tomorrow's leaders and donors, get them out of the house and into your organization. The first step can be unique special events.

For example, in 1981 five of us threw together an all-night party at my small Episcopal church to watch the royal wedding of Prince Charles and Lady Diana Spencer. Two hundred people in the church watched the wedding live from St. Paul's Cathedral on wide-screen TV, sang "God Save the Queen," went to Mass with prayers for the royal family, ate a big English breakfast, then left for work. In the short run we received great press coverage (Chicago dailies and television, cable TV, and Associated Press), had a great time, and netted $250.

Although the income from the party itself was small, it was one of a series of events that helped the church attract fifty-nine new members in a year. Since the average annual pledge is now more than $1,000, the long-range payoff is much higher. Statistics show that 70 to 80 percent of a church's members join because somebody *asks* them; only 7 to 8 percent wander in on their own. Novel events give your members an easy way to invite their family, friends, and co-workers to check you out before they join.

COMMUNITY PROFITS

The value of a good community-based special event will be multiplied beyond the dollars that go to the sponsor. A successful special event can bring in new people with fresh money for food, gasoline, services, and souvenirs.

Every December the Galveston (Texas) Historical Foundation sponsors a Victorian Christmas Celebration called "Dickens on the Strand" (both Galveston and London have a street named the Strand). This festival began eighteen years ago as a thank-you party for volunteers. In 1990, the two-day festival grossed $500,000 for the foundation itself from tickets, tea parties, house tours, the Victorian Costume Ball, and other money makers. The event also provided a great opportunity for other Galveston charities to raise money, so the County Historical Museum presented a "Forest of Christmas Trees," the Trinity Episcopal Church offered an organ recital, and the Ronald McDonald House sponsored a five-kilometer "Run Like the Dickens." The projected economic impact for the entire community (both for-profits and nonprofits) was $12 million.

DISADVANTAGES OF SPECIAL EVENTS

On the downside, special events are labor-intensive.

* They can lose money.
* They can take staff time away from programs.
* They can take fundraisers' time away from asking for individual gifts. One reason volunteers love to do events is they can put off asking for contributions face to face. If possible, try to do both.
* They may distract major donors from considering larger gifts.
* Benefits bring in benefit customers, not members or donors.
* They always exclude someone. High-priced events exclude poor people. Dances exclude people who do not like to

dance. Casino nights exclude people who disapprove of gambling. The only way to include everyone is simply to ask for money. Anyone can give you money, but not everyone can play golf, shoot turkeys, or run five kilometers.

FOCUS

If your *only* goal is to raise money, ask for money. Do not even think about doing a special event.

On the other hand, if your goals include testing the leaders, generating publicity, finding new members, having fun, *and* making money, then by all means consider a special event. Set measurable goals whenever you can, and have a ball!

HOW TO CHOOSE THE RIGHT SPECIAL EVENT

The right event is the one your organization's people *want* to do. Your own leaders already have some ideas from other parties they have attended for other charities. Recruit new people as they move in and bring fresh ideas. If your delegates hear about a terrific idea at the national convention, budget money to send two people to train with the other chapter, and then produce a similar event in your community. Some national organizations publish helpful how-to manuals, such as the American Red Cross's booklet *Be Special—In Any Event!*, which tells its chapters how to do a Swim-A-Cross and other events.

As your group members consider possible benefit ideas, ask them to think about the best dates, prices, and the way the ideas connect to your mission.

CALENDAR

Plan your special events at least a year in advance to get the most ideas and the best volunteers. What are the holidays and events that people celebrate anyway, and how can you use them to spice up your fundraising calendar?

For example, the Zoo Society of the Lincoln Park Zoo in Chicago sponsors an elegant ball near Bastille Day in July that was called "Zoo La La" for France's bicentennial and "Red, White and Zoo" for America's bicentennial. In the summer it puts on a gigantic member picnic; in the fall it offers the Spoo-kyZoo spectacular so 30,000 kids can show off their costumes and have safe fun; in December it sponsors carolling to the animals; and in January it hosts a few hundred football fans on ZooperBowl Sunday in the newly restored 1912 landmark Cafe Brauer.

Christmas and Hanukkah are especially good for selling products. For example, the Hinsdale (Illinois) Humane Society sells holiday cards in sets of thirteen (a "barker's dozen") for $6. They also run "Santa Paws," a chance to have your pet's photo taken with Santa Claus for $12.

The Johnson City (Texas) Chamber of Commerce "lit up" its historic courthouse with more than 100,000 Christmas lights, creating a county-wide tourist attraction to cheer residents and build traffic for local merchants. They sold necklaces for $5 made from Christmas tree lights, an attractive way to make money and promote the courthouse project at the same time.

What date fits best with your group's mission? For example, the Illinois Committee for Control of Handguns sponsors its big dinner every year on Abraham Lincoln's birthday, February 12, because it is a state holiday anyway and the Great Emancipator was assassinated with a handgun. Volunteer fire departments schedule the Fireman's Ball during Fire Prevention Week in October. A project for disabled children used Groundhog Day and asked people to "bring light to the lives of handicapped children."

Use people's normal party patterns. Thirty-nine percent of families eat out on Mother's Day; 24 percent eat out on Father's Day. If you schedule a breakfast or dinner on one of those Sundays, you know you can draw a crowd. Any group can find an occasion for a party in *Chase's Annual Events*, the world's greatest collection of special days, weeks, months, historical anniversaries, and celebrities' birthdays. For order information, see Chapter 14.

Competition for a good date can make you crazy. In some communities multiple fundraisers take place every Saturday night of the year. In New York City there are competing black-tie galas on week nights, and this trend is spreading to other large cities. Some charities "own" certain holidays. It is futile to try to program an event on Valentine's Day if the Heart Association has done its Sweetheart Ball on February 14 for the past fifty years.

Call around and find out when the major competition will be. Big hospitals, cultural groups, and associations for diseases may plan their events a year or two in advance. Many communities have some central clearinghouse for benefit dates; it may be the newspaper, the Junior League, or another organization. Also check with the local and state arts councils, the convention and tourism bureau, and the major political parties. Ask a sports fan for important national and international sporting events, and never underestimate the zeal of sports fans.

Ask your leaders for dates of school vacations, graduation, and significant events in their own lives, such as weddings and anniversaries. Do not schedule your biggest event in June if the event chair is planning her daughter's wedding that month, or a New Year's Eve party if your president's son will be the quarterback at this year's Rose Bowl game.

Even after all these precautions, you can still face competition. In 1988 I cleared the dates for the Horizon Hospice 10th Anniversary Gala in Chicago and found a Saturday night on which no other major charities were having an event. So we booked the big ballroom at a fancy hotel. Unfortunately, I was not the only genius to find the "perfect Saturday," so we ended up with another charity having a party right next door in the smaller ballroom. Learning from this, in 1989 we decided to have the party in an exciting new retail and museum space built into an old river warehouse called North Pier. Since the developer made special arrangements for us to be there, we knew there would not be another group next door.

There is a great advantage to choosing a date that connects to your mission and making it your "own" through repetition, enthusiastic sales, and skillful public relations. Then the rest of the community can plan around your date, rather than vice versa.

However, any negative can be a positive. When the benefit committee of the St. Mary of the Plains Hospital Foundation in Lubbock, Texas, tried to find a date for a gala, the committee members discovered all the Saturday nights were taken by bigger charities and every Saturday afternoon was devoted to college football, an activity that in Texas reaches the heights of a religious experience. So they got creative and decided to use Saturday morning. They sent out a poster-size invitation in New Orleans colors inviting people to a "Breakfast at Brennan's with the Preservation Hall Jazz Band."

The breakfast was novel and made just as much profit as the nighttime parties. It also allowed everyone to support a good cause and still get to the football game on time. St. Mary of the Plains attracted the usual benefit crowd who wanted to be part of a unique event, as well as all the morning people who had never seen an evening socializer. All in all, it was a great way to turn a negative into a positive.

REPEAT

As long as an event is making money, it is best to keep repeating it, so it becomes an important part of the members', the organization's, and the community's calendar. There is a learning curve to starting a new event, so it is best to repeat the event at least three years.

The first year is a learning year; your profits will be lower because your expenses are higher as you learn which vendors and volunteers are the most dependable. Consider the higher expenses as tuition to learn how to do the best event. Keep meticulous records, and ruthlessly evaluate every piece of your event, every vendor, and every idea (especially your own). Prune out the losers, and pump up the profit makers.

Be sure everyone on the fundraising team knows that it will take more than a year to develop a great fundraising event. Otherwise it is easy to get discouraged and give in to the people who say, often correctly from a one-year sample, "This is too much work for too little money." As Clifford Swick, the "Sage of Saratoga," says, "Fools and children judge half-done work." Give every event at least three years to become an efficient money maker.

Solving your first-year problems will often be the key to future success. An arts group in New Hampshire scheduled a concert series in December and January, but every concert was snowed out. The intrepid fundraisers scheduled a new series for February and March and billed them as the "Cabin-Fever Concerts." Their market was eager for any diversion after spending the bleak midwinter indoors, so the concerts have become a dependable money maker.

The second year, you can expect to double your profits; then the growth of the event will mirror the growth of the organization. For example, "run, jane, run" in Fort Wayne, Indiana, began with three athletic events and now features sixteen events, including a dance and a dinner, as well as competitive athletics. The event's profits went up more than 800 percent in nine years, from $10,000 in 1981 to $86,000 in 1990. Through careful evaluation, the Fort Wayne Women's Bureau learned which events, such as basketball, did not work, and took them out. Now they have an event that is connected to their mission and produces a dependable profit, around $85,000 every year.

The ideal system for a big event is to have selected next year's date and chairs before this year's event. That way the 1993 people can intern under the 1992 chairs and learn the ropes. At the big event, you can announce the chairs for next year and put their names in the program. Then the new chairs can get right to work the day after this year's party, and everyone knows whom to call with any good ideas. This system also creates someone with a self-interest to do the nagging to get this year's reports written and turned in.

Some organizations also announce how much money they made at the event itself. You can do this if it fits in with the style of your audience. Other groups do not mention the event total at the party itself, but will include it in the newsletter article and all the "you did a fabulous job!" thank-you notes to the workers and big donors.

PRICE

No matter what price you set, several people will tell you it is too high. Be sure to test this. First, ask everyone on the committee to buy four tickets. If none of your own people will buy tickets at this price, they are not going to sell them either. Change to a less fancy, less expensive event.

In most cases, take complaints about money with a grain of salt. Often a higher-priced ticket is easier to sell. Because people have a consumer mentality, most people think that the more something costs, the better it will be.

CASE STUDY: RUN, JANE, RUN

**run,
jane,run.**

*Since 1976, the Fort Wayne Women's Bureau has been enabling
women and their families to get better jobs, improve their mental
and physical health, and fight prejudice. In 1981 the Bureau's staff
and leaders came up with an idea for a special event to encourage
more women and girls to participate in sports. They called the
event "run, jane, run" to combat the stereotype taught in the old*
Dick and Jane *books, where the boy was told, "Run, Dick, run!"
and the girl was told, "Look, Jane, look. Look at Dick run!"*

*The stereotype of "the weaker sex" is still prevalent in athlet-
ics, although out of date. At the 1928 Olympics, the women's 800-
meter track race was eliminated after many of the women collapsed on the field from exhaustion. Today, only 14.6 seconds
separate the men's and women's Olympic records.* The Fort
Wayne Women's Bureau decided it was time to highlight all the
ways women of all ages are active athletes.*

*In 1981 the Bureau sponsored a run, an award dinner for a
woman athlete, and a rematch of the Fort Wayne Daisies and the
Kalamazoo Lassies, two of the professional women's baseball
teams in the All-American Girls Professional Baseball League
created by frugal Philip K. Wrigley in 1942. He wanted to fill
Wrigley Field and the other ballparks during World War II when
most of the able-bodied male baseball players were in the service.*

*Blythe Hamer, "Less may be more for women," *Chicago Tribune*, March 16,
1986.

With coaching by Jimmy Foxx and "charm" by Helena Ruben-
stein, the women pros filled the parks until, like Rosie the Rivet-
er, they were replaced by the men after the war.

The Fort Wayne Women's Bureau brought back the professional women baseball stars to play a game and tell their stories.
They were so good the story got picked up by Sports Illustrated,
and in 1988 artifacts from the professional women's league were
included in a permanent exhibit at the National Baseball Hall of
Fame in Cooperstown, New York.

This is the perfect event. It is fun, it makes money, and it
promotes the mission of the organization: the well-being and self-
esteem of women. The Bureau also makes an effort to be inclusive
by staging events for men and women, young and old, jocks and
brains. "run, jane, run" now features sixteen events, including a
dance, wheelchair races, Scrabble tournament, golf, and bowling.
Also, a dinner features great athletes like Willye White, the only
American female athlete to qualify for five consecutive Olympic
teams; golfer Carol Mann; marathon swimmer Diana Nyad; and
legendary track star Wilma Rudolph. In addition to tickets and
T-shirts, the Bureau also sells lots of advertising. As with the
Olympics, it gets major sponsors for each event: Fort Wayne
Cardiology sponsors racquetball, ITT Aerospace sponsors volley-
ball, and Central Soya sponsors the aerobics workout. In the first
nine years, "run, jane, run" generated $580,000 for the Fort
Wayne Women's Bureau and gave 23,000 amateur women athletes
a chance to compete.

Having hit on a good idea, in 1984 the Bureau created a new
nonprofit organization to recruit, train, and assist other women's
centers to replicate this event. The new organization, run, jane,
run, inc., trademarked the name and logo, and franchised the
event to other cities. Then the organizers looked for a national
corporate sponsor to underwrite the national expansion plan.

In 1990 run, jane, run, inc. received $150,000 from the Lin-
coln National Group and K&K Insurance Group to be the official
national sponsors of "run, jane, run." Administrative Manager
Carla Trzynka says this funding will enable the event to grow into
Cleveland; Denver; Grand Rapids, Michigan; South Bend, Indiana; and Tulsa, Oklahoma. Today "run, jane, run" is the largest
amateur women's sports competition in the United States.

How to Price the Tickets

Set a basic price for tickets and a special higher price to find major donor prospects. If you ask for more, you will get more. For example, the regular ticket price for the Houston Red Cross's New Year's Eve M*A*S*H Bash is $150. However, for $7,500 you can be the "Joint Chiefs of Staff" and get a whole table.

Let's say you've planned a picnic and softball game in the park for a low-priced family event. Basic tickets are $5. Your categories could be:

Rookie	$ 5
Designated Hitter	10
All-Star	25
Free Agent	100
Hall of Famer	1,000

Most people will still pay you $5 or $10, but you will always get one or two pleasant surprises in the larger categories. Then you can begin to cultivate those people for larger gifts, too.

Make up names for different price categories that reflect your mission. The public-interest law firm BPI uses a knight as its logo to represent the firm's tradition of fighting for the forgotten and defenseless in the courts. At BPI's 1990 Law Day dinner, which netted $150,000, donors could support BPI as one of the following:

Category	Price	Tickets
Saint	$10,000	10 or more
Knight	5,000	10 or more
Good Samaritan	2,500	10 or more
Hero	1,500	10
Squire	1,000	8
Salt-of-the-Earth	500	4
True Friend	250	2

Any group can use the tried-and-true category names such as benefactor, contributor, sustainer, patron, or donor.

WHAT RESOURCES DO YOUR PEOPLE HAVE?

Look at what you have, not at what you lack. One woman at a New York City workshop complained repeatedly how hard it was to raise money in her town, since it had only eight thousand residents. I was feeling sorry for her. When the time came to describe her benefit, she told about the string quartet she had play in her home. I asked, "How many people can you fit in your home?" She said, "Well, only a hundred in the living room, so I put the overflow in the dining room." It turned out she lived in one of the most expensive, exclusive towns on the East Coast, in a historic mansion. The neighbors on her block alone could easily have funded the entire budget.

Who has an interest in your cause? This is the best way to involve celebrities and corporate and civic leaders. For example, *Washington Post* fashion editor Nina Hyde, who has been diagnosed with breast cancer herself, has zealously raised money to fight the disease. So far she has raised more than $1 million from high-fashion designers such as Oscar de la Renta, whose wife died of breast cancer, and Donna Karan, whose mentor Anne Klein died of the same disease, as well as Ralph Lauren and many other donors.[4]

COMPLAINTS

After your committee has researched local events, interviewed the fundraisers, found a good date, set the prices, and come up with a great theme, someone will still complain. In fact, no matter what you do, someone will complain. One of the jobs of the benefit committee chairs is to handle complaints and keep everyone else on track selling tickets.

Complaints are a part of human nature, and they always happen. In 1784 King George III (an ardent Handel fan) decided to bring back the *Messiah* for the Centennial of Handel's birth. (The real centennial was 1785, but the King was enthusiastic, so his people did it early to keep him happy.) The King's committee put together a gigantic benefit concert in Westminster Abbey, and people complained about the presenting of popular anthems in the *church*.

Later, choral groups on the continent complained the music was too dull, so someone hired Mozart to punch it up a little. His version was used in the German town of Halle, Handel's birthplace. Halle did not get around to commemorating the composer's birthday centennial until 1803, because Germans complained that the English had hogged all the glory in 1784. If you go to Halle today, you can see the statue of Handel built with money raised at a benefit concert of the *Messiah* in 1857 featuring the "Swedish Nightingale," Jenny Lind.[5] You just know that someone complained that they should have let the nice soprano from the local chorus do the solos, instead of some foreigner who was not even *from* Halle.

CORPORATIONS AND SPECIAL EVENTS

Some corporations like to underwrite entire special events so they can reach the people who will attend the event. If you're lucky, get some competition going. For example, when Bloomingdale's department store opened in Chicago in 1988, it invited people to pay $225 each to preview the new store as a fundraiser for the Chicago Symphony Orchestra. Bloomie's underwrote all the expenses; the orchestra netted $440,000. Across the street, Chicago's own Marshall Field's sponsored an even more elegant party for only $175 a ticket to show off its newly redecorated Water Tower Place store and benefit the Lyric Opera of Chicago. Field's covered all the costs; the Lyric Opera netted $170,000.

Sometimes companies will buy a block of tickets and use them as incentives for top employees. Other companies use a participatory event, like the March of Dimes walkathon WalkAmerica as a way to get everyone from the mailroom to the executive suite out together for a good cause. The 1990 WalkAmerica made $51 million.

Unfortunately, some corporate donors really hate getting asked for special events. Business leaders get deluged with invitations; they could easily attend a dozen events every night in a big city. What we think is a fun event they see as *work*.

So be careful. If you are asking corporate leaders to support your benefit, make the event truly special, relate it to your mission, and make it more fun than work. No long programs, no guilt, and no preaching. Even better, simply ask for money.

TAXES

Since 1987, the Internal Revenue Service has issued much more explicit rules for the language and arithmetic charities must use to inform your donors of how much money they may legally deduct from their taxable income. Now the charity is responsible for informing the donor exactly what amount goes for the party and what amount goes to the cause itself. So, for example, if the value of the party is $50 a head and the ticket is $150, then the donor may legally deduct $100. The charity needs to say that on the invitation.

For more information on your organization's responsibilities for informing its donors, order IRS Publication 1391, "Deductibility of Payments Made to Charities Conducting Fund-Raising Events," or call the IRS Hotline on Fundraising at 202/343-8900.

On the following page is an example of the inside of the business-reply envelope for the gala benefit sponsored by the wives of the Cubs baseball team for the Family Rescue shelter for women and their children. See how they make it easy to buy gala or raffle tickets, offer donors the option of charging the cost to their credit card, and suggest they bring their credit card so they can bid at the auction. The phone number was for a voice mailbox that collects messages without tying up anybody's work phone or revealing anyone's home phone. Note that this form puts in writing the exact dollar amount that is tax-deductible.

ETHICS

Ethically, you must always be very careful to separate your customers and your members. It is dishonest to claim that your group speaks for one thousand people because one thousand people came to an event. You can claim only to represent the people who say they share your goals—not the customers who eat your dinners or buy your crafts.

GAMBLING

The most controversial kind of special event is any form of gambling. It is a great temptation to put on gambling events

---

Yes, we want to attend the Sixth ANNUAL CUBS WIVES FOR FAMILY RESCUE GALA
Benefit to roast the Chicago Cubs.
Please reserve:

_____ individual tickets at $ 150.00 per ticket

_____ raffle ticket(s) at $ 25.00 per ticket or five tickets at $ 100.00

_____ I cannot attend but wish to make a contribution of $_____ to benefit
Family Rescue, a shelter for abused women and children.

NAME:_____

ADDRESS: _____

_____

DAYTIME PHONE: _____ EVENING PHONE: _____

TABLES LIMITED TO 10   Please list guests in your party:

GUESTS:_____   _____

_____   _____

_____   _____

_____   _____

_____   _____

I wish to be seated with:_____

If you have purchased a table, please indicate how many seats you will be using _____

Payment Options: □ Check enclosed for $_____

Make checks payable to: **Cubs Wives For Family Rescue**

□ Please charge my card for $_____

□Visa □MasterCard   Acct. No. _____   Exp. Date_____

Signature _____

(*Credit card orders must have signature to be valid.*)

Please Respond by Monday, July 16, 1990.   Tickets will be held at the door.

Visa and MasterCard will be   For Information   The Amount of $100.00 per
accepted for Auctions.   Call   ticket is Tax Deductible.

---

because they can raise immense amounts of money. Americans
spend fifteen times more money on gambling than they donate
to churches.[6] Thirty-two states run a state lottery; about $96 per
head is spent on tickets every year. This means that if all the
state lotteries were combined, they would place twenty-first on
the *Fortune* 500 list of the nation's largest corporations.[7]

Since it is inevitable that people are going to gamble anyway, why not get a piece of the pie? Some charities do decide to use gambling as part of their fundraising strategy. Depending on the state laws, charities can choose to make money from bingo, pull-tabs, card games, raffles, or sweepstakes.

What are the negatives? Gambling, more than any other choice of fundraising strategy, attracts people who may be unaware, indifferent, or even hostile to your mission. Gamblers come to gamble. Period. I am convinced you could run a bingo for "Friends of Hitler" and fill the hall with bingo players.

Gambling is an addiction for some people. Remember when baseball star Pete Rose was found guilty of not reporting his income from illegal gambling? Now the general public is more aware that gambling can be an addiction and may lead to criminal activity.

Many religious congregations are opposed to gambling because it brings out the worst in people. The only way I can win is if everyone else loses. Then it is a very short step from hoping I win to hoping that you lose. This is not in the best spiritual traditions of promoting cooperation and mutual aid.

Many community organizations are opposed to gambling as a regressive tax. Poorer people spend a higher percentage of their income on gambling than richer people. If your organization works for economic justice, do not use gambling as a fundraiser.

CONCLUSION

The key to successful special events is attention to detail. For more details on the details, attend as many events as you can, observe the staff and volunteers in action, and then interview the people who run the best benefits. For more advice on special events, get *The Grass Roots Fundraising Book*, listed in Chapter 14.

Special events give you more ways to have more fun, meet more people, and test more leaders than any other form of fundraising. You can meet your social needs and your organizational needs at the same time. For fun and profit, always include at least one or two special events in your fundraising strategy.

"Money will not come in and
surrender."
　　　—*Roy L. Williams,*
　　　Narragansett Council
　　　Boy Scouts of America

Chapter 5

The Smaller Gift

Building Your Base

From time to time, veteran fundraisers will tell you a story
about some old geezer who just wanders into the office, leaves a
shopping bag full of cash (or the deed to the ranch, or a diamond bracelet . . .), and then wanders out. However, purely
spontaneous contributions are so rare as to be ranked as mira-
cles. The reason these stories get repeated is that they are so
unusual.

You are not serving your organization by waiting for
money to come in and surrender. To guarantee a dependable
income, you need to *ask* for money and ask your volunteers to
ask for money.

If you want to raise money and *at the same time* identify the
citizens who care about your cause, you have to ask people to
give money to your organization because they want what it does.
Good people are going to want to pay for the good work your
group does, just as they want to pay for prizes, pastry, and
parties. The fastest, easiest, most accurate way to find the people
who share your values is to ask them for money.

The biggest advantage to asking for money (as opposed to
selling anything) is that you can get more money per transac-

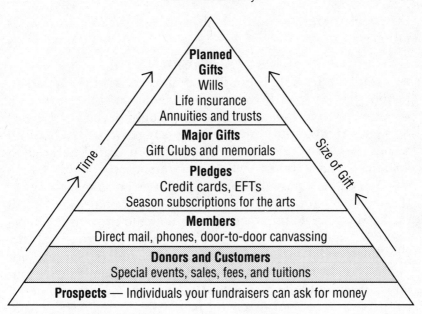

tion. If Darryl bought *everything* at the bake sale, he might spend $1,000. Then if you want him to give again, you have to bake some more. On the other hand, if you ask him to support the worthwhile work your group does, he can give you a small donation the first year, pledge a larger amount the second year, and put your organization in his will the third year. The only limit is your enthusiasm.

Asking for money for your programs identifies the most interested donors, the most committed leaders, and the most desirable issues. Remember, this is building the broad base of givers, some of whom will later make larger gifts and bequests. Let's look at whom you can ask for small gifts to start the campaign, and then we will look at the best way to ask in person.

WHOM CAN YOU ASK?

We know that 90 percent of charity dollars come from individuals. To build a base of dependable, renewable, internally controlled big money, begin your fundraising strategy by finding the broadest group of individuals who can give to your organization.

LIST OF PROSPECTS

Ask your fundraising committee to make a list of the names of people they personally can ask for a donation. There may be a volunteer who recommends that "we" ought to ask "everyone." Smile pleasantly and translate every suggestion like this into second person singular. Then transactions can be traced so volunteers and staff can be held accountable.

You can get started by asking each person to make a list of the names of ten individuals he or she can personally ask for $20 each. Adapt the dollar amount up or down to fit your neighborhood. Ask for ten names so the volunteers need to stretch a little.

These need to be the names of individuals who are not already donors to your group. For right now, do not worry about duplications. Just get each volunteer to write down the names of ten people he or she can ask for money.

PROSPECTS FOR SMALLER GIFTS

Names of individuals I can ask for $20 to become new donors for my organization:

1.	6.
2.	7.
3.	8.
4.	9.
5.	10.

To continue, discuss the following possibilities and add your other prospects unique to your group.

Yourself

The first gift must be your gift. Salespeople say, "You can't sell something you won't buy." That is why marketing people use the products they promote. In the same way, you need to practice what you preach.

The most persuasive fact is always, "I've made a gift; now I'm giving my time to ask you to make a gift."

Your Family and Friends

Volunteers feel strongly in opposite ways about asking their family and friends for money. Many people hate asking their own family members and friends. Volunteers may not want to feel indebted to their family or friends, or they may be afraid that their loved ones will feel unable to say no. So some of your volunteers will flatly refuse to ask their own family or friends.

In that case, simply ask them to trade their list with another volunteer who feels the same way. Clifford can ask Molly's family and friends, and Molly can ask Clifford's family and friends. No one is left out, but your volunteers still feel good about the process.

On the other hand, many people *like* to ask their family and friends. If you feel strongly about this cause, if this group has given you joy and strength, and if the group has made real improvements in your life, of course you are eager to include your family and friends.

In fact, consider it the other way. What if you do *not* ask them? Your brother and your best friend are going to wonder, "Don't you think I have the same values? Don't you think I want the same things you do? Why did you ask everyone else, and not ask *me*?"

Some charities intentionally market to families. The Shelburne Museum in Vermont offers a membership for individuals at $20, adult couples at $30, or families at $40. They also offer a "Grandparents Membership"—$25 for an individual or $35 for a couple—that offers all of the benefits of the other memberships plus free admission for all grandchildren under 18.

Your Neighbors

If you have lived in the community for a while, you probably know many of your neighbors already. If you are active, you may already be part of a block club, tenant association, or civic group. In that case, begin working through the existing structures in the community.

If you are new to the community, one easy way to start recruiting your neighbors is with the list of registered voters, usually free from the county board of elections. The list gives the names of the registered voters for each precinct or township, organized numerically by address, then alphabetically by name. In some communities this list also tells the political party and the age of the voters, so you can easily recruit thirtysomething Republicans or senior-citizen Democrats.

If you are fundraising in a community with many unregistered voters, you will need to make your own list. In neighborhoods with many immigrants, try working through the local clubs, such as the Sons of Norway or the 18th Street Soccer League. Or you can simply go door to door and ask everyone to get involved. Many churches and political campaigns were built this way, and door knocking can work for you, too.

In rural areas raise funds from your neighbors when they come to you. One group in Tennessee signed up members when people came out of the hills and hollers to vote on election day. In Montana the Northern Plains Resource Council began when Bill Mitchell set up his card table in the general store and sold memberships to all the ranchers who came in to buy supplies.

Co-Workers

There are many advantages to raising funds from the people you work with. First, you know they have a job and hence at least *some* income. Second, you may know something more about their interests. If Joy started the recycling collection system in the lunch room, she is a good prospect for an environmental group. If Bob spends every lunch discussing box scores, he is a good prospect for the Little League.

Ask the Chamber of Commerce for the names of the largest employers in your community. These usually include the school system, labor-intensive sites like hospitals, and large manufacturing plants. In the county seat or state capital, it will include all the branches of the county or state governments. Recruit a volunteer for the fundraising committee from each of the top ten largest employers.

Students and Teachers

If you go to school or live in a college town, ask the students to raise money for your cause. Fraternities and sororities often need to organize fundraising events to get their parties approved. Most students and teachers get three to four months of vacation, so they can be great summertime volunteers.

Merchants

As Deep Throat told Watergate reporter Bob Woodward, "Follow the money." Where do your own constituents spend their money? Track where your own dollars go, and then ask those merchants for support.

Also ask the vendors who sell to the organization itself. Every group buys office supplies, insurance, printing, computers, and food. Be sure to ask the merchants who sell to the organization to donate; if they say no, shop the competition.

Even if your community is experiencing hard times, there are still merchants making money. If people are not buying new cars, they are getting their old cars repaired and buying new batteries, parts, and tires. If men are not buying new suits, they are buying neckties. Accessory sales always go up in hard times.

In smaller communities it is vital to recruit a few insiders for the fundraising committee so you are not misled by modesty and underestimate the profits of local businesses. Unlike big-city yuppies, successful people in small towns do not flaunt their wealth through conspicuous consumption. Instead, they try hard to blend into the crowd. One committee from a small town in Kansas laughingly told about the local bank president who always drove a Chevrolet but bought a Cadillac the day he retired.

Professionals

Ask your own doctor, dentist, pediatrician, barber, beautician, veterinarian, lawyer, accountant, or insurance agent. You have to go see these people anyway. They never have any problem taking *your* money; you can simply ask for some of it back.

In smaller communities, compare your lists to avoid duplications. If everyone in your group goes to the same dentist, ask the person with the largest recent bill to ask. If Jack never had a cavity, do not assign the dentist to him; if Rose just had root canal work, she is the one to ask the dentist.

In larger communities, first ask two or three professionals to give to your group, and then ask them to ask other people in the same profession. Structure the campaign so the bankers can be competing with the lawyers and the insurance agents.

Some charities are having great success asking professionals through videotapes. Because doctors are very busy and ethically have to respond to their patients when called, it is often difficult to see them in person to ask for money. The Lakeland, Florida, United Way made a videotape asking for donations and stressing how the money would be used locally. Each doctor could play the tape at his or her convenience. The videotapes produced a 54 percent increase in giving from doctors, almost $20,000 more than the year before.[1]

Other Organizations

Sometimes volunteers will try to weasel out of fundraising by saying, "*I* can't ask for money—I don't have the time!" When you ask for more information, you find out that Monday they drive the carpool, Tuesday is the volunteer fire department practice, Thursday they tutor at the library, Saturday is a birthday party, and Sunday they go to church. Now the same volunteer who just claimed to have no time to fundraise has given you five possibilities for asking for money. Make it easy to ask everyone this person sees. In five minutes he or she can sell a membership if prepared with all the materials.

Other organizations may be able to help you if they see a connection with your cause. A few years ago, the Vancouver Aquarium lost many of its fish through a terrible act of vandalism. In the spontaneous outpouring of generosity to help replace the fish, the police department paid for a fish called a sergeant major, the carpenters' union donated for the sawfish, and parochial school children contributed for the angel fish.

Religious Congregations

Every year almost half of the money given in America goes to religious institutions, including churches, synagogues, mosques, temples, and every religious denomination. About a third of this money is donated back to the community for peace and justice causes.

Your Organization's People

Last, but certainly not least, are your own people. Always ask your own constituents, patients, and clients for money, and ask them to ask for money.

GETTING STARTED

Once the committee has a list of prospects, review the list and develop a strategy for who would be the best person to ask each person on the list. It is often much easier to ask volunteers to go in pairs. For example, if two people go to the same temple, they can work together to ask their friends.

These small gifts are building the base for your overall fundraising strategy. Over the next few years, you can begin asking some of them to make larger gifts and consider a bequest. But you need to start with many small givers. Make your own contribution, and start asking these people for money.

BUILDING THE BASE:
HOW TO ASK FOR SMALL GIFTS

---

1. *Make a gift yourself.*
2. *Research your prospects.*
   a. *How much do they care about your work?*
   b. *How much money can they give?*
3. *Educate your prospects.*
4. *Practice.*
5. *Make the appointment. Ask in person.*
6. *Smile. Make eye contact. Listen.*
7. *Ask for a specific dollar amount.*
8. *Answer questions. Think.*
9. *Ask for the dollar amount again.*
10. *If you get a gift, send a note the same day, thanking the donor for the donation.*
11. *If you do not get a gift, send a note the same day, thanking the donor for his or her time and helpful suggestions.*

BEFORE YOU ASK

There are three things you can do before you ask for money to make it easier for you to ask and easier for the prospect to say yes:

1. Give a gift yourself.
2. Research your prospects.
3. Educate your prospects.

Let's look at each of these.

ACTIONS SPEAK LOUDER THAN WORDS

First, give a gift of money yourself. If you are asking for big gifts, give a big gift. If you are asking for planned gifts, name the group in your own will, trust, or insurance policy.

Giving a gift yourself will guarantee your success as a fundraiser. You may be tempted to say that you can wait till the end of the campaign and then give your gift, but that will not work.

Givers become better askers, and askers become better givers. In the best campaigns the leadership gives at the beginning, and then becomes even more committed through the process of asking for money. Often your fundraisers may be surprised and delighted when their prospects give larger amounts than they gave themselves. Then the fundraisers want to give more to keep up.

If you are asking your mother or your best friend, she may simply reply, "Well, dear, how much did you give?" If you just mumble about your good intentions, she will know this cause is not important to you. You may *say* very eloquently that this is urgent, but if people do not *see* you giving your own money, they will not believe you mean it.

Many charities now videotape sessions in which their volunteers practice asking for money. Videotapes show that if the asker has not made a donation of his or her own money, the asker's eyes will drop when he or she gets to the "close," the part that involves actually asking for the donation. So anyone can tell from your body language whether or not you gave money yourself.

When your organization runs its first fundraising campaign, do your best to get every volunteer and staff person working on the campaign to make a gift before the campaign. You may get 100 percent participation, and if you do, that is great. More likely a few people will make excuses and "wait" to make their gift. Do the best you can to persuade everyone to give, but do not hold up the campaign because of a few stingy people. Launch your campaign and keep track very carefully of who gives at the beginning and who does not. Then keep track of who gets the most donations. After a year or two you will have enough data from your own people to show that the best fundraisers give their own gift first. After five or ten years the connection between giving first and getting the most will be so glaring that you can simply make it a criterion for serving on the fundraising committee.

SHOULD THE FUNDRAISING STAFF ALSO CONTRIBUTE?

Giving to the organization is indispensable for the fundraising staff. If your paid staff is working on a major gifts campaign, they should make major gifts, too, according to their means. If they are working on the planned gifts campaign, they should put this organization in their own will, trust, or insurance plan. Ask ten of the most successful professional fundraisers you can find, and I will bet the ranch all of them have made a serious gift to the place where they work.

The boss can set a good example and make a meaningful gift first. Then make it easy for the fundraising staff to give through payroll deduction, a credit union, credit card pledges, or electronic funds transfers at their bank.

RESEARCH YOUR PROSPECTS

After making your own gift, the second thing that makes it easier to ask is learning more about your prospects. If you are asking your brother, you probably already know his commitments and his financial status. If you are asking the stranger who moved in next door yesterday, you will need to do more research.

You want to find out two things:

1. The prospect's commitment to your cause
2. The prospect's ability to give

Of these two, commitment is more important. This is why volunteers are such good prospects for donations. You *know* they care about your cause.

To get started, work with the people you already know. After you have built a base of believers, you can begin to research people based on their wealth. Of course, the ideal thing is to find someone who loves the group *and* has a lot of money.

To find people with wealth, see the advice in Chapter 8. Use this information to look for new prospects to ask for money. But always begin with your own volunteers, board, and current donors before you ask strangers, no matter how much money they have.

The last thing to research about your prospect is *when* that person has money. When is payday? Senior citizens in the United States get their social security checks on the third of the month. Most other government checks, such as welfare or disability, arrive on the first of the month.

If your prospects are on a payroll, when do they get paid? Most workers get paid either twice a month—for example, on the fifteenth and the end of the month (twenty-four checks a year), or every other Friday (twenty-six checks a year). It is easier for them to say yes if you ask when they get their middle-of-the-month paycheck.

If your constituents live paycheck to paycheck, with the check spent *before* they get it, try to arrange for payroll deduction where they work so you get the money first. This gives them twenty-four or twenty-six opportunities to give you small amounts that will add up to a large gift. This can be collected for your group through the accounting department, the credit union, an alternative payroll deduction plan, or a donor option handled through the local United Way or Combined Federal Campaign.

Some executives are paid once a month, usually on a day other than Friday to even out the work for accounting. Since these people have to plan ahead more, ask them to make a monthly pledge. Again, try to arrange for a regular deduction from the payroll or a monthly pledge on their credit card.

For students, when do they get their scholarships? Most students get scholarship checks at the beginning of each semester. Ask very early in the semester.

Many salespeople are paid a commission on their sales, so they get the most money when they sell the most. Eighty percent of toys are sold during the six weeks before Christmas and Hanukkah; most chocolate is sold before Easter; most houses sell in the summer. Know when salespeople are likely to do best.

Similarly, some professions give big bonuses at the end of the year. Lawyers, brokers, and executives may have big chunks of cash at year's end. Ranchers and farmers make money when they sell their crops. Learn the timetable for harvest and sales in your area.

EDUCATE YOUR PROSPECTS

The last step before you ask for money is to educate your prospects. Sometimes people are already sold on your cause because their children participate in the program, or their parents have the disease, or they personally have a self-interest. If so, asking is easy. If you have a brand-new cause, you may need to educate your prospects.

In 1978 I was part of a group of nine people who started the first hospice in Chicago, a special program of care for people who are dying and their caregivers. The first question in every new group was always "What *is* a hospice?" Some of those early, curious people have been our most stalwart supporters for more than twelve years.

If you are brand-new, get an older group to host your first presentations. When Horizon Hospice was still operating from a card table in the president's bedroom, we hosted events at a local church, university, hospital, and in volunteers' living rooms.

If your program is already up and running, get people to witness the work you do, meet the staff, and hear success stories from your constituents. Throw a party in your building so people can see the neighborhood and meet the leadership. Special events are a great way to attract new people for a fun time while you sneak in a little program on your cause, too.

HOW TO ASK FOR MONEY

To ask for money, begin with your list of ten prospects for small gifts. Then use the following system, which I have copied from sales training. Try out these steps yourself, and then ask your fundraising committee to try them. Most people find it easier than they thought.

EXPECT SUCCESS

Decide you will succeed. Before you do anything else, tell yourself that you are going to raise the money so this great group can do terrific things.

SMILE

Trial lawyers teach witnesses to smile at the jury, because research shows that juries believe a witness who smiles more than a witness who does not smile, regardless of whether or not this person is telling the truth. (Of course, your fundraisers will have the advantage of telling the truth, the whole truth, and nothing but the truth at all times.)

As fundraisers, it is especially important for you to smile and to train your volunteers to smile. You cannot control your emotions; you *can* control your actions. You may feel apprehensive about asking for money, especially if you are new or if you are asking for a large amount. But if you smile, make eye contact, and *act* as though you are enjoying this transaction, the prospects will think you are great—and you will too.

IDENTIFY YOURSELF

Say your name, the name of your group, and what it does. Never assume that your prospect has read or will remember your literature. Always tell the prospect right at the beginning who you are, who you are representing, and what that group does.

EXPLAIN YOUR NEED

Yes, you should say you are there to talk about money. Explain your fundraising strategy and why you need this contribution now.

THE CLOSE

The hardest part to learn is the close. The preceding come naturally, because people tend to like to talk about the groups they like anyway. Actually saying, "I want $20 from you now" can seem a lot harder. Here is how to close:

1. Say the dollar amount you want.
2. Say what it is for.
3. Say why you want this amount now.
4. Engage your prospect in discussion.
5. Repeat the dollar amount.
6. Stop talking, smile, and wait for the prospect to say yes.

Let's look at each of these steps.

Specify an Amount

First, you do need to ask for a specific dollar amount. People cannot respond unless you tell them what you want (assuming this is your first request for their first gift). If the prospects want to give less, they will say so. If they want to give more, you can ask again and ask for more next time. But you have to begin your conversation with a specific amount. No one can write a check for "some" money.

Explain the Use

Say what the money is for. For your first request, it is easiest to ask the prospect to pay dues and become a member. Then you are building the size and political strength of the organization at the same time that you raise money.

If your organization does not have members who pay dues, simply define what the money will buy. For example, the envelope used by the Bishop Desmond Tutu South African Refugee Scholarship Fund specifies what various amounts of money can do for South African children.

Be prepared with such a menu of what their money can buy. If you have researched your prospect, you may be able to guess what he or she will like the most. But people can always surprise you, so have two or three choices ready. Include one choice that seems like a financial stretch, because some donors will always choose the top category because "it's the best." For example, the South African Refugee Scholarship Fund did receive a few gifts in the $10,000 category, their top choice in the mailing. If a *letter* can get $10,000, imagine what you can get live and in person.

Create a Deadline

Say why you need the money now. It is always easier to say "not now" rather than "no." If there is a real urgent need or a real deadline, it will be easier for your fundraisers to get the gift now. Schools create artificial deadlines through homecomings and reunions. If your class is having its twenty-fifth or fiftieth reunion, then the school can create an artificial deadline and ego rewards for you to give a gift now. Any organization can celebrate a tenth, twenty-fifth, fiftieth, or one hundredth anniversary and use the same tactic.

Another strategy for creating a deadline is a matching grant or challenge gift. A major donor, corporation, or foundation agrees to match whatever donations come in by a certain date. Then the fundraisers can urge prospects to make a gift now because the money will be doubled by the match.

Involve the Other Person

Engage the prospect in discussion about your cause. What, if anything, does Mr. Jones already know about it? Has he used any of your services? Does he recognize the problem you are trying to solve? Does he have any questions?

Repeat Your Request

Ask for the dollar amount again. Bring the discussion back to the need for money and, more importantly, what the money will

The Bishop Desmond Tutu Southern African Refugee Scholarship Fund

Yes, Archbishop Tutu
I want to help the children—the refugees—the future leaders of South Africa.

_____
_____
_____
_____
_____
_____

CONTRIBUTIONS ARE IMPORTANT IN SO MANY WAYS:

• $10,000 supports one student for an entire year	• $1,500 pays for airfare from Africa to the United States	• $1,000 pays for one summer's expenses	• $500 buys clothing for a student who arrives with nothing	• $400 covers the cost of books for one year
• $300 provides annual medical insurance	• $210 pays for dental care for one year	• $105 buys school supplies	• $70 provides eyeglasses	• $27.50 allows a student to purchase a calculator

To help you bring the next group of refugee students from Africa I am enclosing my tax deductible gift of:

_____$25 _____$30 _____$50 _____$100 _____$500 _____$1000 _____$ other

My company will match this gift:

_____

(name of corporation)

Please make your check payable to The Bishop Tutu Refugee Scholarship Fund and send it directly with this form in the enclosed postage-paid envelope. We are grateful for your support and appreciate your passing on to a friend any duplicate appeals you receive.

The Bishop Desmond Tutu Southern African Refugee Scholarship Fund
A Program of the Phelps-Stokes Fund
10 East 87th Street • New York, New York 10128 • (212) 427-8100

buy. Say the dollar amount at the beginning, the purpose, the urgency, then the dollar amount again.

Wait for an Answer

Finally, stop talking and wait for your prospect to say yes. For those of us who love to talk, this is the hardest part. But it is the clearest message you can send that you are serious, you want the money, and you want it now. If you are not talking, the prospect has to talk, and probably will say yes.

Yes or No

If the prospect says yes, get the cash, check, credit card information, or completed pledge card. Thank the new donor and give her any recognition materials, such as a membership card, button, or decal. Emphasize how her gift will help the group achieve its goals.

Ask for all the data needed for a new donor's record: name, addresses, phone numbers, dollar amount, and special interests. Pass this on to the fundraising office (or the secretary if your group does not have an office). If the donor wants to volunteer, pass on the name to the volunteer coordinator, organizer, or committee chair.

Especially if the prospect says no, "kill him with kindness." Thank him for his time and ask to leave your brochure and pledge card. If you leave a good impression it will be easier for another fundraiser to ask again next year. Whether you get a yes or a no, send a thank-you note to the prospect.

THANK-YOU NOTES

The thank-you note is the most important tool in fundraising. If you want small givers to become major donors and new volunteers to develop into active leaders, recognize every contribution with a prompt, sincere thank-you.

Ask your fundraising team to tell about the best thank-you they ever received and how that made them feel. Then ask for examples of times when your people worked hard or made a big gift and felt ignored. Make yourselves a list of dos and don'ts from this discussion.

At the very least, each fundraiser can send a personal handwritten note after every meeting with a prospect, thanking him or her for the time, good suggestions, and new leads. Send another handwritten thank-you note when the person you ask sends in a donation. Remember, you want people to join your organization and give gifts for a lifetime. Every thank-you note makes the next request and the next gift easier.

For major gifts, remember to thank the donor and anyone else who helped, such as the lawyer, accountant, or appraiser. For corporate gifts, thank the secretary who advocated your cause and the bookkeeper who helped you set up your accounting system as well as the executive who arranged the contributions. For foundation grants, send a prompt thank-you note for every check and a progress report at least quarterly. Although you know that foundation grants run out after one to three years, the foundation staff make up a tight fraternity, so one good grant maker can recommend your program to another good grant maker.

Mail each day's thank-you notes before the sun goes down. If you are asking for money from corporations or foundations, write the note ahead of time, add a postscript after the meeting, and drop it in the mailbox before you leave the building. If you are working with dozens of volunteers, write short thank-you notes and address the envelopes for each person as he or she signs up, and then mail them so the notes arrive the day after the event. For extra-special efforts on the day of the event, send a second thank-you. If you are chairing a major festival or telethon with thousands of volunteers, create a pyramid to delegate the notes, but be sure each volunteer gets a handwritten note the day after his or her service.

This can be a real challenge to your creativity. I have a friend who organized twenty-six nice old ladies to bake cookies for a special event. Several of these ladies call each other every morning to ask, "Did you sleep well?" and then call again every afternoon to ask, "Did you get any mail?" Then they read their mail over the phone. So my friend knew she had to find twenty-six *different* ways to say "thank-you for baking the cookies." It was not easy, but she did it.

In the same way, your organization may negotiate a major gift such as a piece of property that involves several branches and generations of the same wealthy family. Each person needs to get an equally wonderful and equally sincere but differently worded thank-you note.

No, it is not enough to send a receipt from the office. You may choose to send a form letter and an official receipt from the office (or from the treasurer if your organization does not have an office), but the person who asks for the gift must still send a personal note. If the donation is earmarked to pay or endow the salary of a specific staff person—the first violin, the oncologist, or the professor of Slavic languages—that person could also send a note. Extra notes from the CEO and the top elected officer are great, too.

WHAT IF?

Of course, in real life asking for small gifts is never this tidy. Usually several other questions come up before you get the contribution. Let's look at some of these.

What if they ask a question I can't answer?

Smile, say, "What a good question!" and tell the truth. Never lie and never guess. Remember this is the *first* contribution you are asking for, and if this is a good prospect, you (or another fundraiser) can get future gifts from the same donor for a lifetime. So if you do not know an answer, get the answer and send it in writing the next day. Then you will be ready for the next person who asks this question.

What if I ask for too much?

Prospects will tell you. Imagine the very worst scenario: Your prospect, unbeknownst to you, has been laid off his job. You can ask for any amount, and he will say, "I can't make a contribution now—I'm not working."

This is your chance to use the Golden Rule. Save the prospect's dignity. Just say, "We all know how that is. We've all been out of work at one time or another. Since this is not a good time, I hope you will help us again in the future when you get back to work. Meanwhile, would you like to help out by volunteering on the next event?"

What if I ask for too little?

This one is easier to solve. If you ask for $20 and the person says, "Is that all?" you can always ask the prospect, "Would you like to give more?" or, "Would you like to pledge $20 a month?" If someone gives very easily, you can always repeat the transaction. Be sure you send a thank-you note the same day, and then follow up the next week with a clipping, brochure, or letter. Ask again the next month.

What about controversy?

Controversy is usually very good for your fundraising, because it will clarify the issue and emphasize the urgency of the need. When the Seattle conservatives forced the United Way to expel Planned Parenthood, they were doing Planned Parenthood a favor. Leaders from that organization went directly to local individuals and businesses for support. Result: their donor list went from three thousand to seventeen thousand people, and they made up more than the $450,000 lost from the United Way.

There is an old union song with the refrain "Which side are you on?" Any controversy will get your organization's name out in the public. Most service delivery organizations lose more people from apathy and boredom than from honest differences of opinion. A good fight will help you define who is on your side (hot prospects), who is on the other side (not prospects), and who is undecided, so you can use a fundraising call to raise money and persuade another voter at the same time.

Can you write out what I should say?

Of course, there is a temptation to say, "Just give me the script. If I know what to say, I can do it." Surprisingly, because Americans are *so* generous, a scripted request for money will work, for a while, for small amounts of money. However, if your organization wants to build a permanent, powerful institution, if you are approaching the movers and shakers in your community, or if you are already tired of raising the budget from nickels and dimes, simply reading a script will not work.

If you want to get bigger gifts—the farm, the Van Gogh painting, or the balance of someone's estate (as well as his or her dues, T-shirt purchase, and attendance at the gala)—then you and all your fundraisers need to do more than read the script. You need to do the work ahead of time to feel proud and confident about your organization and the entire fundraising process.

SHOWTIME!

Once your committee has lists of names each person will ask, work as a group to decide what you want to say. Actually act out calling on a person to ask for money. Review your lists of prospects, and set up different pairs of people to act out asking a friend, a neighbor, a co-worker, your doctor, your grocery store manager. This will give half the committee the chance to see how it feels to ask, and half will see how it feels to give. This process should flush out many of the questions so your group can brainstorm to find the best answers.

DO IT NOW

Now the time has come to make all this real—it is time to ask for money. Remember, before you go to ask, give a gift yourself, find out why the prospect would like your organization, and prepare simple materials to share the achievements and needs.

Then it is time to visit the ten people on your list and ask them for money. Like any new activity, it gets easier every call. But even if you are afraid, just do it. There is no other way to find the people who share your values and want to support your group.

No matter how wonderful your organization is, if you do not ask, you will not get. At one of my fundraising workshops, a participant was the executive director of a consumers organization that had just been featured on the TV show "60 Minutes." This show has 29 million viewers every week. She was waiting for the money to roll in, since the broadcast had been very favorable about her organization. Unfortunately all the organization did was wait, and all it got was a trivial amount of money.

The organization could have run an ad in the local newspaper's TV section alerting viewers to watch the show and call the office to make a pledge. Volunteers could have called the group's membership list to ask for gifts. The fundraisers could have organized parties to watch the show with their best donors and prospects and then ask them in person for a major gift. Asking in several different ways could have turned this great publicity into great profits.

If your organization does not ask, not even the best publicity will motivate people to give. You have to ask.

"For all serious daring starts from within."

—*Eudora Welty*
One Writer's Beginnings

Chapter 6

Memberships and Pledges
Do It Yourself

Membership drives are the reality check for an organization. I could move to Fargo tomorrow, rent an office for the Friends of the Fargo Felines, and say that I represent every cat lover in Fargo. Or in North Dakota. Or in the Red River Valley, including all of Minnesota and Manitoba. The way my donors, friends, and enemies measure who my organization *really* represents is by asking, "How many members do you have?"

This chapter will look at why you want members and how to get them by using mail, phones, and a door-to-door campaign. The next chapter will look at hiring professionals to reach a huge audience via the mail, phones, or doors.

Members are people who give you money (usually once a year) because they want to support the mission of your organization. They are not giving money for a T-shirt, or food, or a party. They are giving money because they want the services or results that only your organization can provide.

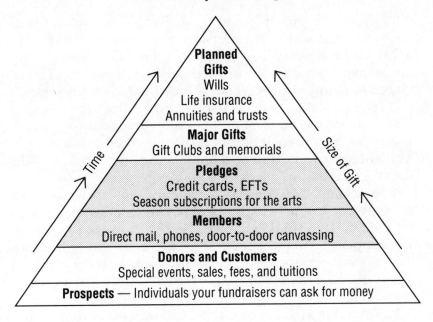

WHY DO IT?

Besides money, there are four advantages to raising money through membership dues. Your organization will get

1. Political power
2. An accurate evaluation of your programs and leaders
3. More people
4. Greater loyalty from your donors

Your organization gains more political power as it obtains more members. Almost every organization will need to influence public policy. If you can tell your state representative that three thousand members of your museum are voters in her district and they all want the culture trolley to go past your museum, she is more likely to vote to fund it.

The second reason for doing a membership drive is that it

will give you a current, accurate, and objective evaluation of your programs and your leadership. Selling memberships separates the fundraisers from the philosophers. Convincing regular people to pay dues keeps you from sinking into a swamp of jargon or taking the easy route of preaching to the converted.

Dues also allow you to "test the turf." Sales tell you which neighborhoods or kinds of people really care about your issues. If they pay, they want it; if they do not pay, they do not want it. You will never waste staff or supplies if they are allocated to the communities that pay dues for your group.

For example, Mike Easter is the star membership salesman of the Roane County chapter of Save Our Cumberland Mountains (SOCM) in rural Tennessee. He says, "Most of the recruiting happened around people working on an issue that they cared a lot about, such as the proposed medical waste incinerators in Roane County, and really the SOCM organization sold itself. People were saying, 'We couldn't have done this without SOCM,' and it was easy to say, 'SOCM isn't something far off; it's us, we're doing it,' and to ask them to join us."[1]

Selling memberships is the only form of fundraising that gives your organization an incentive to grow. New members are also a source of new volunteers. If you sell one hundred new memberships, you can project twenty new names for the annual event and ten new people to actually volunteer and do some work for you. Out of the ten volunteers, perhaps one or two will have the interest and aptitude to become your future leaders.

Best of all, your own leaders are raising money internally for your own programs. This gives you pride, power, and independence. Your organization can with dignity negotiate with any grant maker outside the community, because you know you have enough internal money to walk away from any deal that does not meet your ethical standards. By asking for money, your own leaders will be locked into the organization itself. As Mary Gonzales, Associate Director of the United Neighborhood Organization (UNO), says, "If the people are paying for it, the people are going to do two things: number one, they are going to demand accountability, and number two, they are going to stay in their inner circle, where the decisions are being made, because it's their money on the table.[2]

ANNUAL MEMBERSHIPS

Many groups sign up all their members once a year. School groups, clubs, and parents' associations sell their memberships in the fall. Summer sports clubs and block clubs sell their memberships in the spring. Professional associations often run on a calendar year, renewed in the fall for the next year.

An annual membership drive requires that the membership committee do a lot of intense work all at one time. In reality, the committee's effort takes place in about four months.

Three months before the membership drive, clean up your lists. Take off the people who have moved out, died, or no longer want to be involved. Add the new names. Also add the names of people you are not sure about; at least half of them may be interested.

Two months before the drive, prepare your membership materials, such as receipts, membership cards, buttons, and any other materials you want to sell. Recruit the people to sell the memberships, and make any arrangements you need to reserve rooms or advertising.

One month before the membership campaign, collect prizes for the salespeople. Get the committee together and have a short meeting to practice your sales pitch. Divide up your prospects by geography (Barb and Charlie will recruit everyone west of the river), dues category (Keith and Shannon will sell to the President's Club prospects at $500+), or subgroup (Juanita and Hector will be responsible for all the parents of the pre-schoolers).

Kick off with some unusual visual that will get you on the evening news or the local paper. Sell enthusiastically for two to four weeks, and then have a party and *stop*. Celebrate and announce the chairs for next year's membership drive. They can handle any sales between the campaigns.

MEMBERSHIP CATEGORIES

Create membership categories that relate to your mission. The Friends of the Topeka Public Library uses the following membership categories:

$1,000 (or more)	Lifetime
100 (or more)	Bibliophile
50	Researcher
25	Bookworm
10	Avid Reader
5	Gentle Reader

Each lifetime member gets his or her name on a plaque by the front desk. The last time I was in the Topeka Public Library, librarian Jeff Imparato pointed out that three of the "lifetime" memberships had been given posthumously in memory of a library patron. This suggests some donors will always choose the largest category, so aim high with your top category and make at least one more expensive than a "lifetime" category.

The Amistad Research Center in New Orleans is a manuscript library for the study of ethnic history and culture and race relations in the United States. Ninety percent of its collection pertains to the history and culture of African-American individuals and organizations. The center's membership categories are named for famous African Americans. Here is a sample of what members get at each level:

- Phillis Wheatley Club ($15)—Get the quarterly newsletter, invitations to special events, and discounts on reproductions from the center's art collections.
- Sojourner Truth Club ($50)—Get all of the above and a special-edition poster or print.
- Frederick Douglass Club ($100)—Get all of the above and the annual magazine.
- Harriet Tubman Club ($500)—Get all of the above and are an honored guest at the annual Heritage Banquet.
- Cinque Club ($1,000)—Get all of the above and receive a limited-edition portfolio of facsimiles of the most beautiful and rare manuscripts in the center.

Also, businesses and professional partnerships can join as a Sustaining Partner for $250, Curatorial Partner for $500, or Conservator Partner for $1,000. For more information on big-money gift clubs, see Chapter 9.

PLAN FOR THE NET

Net membership is how many members you have left at the end of the year. In every community people die, move away, or simply lose interest. They may drop out because they change jobs (work nights), get married (had triplets), go back to school (double major), or retire (gone fishing).

Keep track of how many people join and how many quit each year. Then you will know how many new donors you need to recruit. In other words, if you know that 20 percent leave each year and you want 1,000 members each year, you need to start with 1,200 to allow for attrition.

The turnover figure will vary radically depending on your location and constituencies. Most small towns have less turn-over than suburbs; age-specific groups, such as the Little League, have more turnover than institutions for all age groups.

RENEWALS

Most organizations focus their sales drive for memberships in one or two months, but some organizations get members year-round. The easiest system is to put your membership data on a computer, code it by month and salesperson, then generate letters by month. For example, if Gail sells Morgan a member-ship in May, the office sends him a letter the next March saying, "Your membership is about to expire; renew now for another exciting year." If Morgan does not respond, send another letter in April. If he still does not respond, in May give his name (and all the others who have not responded to the mail) to Gail, who sold his membership last May. Then she can reach him by phone or in person to ask him to renew.

If the original salesperson is not available, give the renew-als to someone else in the same neighborhood or category. Renewals are much easier than new sales, so they are a good way to help timid salespeople get started.

REWARD RENEWALS

The Santa Fe Opera attracts fans from all over New Mexico as well as Texas, California, Colorado, New York, and beyond. To encourage repeat audiences and repeat gifts, the opera created the "Encore Club." Those who give four years in a row get an asterisk by their name in the program. An explanatory note reads, "Santa Fe Opera extends special thanks to those individuals and businesses who have contributed on an annual basis for the past four years. Such dedication and loyalty are deeply appreciated."

The Denver Symphony gave its season subscribers purple buttons that said, "I've renewed—have you?" This way, the people who renewed first could urge everyone else in their row or their box to renew. Think of ways to reward your members who renew.

FUNDRAISING BY MAIL, TELEPHONES, OR DOOR TO DOOR

You can get the most money by asking for money face to face. But even the most stalwart fundraisers have limits on how many people they can visit in person. Phones, mail, and door-to-door canvassing using volunteer solicitors will enable you to reach a large number of people for small gifts. Then you can use other strategies to get them more involved and giving larger gifts.

MAIL

According to a survey conducted in San Francisco, 71 percent of the respondents said the best part of the day was when they got the mail. This tells us two things:

1. Mail is very important to most people. You can use it to educate and motivate your public.
2. These people need to get out more! Nonprofit organizations can fill that need when you ask people to join up and march, pray, tutor, party, sing, build, organize, serve, clean up, or fundraise with you.

Volunteer Mailing

When nine volunteers started Horizon Hospice in Chicago in

1978, it was the first hospice in Illinois and one of a handful in the United States. There was nowhere to buy or borrow a list of hospice supporters, so we had to begin to build a base of supporters with the names of the people we knew. The president asked every board member to address an envelope to each name in his or her own personal address book, and then to write a note like, "Hospice is an idea whose time has come. I'm supporting it this year—I hope you will too." We were careful to get an address for every person who attended our open meetings, speeches, and parties, and then mailed information to these people. Also, we tested small lists from other organizations; these were the least successful. Music lovers and sports fans did not respond to a request to help people die pain-free and alert.

However, our own friends, families, and co-workers responded generously. Over the years, we have collected more names at every meeting, benefit, and speech. The executive director and the president are very good about asking all board members to provide new names at least twice a year. As the table below shows, because of careful work on the list and personal effort on addressing and notes, we have seen the profits grow slowly but steadily each year.

HORIZON HOSPICE DO-IT-YOURSELF MAILING

Year	Holiday Mailing Income
1980	$ 7,000
1981	8,000
1982	13,000
1983	20,000
1984	22,000
1985	29,000
1986	36,000
1987	36,000
1988	38,000
1989	76,000

The hospice mails a simple piece that is usually a photo of a patient and a volunteer, an explanation of the services offered, the results (60 percent of the patients are able to die in their own homes; the national average is 20 percent), and the patient census and description. Each letter includes a reply card asking for the cost of one day's care, and a reply envelope. The office staff have computerized the donor list so they can print out a list of donors for each board member. All of the envelopes are addressed by hand by board members and volunteers, with handwritten notes to people they know.

You can see that with hard work and a good cause, even the smallest effort can grow to significant numbers. Especially with a new cause that was virtually unknown in the United States, mail was an effective way to reach and educate many new donors.

Year-End/Holiday Mailing

Even the smallest group can send at least one mailing a year during the holidays. Statistically, November is the most profitable month for mailers,[3] proving once again the benefits of competition. Ask all the board members and key volunteers to bring in their lists of names in the summer, and get them on a computer.

Meanwhile, ask the staff to compile statistics on the organization's results and recruit volunteers to take photographs, write, and design your package. Proofread everything out loud twice. Print the letter and envelopes in early September, and then organize addressing parties in early October, so the mailing can go to the post office in late October.

Be sure you code each return so you know which lists to use again next year and which ones to replace. The easiest system is to stack the reply cards and run a wide felt marker down the side of the stack. Use a different color for each list. It will leave a faint line of color on one edge of the card; most readers will never notice it.

As the mail comes in, record the contributions, send a receipt and a thank-you note from the office, and then notify each board member so he or she can also thank the donor. After two months, analyze what worked, and send the final results to each volunteer with another thank-you note.

Every group can mail at the end of the year to take advantage of donors who get extra bonus money at the end of the year, such as law partners, executives, and salespeople. Mailing in November will keep your group's name and achievements before the people who wait till the end of the year to make their tax-deductible donations. Remind them about your terrific organization.

How Often to Mail

Most organizations can, and should, mail more than once a year. Some mail-order catalogs and political parties mail as often as fourteen times a year. In the fundraising frenzy that occurs the year before a presidential election, the major political parties have mailed as often as every ten days in order to wring every possible dollar out of their donors. Then that sum will be matched by the federal government in January of the election year.

Obviously, volunteer groups would burn out their donors if they mailed thirty times a year. But you can mail at least four times a year asking for money. Here's the easiest system:

1. Mail in November for the year-end/holiday mailing.
2. Send your annual report in January or February (the third best month).
3. Ask members to renew their memberships or increase their annual gifts ten months after the date they first gave.
4. Mail a letter relating specifically to your issues or to a date connected to your cause. For example, hospices and veterans' organizations mail near Memorial Day; literacy and tutoring groups mail in August to arrive with the "back to school" advertisements.

If you want to mail more than four times a year, simply plan for each mailing to highlight different issues or needs. Fundraising mailings can be planned to add to a regular newsletter or to alternate with the newsletter.

Connect to Your Mission

Americans get the most mail near Christmas and Hanukkah, so think about other holidays that fit in naturally with your issue or constituency. For example, the Minnesota Women's Fund sent a letter in May that was connected with Mother's Day. It says, "As we prepare to honor our mothers, and be honored by our children, it is a good time to think about the world in which we live the other days of the year." The letter goes on to describe the needs of women and girls in Minnesota and to ask for "an investment in the girls and women in Minnesota. When the flowers of Mother's Day have faded, your investment in the future of girls and women will continue to grow."

It is more effective to mail more than once a year because it is so easy to discard or misplace even a good letter for a good cause during the hectic holidays. If you mail at other times of the year, too, you can take advantage of less competition in the mailboxes, other income patterns (income tax refunds February to May, farm sales at harvest time, scholarships in September and January), and just random luck.

Repetition is good for raising money. Remember, your organization is competing with every other product for the public's money. If people see and hear commercials twenty times every *day* for beer, hamburgers, and gasoline, how much impact will you have if you ask for your group only once a year?

DIALING FOR DOLLARS

It is most effective and most fun to do fundraising phone calling in a group. First the planning committee culls through the organization's donor cards, takes out any card marked "Do not call," and then prepares a duplicate set of cards with name, address, phone number, amount of the last gift, suggested amount for this gift, and issue interest. This can be done easily with a computer or laboriously with a team of volunteers.

With new technologies, telephones are everywhere. Be sensitive to local customs. In Los Angeles and Houston, for example, it is normal to call people on their car phones because it is normal for people to be in traffic for hours every day. In most other communities, the use of car phones is limited to family emergencies. One Florida organization unfortunately antagonized its best donor when an overeager fundraiser called him on his *boat*. Use a little common sense and a lot of restraint when making up the cards to call for contributions.

Then recruit a team of callers. Colleges and universities try to recruit alumni from the same age groups. Politicians recruit people from the same precincts or townships. Everyone looks for a few veterans with experience and a few rookies with enthusiasm.

The key to success is making it all fun. Have a lot of production prizes. Ask celebrities to stop by. Keep each night short, and your volunteers will be glad to help again next year.

My college does a volunteer phone solicitation every year at an advertising agency. We call names from our graduating class, ask for donations, and then we all adjourn to the saloon in the basement to reminisce. It is easy to get volunteers year after year because the college makes it fun, it is only three hours, you get to see old friends and make new friends, you know the cause so the rap is clear, and they give lots of prizes: best amounts per hour, most gifts, largest gifts, rookie of the year, and most valuable player.

Volunteer phonathons also work very well when your group needs to raise a lot of money quickly. They are a staple of civil disobedience campaigns. Volunteers get on the phone and say, "Henry David Thoreau is in jail because he refused to pay the poll tax. We need to raise bail tonight to get him out!" Once you get the leader out of jail, you can use the phone, mail, and door-to-door campaigns to ask for money to support your campaign to fight the unfair tax.

VOLUNTEER CANVASSING

For decades, door-to-door canvassing by housewives was the backbone of raising money for disease prevention and cures, mental health, the hospital, and civic causes in middle-class neighborhoods. As the majority of American women went to work outside the home, "passing the envelope" fell to the minority who were full-time homemakers. In wealthier neighborhoods residents did not want to bother with a fundraising technique that raised only a few dollars per transaction; in rough neighborhoods it was not prudent to ask volunteers to walk through gangs with an envelope full of cash. More and more, this valuable fundraising technique has been replaced with special events, mail, and telemarketing to reach the same households.

However, going door to door still can be a very effective way to reach households who do not respond to mail or phone. Since your volunteers are talking face to face with the public, they can find hidden treasure. A canvassing coordinator for the Heart and Stroke Fund in British Columbia, Canada, told me about motivating her newest volunteer to go door to door in February, Heart Month. The young volunteer was discouraged after one block with no donations, but the team leader told her to try one more block. On that block, a man greeted her with "The Heart Fund—great! I've been waiting for you to visit: I'm a member of the 'Zipper Club'!" (This is the fellowship of men who have had open-heart surgery; the stitches and staples leave a pattern like a zipper down the middle of the patient's chest.) He gave her $500 at the door.

This man believed he was alive because of heart research; he did not need a hard sell. But the important fact is he was "waiting" for the charity to call on him. He may be one of thousands of people who will not give through the mail, or come to parties, or buy products. But if you ask him in person, he can tell his story and begin a relationship with the group.

Most volunteer canvassers will get $5 to $50 at the door. But every campaign will have a few pleasant surprises of getting larger gifts or hearing stories of how your organization changed their lives. Those surprises help make door-to-door canvassing worthwhile.

Your fundraisers can plan a safe way to meet your neighbors and ask them for money. Especially for community organizations, it is vital that you make the effort to reach every neighbor. A door-to-door membership drive will build your budget and your political power at the same time.

Door-to-door canvassing by volunteers is especially good in very low-income areas where residents may not have telephones or reliable mail service. There is no cost for phone calls or postage, so even the poorest people can sell memberships with no expenses. It is also the ideal way to sell memberships in a community with a large number of immigrants who do not speak English. Volunteer canvassers who speak the languages and dialects of the community can sell memberships, introduce your organization, and assess current neighborhood needs at the same time.

PUTTING IT ALL TOGETHER

First, ask your volunteers how they want to raise money from the public. Then look at your calendar and plan how to space the campaigns. Adapt this to fit your own community.

For example, you could send a team of volunteers door to door once in the spring and once in the fall; telephone for donations in the summer in the South and the winter in the North, when people are more likely eager to be indoors; then mail four times in between. This gives you seven ways to ask your neighbors for money and find your supporters. It also gives you three different ways for people to volunteer. The shy people can work on the mail, while the more outgoing volunteers can telephone or go door to door.

PLEDGES

"We mutually pledge to each other
our Lives, our Fortunes and our
sacred Honor."
—*The Declaration of Independence*

According to a Gallup survey of American donors, 38 percent of the contributors said they wish they could have given more. Pledges are the perfect strategy to make this happen. A pledge is a commitment to pay a specific amount of money each week, month, or quarter for one or more years.

The most common pledge is the weekly pledge for a religious congregation. In most congregations, pledges are solicited in a tightly organized "stewardship" campaign in the fall. The most enthusiastic fifth of the parish make their pledges first; then each of those people asks four other families to make their pledges. In a month, the campaign is over, and everyone has been asked in person. The obvious advantage that religious congregations have over other nonprofits is that they see the pledgers fifty-two times a year.

For most charities, the ideal way to ask for pledges is via the donor's credit card. In this case, your fundraiser can arrange to use the major credit cards issued through your bank. If there is more than one bank in your community, shop around for the best deal. Just like a store, your organization will pay the bank a small percentage, usually about three to five percent, for servicing the credit card accounts. It is well worth the fee, because you can use the money the next day, rather than waiting weeks for checks to clear. Having a credit card option will also increase sales on all your special events or any other time you sell merchandise.

With credit cards, your fundraisers need to ask only once, and you keep getting the pledged amount every month until the donor tells the company to stop payment. You get the pledge even if the donor moves away. Credit cards are the most popular tool for telephone canvassers to get monthly pledges or to sell season subscriptions. A donor who will give someone $10 to $25 at the door will pledge twelve times as much over the phone via his or her credit card.

For further lessons, watch the next time your public television station does its membership drive. Many stations now offer donors four credit card options and urge viewers to call in because it will take only "one minute to become a member." This is why credit cards are the payment plan of choice for younger professionals.

When I was in Kansas City, I picked up a brochure at the Nelson-Atkins Museum of Art, one of the outstanding art museums in the world. (It owns what is considered the finest collection of Chinese art outside of China.) The brochure is called "An Hour with the Masters" and gives patrons the quickest route to see the top fourteen objects in the museum.

I'm sure "An Hour with the Masters" grew out of dozens of people walking in every day and asking, "What can I see in an hour?" The customer is always right. If they want speed, give them speed. So if your donors want to sign up in one minute, give them a credit card option.

While young people like to give via credit cards, older people prefer to use electronic funds transfer (EFT). This is the way the federal government sends out social security checks under the name "direct deposit." Money is sent electronically into bank accounts, so nothing can be lost, stolen, or delayed. In the same way, you can offer your donors the option of making payments directly from their bank to your bank through the magic of electronics. More and more people are paying their utility bills, bank loans, and mortgages this way; they can make payments to good nonprofits this way, too.

For performing arts groups, season subscriptions serve the same function as pledges. Rather than depend on fickle single-ticket buyers, you can presell the entire season to subscribers. For hundreds of ideas to sell season subscriptions, see Danny Newman's book *Subscribe Now!*, which is listed in Chapter 14.

PAYROLL DEDUCTION

In 1943 the federal government began withholding social security and federal income taxes from worker's paychecks. Soon fundraisers used the same strategy to collect money directly from workers' paychecks for charities. Today workers give more than $2 billion through their paychecks to the United Way, the Combined Federal Campaign (CFC) for federal employees, and hundreds of smaller campaigns. Your organization can consider all three of these strategies.

The payroll deduction strategy is good for charities because the money is handled for you through the payroll department of the workplace, all of your target market is employed, and a pyramid structure is already in place to run the campaign. It can be very difficult to get accepted into new workplaces, but once you are in, this approach can be a dependable source of money.

UNITED WAY DONOR OPTION

Some organizations collect pledges through a donor option program of the local United Way. United Ways raise 94 percent of their money through payroll deduction, so they are the best place to start. Your opportunities will be different for each of the 2,300 United Ways in America. Some allow only their own health and human service agencies to ask for gifts through their payroll deduction plans. Others will allow any 501(c)(3)charity to ask. Ask your local United Way for its rules for donor option, and then ask a charity that uses payroll deduction through donor option for the unwritten rules. (See Chapter 13 for more on getting allocations and grants from the United Ways.)

COMBINED FEDERAL CAMPAIGN

The Combined Federal Campaign (CFC) is the nation's largest employee charity drive. It is how federal employees—both military and civilian workers—give at the office. In 1989 more than four million employees gave $186 million through 550 local CFC campaigns. Of course, the largest by far is the campaign for the Washington, D.C., area, which raised $28 million for 530 national and 800 local agencies.

To get the rules, application, and calendar for the Combined Federal Campaign, contact the Office of Personnel Management, Office of CFC Operations, Room 5532, 1900 E Street, NW, Washington, DC 20415. National organizations must apply to the national office. For local campaigns, either ask the national office to send you the address for the Local Federal Coordinating Committee (LFCC) or ask one of your members who is a federal employee to find the name of the LFCC. Ask the LFCC for the rules, applications, and calendar.

These materials are all written in bureaucratic jargon. Get someone involved in your local CFC campaign to help you understand the application process and walk your application through. If you decide your organization should get donations from federal employees, you can apply in the spring. If accepted, you will be included in the campaign in the fall.

Ninety-five percent of these campaigns are managed by the local United Way. But even if you are not a United Way agency, your organization may still ask for employee donations. Since the Combined Federal Campaign was opened up to more agencies in 1987, about 40 percent of the funds go to the United Ways and their member agencies, while the other 60 percent go to non–United Way charities, including more than $20 million for nontraditional social justice and environmental groups.

The Combined Federal Campaign is a model of open donor options. Federal employees may give to as many as five charities through payroll deduction, and they are offered a huge list, including groups on both sides of issues, such as the gun control groups and the National Rifle Association, pro-life groups and pro-choice groups, and groups that raise money for either Palestine or Israel.

STATE AND LOCAL GOVERNMENT CHARITY DRIVES
About twenty states and many more cities and counties permit their employees to use payroll deduction to make donations to the charities they want to fund. Some of these are accessible only to the United Ways or other fundraising federations; others are open to all charities in the community.

To learn how to participate, ask one of your members who is a state, county, or city employee to obtain the name of the person who handles the charity campaign from the person who handles payroll deductions. Ask how your organization can apply. Then check with other local charities that get employee contributions to find out the best strategy for getting the most gifts.

ALTERNATIVE PAYROLL DEDUCTION PLANS
The United Ways and the Combined Federal Campaigns have now been joined by dozens of smaller fundraising campaigns that allow donors the choice of giving to programs for the arts, health care, social action, women and girls, and minorities.

If your organization cannot get payroll deduction gifts through the United Way, consider working with an alternative plan. The alternative payroll deduction plans are now raising more than $200 million a year and growing at about 10 percent every year. These all use the same strategy of asking workers to designate a specific amount from each paycheck. Since workers will give a little bit twenty-four or twenty-six times a year, even small amounts will add up to major gifts.

The charities (outside the United Way) that raised the most money through payroll deductions in 1989 were the National/United Service Agencies ($17 million), the United Negro College Fund ($4.8 million), the Brotherhood Crusade/Black United Fund located in California ($1.2 million), the Cooperating Fund Drive in Minnesota ($560,000), and the Black United Fund of New Jersey ($560,000).

Contact the largest workplaces in your community to find out which campaigns they allow to solicit their workers. Then ask the people who run those campaigns how your organiza-

HOW NOT TO ASK FOR MONEY
THE MOST COMMON
MISTAKES

1. *Not asking.* It would be nice to think that if you just do a terrific job for a terrific cause, folks will take notice and offer to contribute. Forget it.
2. *Not asking family and friends.* Remember who bought most of your Girl Scout cookies?

3. *Beating around the bush.* Don't fall into the stereotypically feminine tactic of hinting at what you want. ("We are *so* broke I don't know where next month's rent is going to come from. Oh, what a lovely diamond ring!")
4. *Being dishonest.* For heaven's sake, tell the truth about what you're doing and what you really need the money for, even if it's to bail out a mistake. Anyone who's

accumulated enough money to give away understands the ups and downs of doing business.
5. *Begging, apologizing, or demanding.* Funders need to be convinced that you believe in the project, and that their participation would not be charity or an obligation, but, yes, a privilege. Don't forget to mention money that you've contributed.

6. *Not knowing the financial side of your program or business.* If you're talking money, you'd better know what you're talking about.
7. *Having too low a budget.* Women tend to ask for less than they know is needed because they can't believe anyone would give

them, say, $10,000. Well, a funder is much less likely to give $5,000 for a project that obviously calls for more than to give the $10,000 needed to do the job right.
8. *Underestimating giving potential.* Aim high—that's what negotiating is all about. They may even be flattered that you think they're so wealthy.

9. *Calling yourself out after only two strikes.* That third person (or the third pitch to the same source) just might be the breakthrough. Try another angle. People admire perseverance.
10. *Taking yes for an answer.* If they gave money once, pitch them again. They believed in you once, they'll give again. And again . . .

Source: *Ms.* magazine, April 1980

tion can be included. If there are no campaigns already organized, meet with the CEO of the workplace and ask him or her to allow employees to give to your organization through payroll deduction.

CONCLUSION

Selling membership is the only form of raising money that builds your organization's political power at the same time that it builds your budget. If you want more people, more volunteers, more voters, more leaders, and more decision makers on your side, always begin your fundraising strategy by asking people to pay dues to your group.

Chapter 7

Memberships by the Professionals

Mail, Phone, Door to Door

If you have a cause that appeals to the emotions and a very large market, your organization can hire a firm to reach your audience through the mail, phones, or door-to-door canvass. This strategy is both an art and a science, and it is well worth investigating. Even with a terrific board of directors, great volunteers, and a professional fundraising staff, your organization would be prudent to hire a special consultant for direct mail, telemarketing, or door-to-door canvassing. All of these strategies require attention from an expert in the current laws, technologies, and creative trends. If you want to ask a few thousand people in your own state to join or donate, review the techniques in the last chapter for doing it yourself. If you want to mail to a million names or knock on all the doors in California, hire a specialized consulting firm to help you.

HOW TO HIRE A CONSULTANT

If your staff and leaders decide they want to launch a new campaign and want outside advice, first decide *exactly what you want*. What is your dollar goal, who from your organization

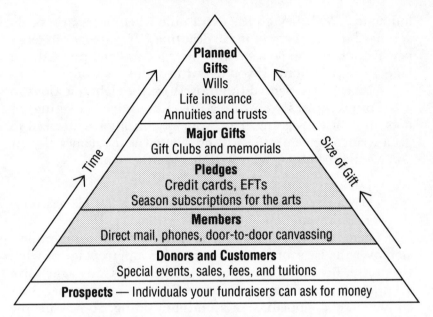

will supervise the consultant, and who will give written approval for each decision? Make a list of what you want and do not want in working with a consultant.

Then ask your national network and local allies to recommend good consultants. Many of the Foundation Center Cooperating Collections maintain files of consultants who work in your community. (See the list of Collections in Chapter 13.) Also read the advertisements in the trade press and shop the vendors at conventions.

Interview three to five firms in person. A direct mail program or a capital campaign may take three to five years to make money, so be sure you will be hiring a firm with similar values, style, and politics. Most firms send out the charismatic founder/ boss to sell you their services; demand to meet the other individuals who will work with your people throughout the campaign.

Satisfied customers are always the best recommendation. Ask for references from the firms' repeat customers. Remember you want a firm that will make money and make your life *easier,* not more complicated. Ask the references if the consultants deliver their work on time and on budget. Do they handle follow-up? Will they go the extra mile when necessary, or do you need to nag them to make deadlines? If you want to test a new firm, hire it to do a small project for you and proceed to a bigger campaign only if you're satisfied with its work.

Also ask experienced fundraisers for the right questions to ask. For example, if you hire a direct mail, telemarketing, or door-to-door canvassing firm, your organization will need to get a written agreement regarding who owns the names of your donors and members. Who will manage the names?

ETHICS

Never pay a percentage. Pay the consultant a flat fee based on the work you want done.

There is a great deal of turmoil in the fundraising profession over the issue of paying consultants a percentage of what they raise. Because Americans are *so* generous, any aggressive salesperson can sell a good nonprofit cause much easier than cosmetics, encyclopedias, or aluminum siding. So new people are flocking to fundraising, offering unsuspecting nonprofits "no-risk" deals to raise money on a percentage. This is obviously great for any aggressive fundraiser but probably not great in the long run for your organization.

Fundraising is simply asking for money. If you hire someone on a percentage basis, he or she will say anything to get the largest possible gift. The consultant can burn out your market, get his or her commission, and then move to a new community and do it again. Then next year, or five years down the road, when your own staff or volunteers try to go back to the same donor, their calls will not be returned because he or she was pressured by the aggressive consultant pushing up his or her percentage.

Most states now regulate professional fundraising firms. Get the current regulations from the attorney general's office and be sure the firms you interview know and comply with all state and federal rules.

There is a professional association for the businesses and consultants who specialize in direct mail and direct marketing for nonprofits. For the list of members who ascribe to its code of ethics, contact the Association of Direct Response Fundraising Counsel (ADFRC), 1501 Broadway, Suite 610, New York, NY 10036; 212/354-7150. It also offers a free brochure called "What Your Organization Needs to Know About Direct Mail Fundraising," that is a good introduction to direct mail.

MAIL

Direct mail is still the most effective way to tell your organization's story to a very large audience. Experts claim that a mailing on an average draws ten times as many responses as newspaper ads and one hundred times as many as television ads.[1] Current technology allows mailers to target specific markets, whether by location, such as Congressional districts, or by demographics, such as forty-year-old Asian-American.

Mail is the most common way that most middle-class people are asked to donate money. According to a 1990 Gallup survey, 30 percent of the people who gave to a charity for the first time did so because they received a letter asking them to give. Anyone who is "mail responsive"—that is, buys or gives through the mail—knows that the amount of mail has exploded in the last ten years. If you give to a whale, you will be on the list for the dolphins, the manatees, and the prairie chickens. In 1989, 92 million Americans mailed in a total of $183 billion to their favorite catalogs and causes.[2]

It used to be that a nonprofit group could start a mailing on its conference room table for $5,000 and make money in a year, just as entrepreneurs could once start a mail-order business on a kitchen table. Those days are gone. With increasing costs and increasing competition, nonprofits need at least $30,000 of seed money and three years of lead time to get into the mail and see a profit. But it is worse for the mail-order catalog companies. Today it takes $5 million and 5 years to start to make money from a mail-order catalog.

To survive the competition, most nonprofits cannot run a successful large direct-mail program alone. You need a savvy, experienced, ethical specialist to guide your campaign from year to year.

Think of going into the mail as going into business. Just as you do not open a store one or two times a year (and make money), you cannot mail sporadically and make money. Direct mail must be an intentional strategy to mail over and over to a mass audience to find the tiny minority who will support your cause.

If you need cash to spend in the next three years, do not even consider direct mail. To produce cash quickly, choose another strategy, especially asking for money face to face. However, if you can budget to wait three years before you see a positive cash stream, look into direct mail.

Also, do not consider direct mail unless you have the seed money to launch the program, probably about $30,000. If your organization does not have the funds to begin this strategy, it will not have the funds to handle success. A good direct-mail campaign will produce more members and donors who will cost more to serve effectively so they will renew year after year.

Again, do not be tempted by a consultant who offers to begin your organization's direct-mail campaign by taking a percentage out of future profits and thus requiring no up-front investment from you. Successful direct mail depends on your members and donors giving repeat gifts year after year. A consultant working on a percentage is going to be looking for quick hits rather than loyal donors who can become a dependable funding base. If you do not have the money to start the program, focus on low-overhead fundraising strategies, especially asking for money face to face, until you do. Then hire an experienced consultant who will work for a flat fee.

PROSPECTING

The way to understand direct mail is to think of it as *prospecting*. It is like looking for gold. Somewhere in all of the lists are a few people who will give to your organization. The purpose of direct mail is to systematically look for them, then find out what they like best, and find a way to keep them giving to you.

The standard goal for a first mailing is a one percent return, but it can be less. It happens this way:

- 92 percent of the people never open the envelope. In other words, 8 percent of the people open the envelope.
- Of these, half, or 4 percent, read past the first paragraph.
- Of these, half, or 2 percent, read to the end of the letter.
- Of these, half, or 1 percent, take the action you want—send money.

Because of increasing costs, when only 1 percent (or less) of the people respond to you the first year, you cannot make money. All the money that comes in has to be reinvested in more prospecting. So if you want to make money in mail, you need to fundraise from some other source for venture capital up front to pay for experimenting the first year or two.

The way this turns into gold is through the people who renew. Every year you keep a donor, you get a higher percentage of renewals. Only about 50 to 60 percent of donors renew the first year, and 60 to 70 percent of donors renew the second year. However, by year five 83 to 90 percent of donors renew, and by year eight 87 to 91 percent will renew.[3]

You need a professional direct-mail expert in order to get donors to respond the first time (by opening the envelope, reading the letter, and sending a check) and to keep responding every time you mail to them. Because there are so many factors in keeping costs down and returns up, you need to hire someone who knows the best vendors, the current postal regulations, and what is working now.

Within the mailing are several areas of concern. What can you honestly and ethically say your organization will do? How will you say it? Mail is emotional, not mental. That's why it works best when people are angry. Environmental groups made a fortune in 1989, thanks to Exxon wrecking the *Valdez* in Alaska; pro-abortion and anti-abortion groups both made money after the Supreme Court's *Webster* decision that threatened safe and legal abortions for the first time in sixteen years. If there is a hot issue in your field, you can mail and make more money.

Save all the begging letters you receive for a month (a week if it is November), then open them all up and consider the pieces that make up a typical direct-mail appeal:

- The outside envelope
- The letter
- Other copy, such as photos (the Statue of Liberty), clippings, brochures, or ballots
- Premiums, such as decals, membership cards, or address labels
- Gimmicks, such as balloons you need to inflate to read the message or (my personal favorite) a shower cap with the outline of a hand on it sent by a preacher so you can wear the cap and pretend he is laying his hand on your head
- The reply card
- The return envelope

One reason mail is so wonderful is that every element of the package and every list can be tested. You never need to guess about anything. Continue using the letters and lists that work, and discontinue the ones that do not work, even if you like them a lot. This is a terrific lesson you can apply to all your other fundraising strategies.

For example, when direct-mail professional Kay Partney Lautman tested a letter to raise money for the Vietnam Veterans Memorial Fund in Washington, D.C., she mailed to both conservative and liberal lists at first. The conservatives gave 70 percent more than the liberals, so of course she kept mailing to that kind of list.

WHAT WORKS

To be effective in asking for money through the mail, you need to have an issue that your readers feel strongly about. Controversy is excellent, and any high-profile news campaign will help you a lot. Remember, you do not have committed volunteers and staff asking in person. All you have is a piece of paper to do the asking for your group. The hotter the issue, the easier it is to raise money via mail.

Professional direct mail works best for a controversial cause, an emotional cause, or a project identified with an appealing leader. If you use a do-it-yourself mailing by your own board members, you can get a 10 to 30 percent return because they are writing a personal letter to their own friends. The best direct mail simulates the same kind of person-to-person contact. One of the most effective letters was the Katharine Hepburn letter for Planned Parenthood. She was believable because her own beloved mother had worked shoulder to shoulder with Margaret Sanger, the founder of Planned Parenthood. The Hepburn letter to get new contributors raised almost $5 million from 170,000 new donors.

In the same way, the Bob Hope letter for the Vietnam Veterans Memorial Fund was so successful it laid the foundation for the entire fundraising campaign to build the wall. Because of his enormous popularity from television and fifty years of valiant efforts for American servicemen and -women, Bob Hope could get the massive response needed. His postscript read, "If you can give $20, it will sponsor the name of one Vietnam war veteran who gave his life in service to our country. We intend to inscribe every single name—57,661, to be precise. A lot of names—a lot of lives. Won't you please help us to begin by sending your tax-deductible gift of $20, $40 or more today?"

Different causes will get different results. For example, mail does very well for environmental causes, the homeless, and cancer. It is less effective raising money for inner-city youth, hospitals, and little-known diseases. Mail does well marketing memberships for zoos and aquariums; it is less effective asking for contributions for zoos.

Luckily for us, the creative genius who wrote this letter, Kay Partney Lautman, got together with her equally talented colleague Henry Goldstein and blabbed all of the secrets of direct mail. Their book, *Dear Friend: Mastering the Art of Direct Mail Fund Raising*, tells you everything you need to know from the pilot mailing and renewals to computers, the post office, and consultants. In any fundraising business that can be a money drain the first three years, a little knowledge is a dangerous thing. This book will give you the best grounding in the basics to decide whether this is the strategy you want to use to ask for money for your organization. See Chapter 14 for order information.

Give through the mail to all of your competitors, so you will know what their letters are saying. Ask family and friends from other cities to send you letters they like, and ask your board and staff to save all the fundraising mail they get. Note the formats and contents that are working for other fundraisers. For example, fancy packages and gimmicks are a thing of the past; today simplicity works best.

I used to get mail handed down by my ninety-five-year-old landlady, who had voted straight-ticket Republican in every election since Harding. Even when I did not agree with Ronald Reagan, I was always dazzled by the brilliance of his fundraising letters. Of course, not everyone can mail from the beaches of Normandy on the anniversary of D-Day, but every group can get million-dollar ideas to think bigger and ask for more.

PHONES

Telemarketing—asking for money by calling your donors and prospects on the telephone—is one of the mysteries of fundraising. I lead fundraising workshops for about two thousand people every year. The vast majority of these people have chosen a career working for a nonprofit. They are people with big hearts and generous habits. Yet when I ask them what type of fundraiser they hate most, their most frequent response is getting called on the phone. At suppertime. By someone obviously reading a script. Or worse, by a computer. Twice in the same night.

Yet telemarketing makes millions of dollars for the groups that use it well. Traditionally it has been used extensively by colleges and universities, which use high-energy students with a clear self-interest.

Today telemarketing is used extensively for sales, politicians, performing arts groups, and consumer organizations. It is usually most effective when used in conjunction with television documentaries, direct mail, or a door-to-door canvass. The advantages of the phone over mail is it is more personal, there is two-way communication, and prospects can be persuaded to give larger amounts, especially by using their credit cards. The advantage over a door-to-door canvass is that it is easier to hire people because it is an indoor job, callers can make more money, and the skills are more transferable to other jobs.

Successful fundraisers can reach more prospects faster by the phone than by any other fundraising strategy available today. The telephone is terrific for truly urgent causes, prompt response to legislation or court rulings that affect your donors, or taking advantage of a breaking news story.

Some of your prospects and donors will just love being called on the phone. Ask any successful phone canvasser, and he or she can tell you stories of their donors who look forward to their calls every year. When Kim Simmons was a telephone canvasser for the Illinois Public Action Council, she was so popular with the people she called that one woman not only sent in a generous donation each time Kim called but she invited Kim to her daughter's wedding.

The telephone makes it easy for new friends to donate or join. Donors do not have to find an envelope, a stamp, and a check; they simply dial the phone and presto—the deed is done.

Telemarketing enables you to reach younger donors and members, who like the speed and ease of using the phone. You get a proven way to expand your base beyond the names you have now.

CALLING IN—800 AND 900 NUMBERS

Some nonprofits are now experimenting with using 800 and 900 phone numbers because this fundraising strategy is donor driven. Unlike telemarketing, where your fundraisers call your own list of donors and prospects, with an 800 or 900 number, you make your market aware of that number. Then the people who want to give call *you.*

With an 800-area-code number, the charity pays all of the costs; then your fundraisers ask for a commitment that will be charged to the caller's telephone bill or credit card. (Pledges promised to be mailed in have a much lower response rate.) The advantage of using an 800 number is that more donors are more familiar with it, and it can reach every U.S. phone. (In the near future, better technology will also allow calling to Canada and Europe.) There is no cost to the caller.

The disadvantage is that all costs are covered by the charity, so partisan causes can be victims of jamming by the opposition. An 800 number is easy for your friends to use and for your enemies to abuse.

With a 900-area-code number, each caller is charged a fee that is a specific amount per call. After the phone company deducts its charges, the charity gets the balance. The advantage of using a 900 number is that the call is charged directly to the person who calls. Unlike direct mail, start-up costs are very low since the telephone costs are deducted by the phone company from the caller. Because the phone company handles billing, there are fewer administrative expenses for the charity.

Enemies of the agency cannot afford to jam your 900 phone lines. Some systems allow "branching," or giving the caller several choices; for example: "Please punch 1 for more information on legislation, punch 2 to order our guide to dangerous pesticides, or punch 3 to make a donation." This feature enables a charity to inform, advocate, and raise funds from the same audience.

The disadvantage of 900 numbers is they have an unsavory reputation because of widespread use of 900 numbers by phone-sex businesses. Not all of your prospects can use a 900 number. Some rural communities block all 900 service, many parents block 900 numbers on their home phones, and according to the *Wall Street Journal*, 900 numbers are blocked from 60 percent of business phones. There is almost no way for a caller to change his or her mind; the charge goes on your bill six seconds after the connection.

If you want to consider telemarketing as a fundraising strategy, ask at least three other charities to recommend the firm they use. Check out the telemarketers in action to see if this is how you want to reach your donors. A great deal of experimentation is going on now with new ways to use 800 and 900 phone numbers, especially in conjunction with television. As homes become wired for fiber optics in the next decade, there will be another leap of what is possible through telephones and television. Keep an open mind about phones, and investigate how your organization can use this strategy now or in the future.

DOOR-TO-DOOR CANVASSING

Professional door-to-door canvassing has been the backbone of fundraising for consumer and community organizations for twenty years. The Citizen Action canvassers alone now market two million memberships every year in twenty-nine states. Canvassing is the most personal of the professional mass-marketing strategies and gives your fundraisers the chance for the most two-way communication. Prospects can be asked to do much more than just give money. An effective door-to-door canvass will also get petitions signed, get letters written, and find new volunteers.

Weather, surprisingly, is not a factor. That is because door-to-door canvassers are true believers; they believe in their cause heart and soul. Canvassers in the Midwest go out in the summer when it is 100 degrees in the shade and in the winter when it is 30 below.

The door-to-door canvass is a great entry-level job for any young person who wants to consider a job in fundraising. If you can sell memberships at the door, you can raise money in other ways, too.

As with mail, professional door-to-door canvassers saw enormous growth in competition in recent years. Today there are twenty canvasses operating every night in San Francisco and Boston, and multiple canvasses in every large city and college town.

Even the best door-to-door canvass does not work well in very low income or very high income neighborhoods, so you need to combine it with other strategies to reach low-income and wealthy donors. Like mail and the phone, door-to-door canvassing needs a "hot" issue with wide popularity, so it works best for emotional issues like stopping a local toxic waste dump.

COMPLAINTS

Complaints are inevitable. No matter what fundraising strategy you choose, prospects will complain. However, it seems as though more people complain more often about phone, mail, and door-to-door canvassing.

Some organizations simply take out all their big ($1,000+) donors from the lists for mail and phones. Most of these people are naturally exempt from the door canvass, since wealthy neighborhoods and buildings have not been profitable to canvass. If you are good at using your computers to segment your market, you can specify which strategies to use for each donor.

Since complaints are a part of fundraising, you need to plan to meet them. Let's look at each one.

PHONES

Ask people to name why they hate fundraisers, and nine out of ten will say, "They call me at dinnertime. I hate it when I have to answer the phone in the middle of dinner!"

Disregard the obvious response, which is "Don't answer the phone." Instead, ask people to tell you the best time to call, and put that information on their donor card. Some jobs will not let employees get calls at work; parents with new babies may not want to have naps interrupted at home; families with teenagers may have *no* good time to get through on their home phone and prefer to get calls at work.

The customer is always right. Ask each person when and where to call, then follow those instructions rigidly.

Some phone campaigns now head off complaints by mailing their best donors a postcard in advance. The card alerts donors to the call and offers them two ways to avoid the phone call: mail in this year's contribution before the call or call the 800 number now and pledge.

MAIL

Some of your donors will go berserk over multiple mailings or misspelled names or late mail. In any case, answer their complaints with a gracious letter and then be sure to meet their wishes.

Ask your donors what mail they want to receive:

- One mailing a year—only their dues renewal or annual gift.
- Mail on specific issues. For example, they want to get the mailings on the health clinic, but not on the senior citizens; they want the mailings on international missions, but not on the local soup kitchen. Or vice versa.
- Send it all. They are curious about everything, and they will respond when they can.
- Nothing. Never send anything. They do not want to get any mail ever, about anything.

It does not matter what the donors choose; honor their choice. If they do not want to be asked through the mail, you can choose different ways to ask.

If any members feel strongly about receiving mail, suggest that they register their name and address with the national association that maintains a "Mail Preference Service" used by the largest for-profit and nonprofit mailers. Individuals can write to the Direct Marketing Association, 11 West 42nd Street, P.O. Box 3861, New York, NY 10163-3861. The file is updated quarterly, so it will take three to six months to get one's name off mailing lists.

DOORS

For a door-to-door canvass, people will again complain about the time of day, interruptions, or other annoyances, such as frightening their dog. Most people are nicer in person, but someone will still want to complain to the canvasser or to the office. Apologize and mark the card, "Do not canvass at the door."

For any complaint, the president of your organization can send a written apology the next day. Simply say, "Thank you for letting me know of the frustration you experienced. . . . Please accept our personal apologies." Then say what action you have taken, and apologize again: "Again, Mr. Jones, please accept my apologies for the inconvenience caused."

WATCHDOGS

Two independent organizations have created a set of standards to evaluate charities and advise donors. Conforming to these standards will give you an outsider's endorsement to assure donors and prospects that your organization is well run. For free copies of the standards, write the National Charities Information Bureau, 19 Union Square West, New York, NY 10002 or the Council of Better Business Bureaus' Philanthropic Advisory Service, 4200 Wilson Boulevard, Arlington, VA 22203.

A charity is regulated by each state where it operates, usually by the attorney general as a charity and by the secretary of state as a corporation doing business in the state. Some cities may also require licensing for door-to-door canvassers or for some special events, such as raffles. Of course every charity must scrupulously obey all laws. In addition, set your own internal standards for ethical fundraising. See Chapter 12 for more on writing your own policies on raising money with integrity.

It is important to see the big picture. No matter what you do, someone will complain. Or maybe a dozen people will complain. This is no reason to stop a strategy that enables you to tell your story to tens of thousands of people each year. Respond promptly and courteously to all complaints, but do not stop a big campaign because of a tiny minority of the whole list.

CONCLUSION

Combining mass marketing strategies can make more money because your donors and members are asked more often in more different ways. Your program and fundraising goals will determine the best mix of strategies. For example, a very urgent issue could benefit from use of Western Union mailgrams that have been proven to be the first piece of mail opened 50 to 70 percent of the time. More complex issues may require a longer letter and visual aids to help members understand the issue and why money is needed.

Direct marketing enables your organization to tell its story to millions of people and motivate thousands of them to join you. In addition to raising money, all three of these fundraising strategies can be used to educate the public on your issues, ask them to take action, or get out to vote. Mass fundraising appeals give more voters more information and hence help them to be better citizens. Richard A. Viguerie, president of the direct marketing firm The Viguerie Company, points out, "In 1960 there were 50,000 contributors to the Nixon-Kennedy election; in 1988 there were two million."[4] Mass fundraising is one of the best tools to make democracy work and raise money at the same time.

"Always bear in mind that your own
resolution to succeed is more
important than any one thing."
                    —*Abraham Lincoln*

Chapter 8

How to Find the Big Givers

America is still the land of opportunity. There are now more
than a million millionaires and even sixty-six billionaires in
the United States. The number of affluent African Americans
doubled between 1982 and 1987. Of course, prosperity varies by
community and constituency. It is a lot easier to find rich folks
in Boca Raton or Beverly Hills than it is in the South Bronx or
on an Indian reservation. Only 2 percent of Native American
households reported income exceeding $50,000 in 1980, com-
pared to 20 percent of all American households.

It is common sense that rich people are going to support
first the politicians who keep them rich and the charities that
make their lives nicer. However, do not reject the idea of asking
for money from major donors simply because your organization
is new, controversial, or unorthodox. *Every* organization can
include an economic mix of prospects in its fundraising strategy. Let the wealthy know how great your group is, and give
them a chance to support you, too.

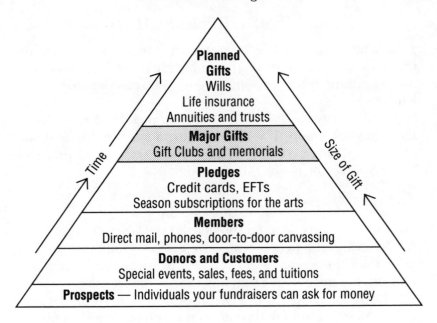

DEFINE MAJOR DONOR

First of all, define what is, for your organization, a major donor. Some grass roots groups consider any donor who gives more than $50 a major donor. Other groups put the trigger at $1,000. It does not matter what you choose, but your organization must be intentional about the size of gifts it wants to get.

After you set the dollar size of a donor, then do the research to learn where you can find people who can pay that amount and more. Giant charities employ full-time professional researchers. Smaller charities make donor research one of the jobs of the director of development. Volunteer groups can make donor research a job for one or two people who are too shy to ask for money.

Give the researchers a specific goal. Let's say your organization wants to get major gifts from fifty donors this year. Assuming one in five says yes, the researchers need to find 250 prospects.

INSIDE RESEARCH

First, and always best, are your own donors. Who loves the organization? Who has seen his or her children flourish because of this group? Who has volunteered? Who has donated consistently?

The best place to look is your own membership and your list of annual donors. If you do not have a membership that pays dues or a donor base that donates every year, build that base before you do the major gift campaign.

YOUR DONOR BASE

On your own lists, look for (obviously) the largest gifts and (not so obviously) the people who have given to you every year for more than three years. Even small gifts, given consistently, can indicate the possibility of giving a larger gift if asked.

Look for people who give an odd amount of money, like $27 or $358. An odd dollar amount can be a clue the donor is allocating his or her total annual charity budget among several nonprofits. This suggests the donor plans his or her charitable giving and your group is already on the short list of good organizations. Look for the best addresses, multiple addresses (summers in Lake Wobegon, Minnesota, and winters in Lake Okeechobee, Florida), the names of the local aristocrats, celebrities, and entrepreneurs, and other indications of commitment or wealth.

For new organizations, you have to start with your own board and active volunteers, and then branch out. For older organizations, look for second- or third-generation members and multiple members from the same family.

Then ask the grapevine who won the lottery, inherited money, sold the ranch, or made a fortune by inventing a better mousetrap. For old money, look for people who went to elite schools, belong to private clubs, or summer and ski at exclusive resorts. For new money, look for the entrepreneurs, especially minorities, women, and immigrants, who want to leverage an entree into the established (white-male-Anglo) power structure.

You can also tailor your research to match the mission of the organization. Historic preservation groups can check the historical society and genealogical society to find the people with deep roots in the community. Environmental, hunting, and fishing clubs can find wealthy outdoorsy types by checking the state department of motor vehicles for owners of campers and recreational vehicles and the state department of conservation of game and wildlife for owners of boats and yachts.

OUTSIDE RESEARCH

Charity begins at home. The first place to look for major gifts must be your own board of directors, active volunteers, and senior staff. Do not think that total strangers will support your group if the cause is not compelling enough to get your own leadership to give.

After you get support from your own leadership and your own donors, then you can research outsiders who share a commitment to your cause and are able to make a large gift. All these research sources, from corporate annual reports to divorce court records, are legal sources of information available to the public. Reading them is how gossip magazines, venture capitalists, opposing lawyers, political parties, and giant charities collect their ammunition. They can help your organization, too.

Review the list of suggestions for finding small individual donors in Chapter 5. We will discuss researching corporate donors in Chapter 11 and foundations in Chapter 13. The following paragraphs describe some other places you can find out more about possible major donors.

MAGAZINES

Town and Country runs a feature called "The Most Generous Living Americans," naming donors of more than $10 million up to the man who has given more than $300 million—Paul Mellon. The *Fortune* 500 issue tells which corporations are making money; the *Inc.* 100 tells about the 100 fastest-growing small companies; the *Forbes* 400 tells about wealthy individuals. Most cities have a city magazine that does an occasional article on the fifty richest people in town and covers the social whirl of the elite. Trade magazines all include a gossip column on people in the business.

NEWSPAPERS
Follow the *Wall Street Journal*, local business papers, and the daily papers in every community where your prospects have homes. Assign someone to clip, file, and key into your data base current information from the business section, news, and gossip columns. Although there is no longer a "society page," most papers have replaced it with a "style" section that will report on clever, expensive, or star-studded gala events.

Assign someone to track the obituaries and key this data into your data base daily. My dear sainted father used to say that the obits were the Irish sports page; if he got through the *F*s and did not see his name, he knew he had to go to work. Obits can tell you about family relations, religious preference, and memorials.

REFERENCE BOOKS
Ask the librarian in the reference room or the researcher for a big charity to give you more ideas. You can get started with *Who's Who*, including the regional versions like *Who's Who in the Southwest* and professional versions like *Who's Who in Banking*. These are fun to read and tell you about your prospect's jobs, schools, family, clubs, religion, political party, military service, awards, and other information. Also check Standard and Poor's *Register of Corporations, Directors and Executives*; Moody's directories; and state as well as local professional directories for lawyers, accountants, and other professions. In twelve cities you can check out old money in *The Social Register*.

NONPROFIT SOURCES
Many wealthy people give away money from their own checkbook, through one or more foundations, and also through their job. Check out philanthropists by name in the *Foundation Directory* and the *Corporate Giving Directory*. Ask all your volunteers to bring into the fundraising office copies of the donor lists from other charities' programs, newsletters, and annual reports. These can tell your volunteers who is giving how much to the competition and may remind them of a good prospect they already know. It is futile to cannibalize these lists

if the names are all strangers to your volunteers. If none of your leaders know any of your community's current major donors, work on recruiting people with wealth or power for your board before you launch your major gift campaign.

PUBLICLY HELD COMPANIES

If your prospect is a director, officer, or major stockholder of a publicly held corporation, you can find out more about his or her assets, income, and retirement package through the annual reports and 10-K forms required by the federal government.

The Securities and Exchange Commission (SEC) requires that publicly held companies publish an annual report. These reveal the largest stockholders, salaries of the officers, and retirement benefits. If you know Mr. Smith retired from the Widget Corporation in 1989, get the corporation's annual report for that year to learn his retirement package. The SEC also requires a 10-K report that will tell you stock holdings of officers and directors and other data. If a private company is sold to a public company, the 10-K will tell you the selling price.

There has been a lot of news about illegal "insider" dealings, but more than 99 percent of what insiders do is legal, and that information is also retrievable for fundraisers. For the SEC, an "insider" is an executive, policy-making officer, or director of a publicly held company, the head of a subsidiary of that company, or an investor who owns more than 10 percent of the stock. A computer data base called Invest/Net keeps track of all purchases and sales of stock in the eleven thousand companies filing with the SEC. It also records all the filings for banking insiders with the Federal Deposit Insurance Company (FDIC), the Office of Thrift Supervision, and the Comptroller of the Currency for American financial institutions. For Canadian fundraisers, Invest/Net tracks the two thousand Canadian companies on the Toronto stock exchange. Invest/Net keeps track of deals every day. You can buy the service yourself or retrieve it through other on-line suppliers such as Dialog and Dow Jones News Retrieval, often available at the public library through the computer-assisted reference center.

The Invest/Net Group can also match the names in your

data base against its list of 150,000 corporate officers, directors, and major shareholders; create a complete trading history back to 1983 for a specific person; or pull the names of every officer or director who serves on the boards of publicly held companies with your prospect. This can help you find allies to persuade your prospect to give to your organization. For this and other computerized research services, see the advertisements in the trade magazines, shop the vendors at fundraising conferences, and ask local researchers who they recommend.

This kind of research is especially valuable for large national organizations with many constituents who move or change jobs often. For smaller organizations, fundraisers can get accurate current data on the real net worth of local business, professional, and civic leaders so you do not underestimate a prospect's ability to give.

COUNTY OFFICES

After an estate is probated, probate court files are public information. If you suspect someone has inherited wealth, write the county where the estate was probated. Ask for the will and the inventory that tells you about real estate, stock, and other property. Today shrewd planners avoid probate by setting up trusts for one or two future generations, but probate court is a good source for the others.

If someone's divorce became final today, the information about it is available at the clerk of court's office in the county of residence. Court records can include financial statements and even IRS returns. However, remember that divorce lawyers specialize in hiding the assets of the party they are representing, so always assume this information is *very* conservative.

The county treasurer or county assessor will have data on property owned in that county, including its assessed value and taxes.

If your prospect contributes to political candidates, his or her donations may be public information, depending on the size of the gift and the integrity of the campaign office. (Bags of cash on election day are not yet a thing of the past in Chicago, Texas, and other bastions of participatory democracy.) Legal contributions to local city and county candidates are recorded by each campaign and available at the county board of elections; records of donations to candidates for state office are available through the state board of elections in your state capitol. Most states require disclosure of gifts of $100 or more.

At the federal level, records of donations larger than $200 per year to candidates for president, senator, or member of Congress are available from the Public Records Office of the Federal Elections Commission (FEC). Your researcher can retrieve data from 1978 to the present by donor's name, city, state, zip code, or amount. You can also retrieve data for Political Action Committees (PACs). For more information visit the FEC's Washington, D.C., office, or call 800/424-9530.

Especially look for donors who gave to politicians who ran on issues defined by your organization. If the politician won, remind your prospect that the politician won because your group cut the issue for the public. (It doesn't hurt to have a letter from the elected official saying this.) If the politician lost, remind the prospect that electoral politics gives, at *best*, a 50-50 chance of winning, whereas a terrific organization like yours is out there fighting for the citizens every day, regardless of who is in City Hall or the White House.

CAUTIONS

Assume that any research using books or data bases is incomplete and out of date. Especially families with old money pride themselves on avoiding publicity. They find ways—get married, change their names, move to Montana—to stay off these lists. Merry pranksters have been known to fill out the *Who's Who* questionnaires with the names of their pets and other nonsense.

Doing research *is* a way to expand your prospects beyond your own list. Just be sure you take anything in print with a grain of salt. Whenever possible, verify your research with insiders who know the prospect.

Do not be misled by people who flash a lot of cash. With easy credit, almost anyone can *look* rich. I knew a salesman who dazzled his clients with a $80,000 sports car. He confessed to me that it was 102 percent financed; he even financed the license plates. On the other hand, there are people worth millions who drive the same compact car for fifteen years.

Actually most of the millionaires in America are not flamboyant movie stars or sports idols; they are boring types who go to work every day. Demographic research tells us that the average American millionaire is John Doe, age fifty-seven, who has been married for thirty-two years to the same woman, owns a highly productive small or medium-sized business, has two children, and works ten to fourteen hours a day, six days a week.[1] There are now more than one million millionaires, only about 1 percent of the population, but they hold 33 percent of the private wealth, 60 percent of the corporate stocks, and 9 percent of the real estate. Nearly twice as many are in sales or marketing than are doctors. They do not work for big corporations, but instead own their own business or a share of a private company. Less than 1 percent are movie stars, entertainers, athletes, or (har-de-har) writers.[2]

Your goal is to find the people who share your values and to give them a chance to help your organization. Always begin with a broad base of annual givers, and then add on the wealthier people who can and will give more if you ask them. According to the U.S. Census Bureau, about 2.2 percent of U.S. households have incomes greater than $100,000. These households each gave about $3,000 to charity in 1989 and will give more in future years. It will take time to find, educate, encourage, and involve these people, but on the other hand, how much time will it take to sell three hundred $10 memberships? You need and want both large and small donors.

RECORDS

It is vital to keep up-to-date records on all of your donors and to collect more extensive information on your best prospects. Several excellent software packages are designed just to help you track and retrieve donor information. These range in price from $35 to $8,000. Attend two or three sales demonstrations to see what the biggest packages offer, and then interview local fundraisers to see what they recommend. Be sure to talk to both the director of development and the person who actually keys in and retrieves the data.

Get your donor data on a computer from day one, because one of the best indicators of a major donor prospect is repeat gifts over several years.

Back up the information every day, and always keep two duplicate sets of the data outside the office. I like to use the "odd-even" backup system. On the odd-numbered days, you back up the data on your odd disks, and on the even-numbered days you back up the data on your even disks. Then if the worst happens, and the office burns down while you are at lunch, destroying the hard drive, the original disks, and one set of backups, you have another set of backup disks that are at most one day behind.

If your records are not on computer now, make this your priority for the next month. Start today. Hire temporaries or high school and college students to key in your data. Even with the most zealous volunteers, you cannot compete in today's fundraising market doing paper retrieval. A manual system is too fragile and too limited; learn to like computers.

For more advice, contact the data-processing people at the best charities in town and shop the vendors at national conventions. Thirteen cities now have technical assistance providers who specialize in knowing the best computers and software for nonprofits. These members of the Technology Resource Consortium (TRC) are not pushing any particular brand of merchandise; they allow nonprofits to try out a variety of equipment and software and help you analyze which system is best for your current and future needs. For a list of TRC members, send a self-addressed, stamped envelope to the Information Technology Resource Center (ITRC), 59 E. Van Buren, Suite 2020, Chicago, IL 60605. You can also get advice from local technical assistance providers, some United Ways, user clubs, dealers, and manufacturers. Or hire a hacker, someone who loves computers. Someone who enjoys working with the computer can infect the rest of the office with a good attitude, too.

Do not buy *anything* until you check with your national organization. Make sure the hardware and the software are compatible with the system your state and national offices are using or will be using next year. Many national organizations can purchase what you need at a deep volume discount, so ask your national office before you go crazy and pay retail.

PROFESSIONALS AND VOLUNTEERS

Prospect research has become such an important part of successful fundraising that it is now recognized as a profession, complete with a professional association to advocate for access to public information and to uphold ethical standards for confidentiality of private information. (See the listing at the end of Chapter 3 for information on the American Prospect Research Association.) As the Information Age continues, the ability to access, retrieve, and analyze data on donors and prospects will become more and more critical.

Although the field is becoming more professional, the best prospects remain your own leaders and the people they know. Surveys and fundraising war stories all show that donors make a big gift because they care passionately about the cause. Of course interest in tax benefits, status, and possible short cuts to heaven are always at work, but most big givers give because they want to give. All the data bases in the library cannot replace one local insider who has the trust of the people you want to reach, because he or she will know the stories that make a difference.

For example, volunteer Margaret Standish is working in Boston's Back Bay Area to preserve and protect the Commonwealth Avenue Mall. This landmark, built on the model of the great French esplanades, is not a shopping center but a landscaped area between two boulevards that contains the largest urban stand of elm trees in the United States.

One elderly woman gave the project $1,500 to buy a new maple tree in memory of her husband; it will shade the park bench where they courted sixty years ago. Many of the project's donors have personal reasons to care about the area; their individual support will leverage a six-figure gift from a major Boston business next year.

Romance and memories are not, and never will be, in the legal records. So successful prospect research needs teamwork between your professionals who know what is in the documents and data bases and your veteran volunteers who know what is in the hearts and souls of the donors.

The following sample shows some of the information that is useful to collect and retrieve. The better software will allow you to cross-index and update data in multiple files. So on the John Adams file, it will say, "husband of Abigail Smith Adams, father of John Quincy Adams, and grandfather of Charles Francis Adams." When any of these files changes, so will all of the others.

PROSPECT RESEARCH FORM

Devise your own form to record information you learn about your best prospects. Add anything else that your organization or your national office wants.

PROSPECT RESEARCH FORM

Name _____ Birth date _____

Spouse _____ Birth date _____

Business/profession _____

Address _____

(Do we have matching gift forms on file?)

Title _____

Phone: Office _____ Car _____

Secretary _____

Phone _____ Fax _____

How long at this job _____

Previous employer _____

If retired, year retired _____

Residence: Summer (dates) _____

Address _____

Phone: Home _____ Car _____

Winter (dates) _____

Address _____

_____

Phone: Home _____ Car _____

Directorates and other companies:

1.

2.

3.

(Do we have matching gift forms on file?)

Estimated annual salary _____

Bonuses _____

Estimated profit from business: $ _____

Other sources of income:

1.

2.

3.

Estimated net worth:

Other evidence of wealth:

Education:

School/College/University	Dates Attended	Degrees
1.		
2.		
3.		

Military service _____

Religion _____

Political party _____

Organizations:	Offices Held
1.	
2.	
3.	

Clubs:	Offices Held
1.	
2.	
3.	

Who knows this prospect?

Name   Relationship

1.

2.

3.

Interest in our program:

Giving history:

Last Gift $\$$_____ When _____ Why _____

Largest Gift $\$$_____ When _____ Why _____

Cumulative Total: $\$$_____

Years given: 19____ to 19____

Volunteer history:

Local	State	National	International

Board

Committees

Special abilities

Program interests

Children:

Names	Birth Dates	Remarks (Schools, Marital Status, Role in Family Business)

1.

2.

3.

Attorney: Name _____ Phone _____

Financial adviser: Name _____ Phone _____

Banker: Name _____ Phone _____

Researched by _____ Date _____

"The first gift I made when I came
into possession of my small estate was
a thousand dollars to the library of
Rockford College, with the stipulation
that it be spent for scientific books."
[$1,000 in 1883 = $12,800 in 1990]
    —*Jane Addams*
        Twenty Years at Hull
        House

Chapter 9

The Big Gift—Now

Some years before she died, Lila Wallace remarked that she
knew her will by heart: "I, Lila Acheson Wallace, being of
sound mind . . . spent it."[1] She spent it locally and globally. Her
money renovated the Great Hall at the Metropolitan Museum of
Art in New York City; restored the flower gardens at the home of
artist Claude Monet in Giverny, France; and preserved the villa
of art critic Bernard Berenson in Tuscany, Italy.

Of course, she had plenty of money to spend, since she had
married the boss of the *Reader's Digest,* the world's most popular magazine. As the daughter of a painter and a Presbyterian
minister, she knew the importance of both beauty and giving to
the things that matter. Before she had money, she spent her *time*
for good causes, teaching high school, working for the YWCA,
and serving as a traveling organizer in World War I, setting up
recreational centers for women factory workers. She became
what fundraisers call a "good prospect"—someone who has the
experience, know-how, values, vision, and means to make a
major gift to an important cause.

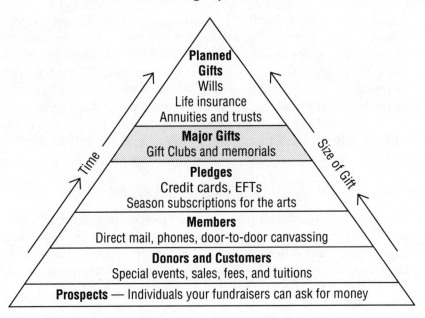

You can find good prospects to give major gifts to your organization, you can learn to ask for big gifts, and you can teach others to ask for large contributions. Asking person to person for big gifts is the fastest way to raise the most money with the least expense. When you ask openly and sincerely for a big gift, you are giving the donor an opportunity to make a big difference in your organization's work. Making a big gift makes the donor feel proud. You get the gift of his or her money; the donor gets the gift of self-esteem.

Do not project your own financial limits onto other people. You may be getting a salary in five figures, but the average CEO in America was paid $1,856,697 in 1989.

Maybe the most that you can give Spelman College is $220 or $22,000, but Bill and Camille Cosby can (and did) give $22 million. Practice what you preach. If you believe that all people have something important to give to your organization, act as though you mean it. Ask the people who can give time to give their time, and ask the people who can give major money to make a major gift.

You are competing for the disposable income of each donor. Should a yuppie buy a sports car for $80,000 or give the money to your group? Should an entrepreneur buy a summer place for $500,000 or give the money to your group? Should a tycoon buy a new plane for $2 million or give the money to your group? Have the courage of your convictions. Your organization will make the world better; you deserve this money just as much as, or more than, manufacturers of luxury goods. Believe you're worth it, and ask for it!

WHO CAN ASK

The best askers are people who have personally made a major gift to this cause. It is much easier if the fundraisers also have experience from other major fund drives and have either wealth or status themselves. However, almost anyone can learn to ask for major gifts if the person has the courage of his or her convictions.

It is ideal to combine one person who has personally benefited because of your work and one who has the confidence to ask for the gift. Do not feel you have to be limited to two people, nor should you always take the same two people. If your first team does not work out, be sensible: send another team. One time a donor did not click at all with my partner and me, two boring middle-class white people, but really liked the next pair, a black pregnant lawyer and a priest. *They* got $35,000. Avoid using children of the prospect; kids cannot close on their own parents. However, they can open the doors for other people to ask.

SKILLS

Successful fundraising requires volunteers who can do three things: listen, think, and ask. Good listeners will collect invaluable advice to improve your programs even when they do not get a gift. Although we can all name names of the exceptions, most people did not get rich being stupid. Be eager to get good advice from the experts at making money.

Second, you need volunteers who can think. Someone

simply reciting the script will never raise big gifts. Volunteers who really care about their organization and really want to get a gift will find solutions that are profitable and ethical for both parties.

Third, you have to ask. The prospect cannot respond unless he or she knows what you want. If you know what you want and say what you want, the prospect will admire your sincerity and simplicity. You both know why you are there—ask.

USE THE CEO

Although volunteers are the best at asking for major gifts, this also has to be a major part of the job of the CEO. If you are the boss, at least half of your time should be spent cultivating current and future donors and asking for gifts. More is better, and full-time may be necessary if your group is in debt.

When Beverly Sills took over as CEO of the New York City Opera, the opera raised $5 million and spent $6.5 million the first year. Then its warehouse burned to the ground. The company lost $10 million worth of costumes and settings; the insurance company paid $1.5 million. Then the unions went on strike. (And you think you have problems?) Beverly Sills could have filed for bankruptcy; many people, including her own husband, encouraged her to do it. Instead, she determined to succeed.

She focused all her energies full time on asking for big gifts from the city, corporations, and mostly major givers. As she jokes, "I got the reputation of being the most expensive breakfast in New York."[2] Results: she got the financial support she needed and in five years had the company in the black with a budget of $20 million a year. Of course, she did not do it alone. She also had excellent professional counsel and many high-powered friends to help. But it was her resolution that made it possible.

Every CEO must care heart and soul about fundraising, especially working with the people who can give you major gifts. Even if you are not a world-famous prima donna, you can make the effort to meet with a major gift prospect every day.

Put major-gift fundraising first on the CEO's work plan every day. Any committee can recruit members and put on special events. The leaders, and the people who want to be leaders next, need to focus on getting the big gifts.

BEFORE YOU ASK

Unlike asking for smaller gifts, asking for large gifts will take several meetings as you develop trust with the prospects, learn what they want to do, and devise the best way to meet their goals. Because this is a long-term process, your fundraisers need to be prepared before they begin to ask for major gifts.

MAKE A GIFT

Before the first meeting, the people who are going to be asking for major gifts must make a major gift themselves. Board members, volunteers, and senior staff can make a one-time gift or a multiyear pledge. Many charities make it easy for paid staff to make a major gift through payroll deductions.

The organization's president, the chairperson of the major-gift campaign committee, and the CEO must show leadership by making a major gift. If necessary, look at your own list of where you make charitable gifts. If this is the year you want to make a major gift, cut out the $25, $50, and $100 gifts to groups that are less important to you, and combine the amount in one major gift to the organization.

Even better, practice what you preach and change your habits to improve your life. Then donate the money saved to the major-gift campaign. Quit smoking and give $1,000 to a nonprofit hospital or the Lung Association; wear a cloth coat rather than fur and donate $15,000 to the Humane Society or the zoo; ride the bus rather than buy a new statusmobile and give $40,000 to Mothers Against Drunk Driving or the group organizing for better access for disabled people on your city's mass-transit system. You get the idea.

People believe what they see more than what they hear. It does not matter what you say—if volunteers and donors do not see the leadership making major gifts, they will never believe this is important or urgent. Making your own big contribution is the most important step to guaranteeing your success in asking for big contributions.

PRACTICE ASKING

After you have made your gift, practice asking for a major gift. Act out saying, "We want you to give $1,000" (or $1 million, or the balance of your estate, or whatever your goal is). Practice smiling, making eye contact, and listening. Brainstorm in a small group to come up with possible tough questions you might be asked, and rehearse the most effective honest answers you can give.

Having the team of people who will ask for large gifts act out a request will show you each person's strengths. Then you can match the best storytellers with the best closers.

Videotape each person doing the ask. Especially if you will be involved in a very long campaign, will be asking for very large gifts, or will have only one chance to solicit a key donor, videotaping is a great tool to use to improve your skills.

ATTITUDE

If you perceive any negative attitudes about asking for money from rich people, this is the time to discuss them frankly. Some volunteers are terrific at organizing events and selling memberships but not good at asking for major gifts. For whatever reason, they can not get over their anger toward rich people. This is *not* the time for amateur group therapy. It is the time to find any volunteers who manifest negative attitudes toward major donors and assign those people to different fundraising committees.

As with any minority group, major donor prospects can be sensitive to language they perceive as offensive. Most rich people hate to be called "rich people." Patricians talk about "people with wealth" or simply "the right people." Rich good old boys say "Bubba has a bunch of money," and the top financial advisers call rich people "high net-worth individuals." Some very wealthy, very conservative, and very old-money people

cannot bear to discuss money at all and instead will use eu-
phemisms like "Mary's trust fund" or "Bill's portfolio." Check
your own language and attitudes to be sure you are speaking
and acting in a way that respects your donors.

ASSEMBLE TRAINING MATERIALS

Prepare a kit of materials for the volunteers and staff who will
be asking for money. This can include a brief history of your
organization, highlights of its most outstanding achievements,
the need for this particular request, and the way it fits into the
big picture of the organization. Include a menu of funding
needs and the opportunities for recognition—for example, for
$5,000 you get your name on a chair; for $50,000 you get your
name in the lobby; for $5 million you get your name on the
theater. Remind volunteers about the tax advantages of giving to
a tax-exempt nonprofit organization. Include the names and
numbers for leadership, the fundraising staff, and the organization's legal, insurance, and tax advisers to help with complicated gifts.

Give a simple step-by-step list of *exactly* what you want
volunteers to do, including the reporting, paperwork, and
thank-you notes. Include all of the organization stationery,
envelopes, and brochures they will need.

Also spell out what volunteers may *not* do, such as offer to
rename the college for a donor. For larger institutions, specify
the name of one executive who will approve and sign all agreements.

It goes without saying—but say it anyway—that all information about a prospect's personal or financial circumstances
will be held in strictest confidence by the volunteer and the
organization. Major donors will need to feel they can tell you
about their wishes and fears about money, their own future, and
the future of their loved ones. Fundraisers who earn a reputation for complete discretion will get the most repeat major gifts.

RATE YOUR PROSPECTS

The last step before approaching the prospects is estimating
how much money they can give and how much you can ask for

at this time. Convene your committee, including people who know the prospects and a few people who have had experience rating prospects for other campaigns. Assign a specific dollar amount for each prospect so it is easier for both the asker and the askee.

Aim high. It is flattering to the prospect to be asked for a large amount, and people like a challenge. If it is too high, do not worry—the prospect will suggest a lower amount.

Setting dollar goals in a group assures that prospects who are committed to your cause and have the ability to give are not deprived of the joy of giving a large amount to your group. This saves everyone from the fainthearted, who will want to murmur, "Any amount will be appreciated." Since the group has set specific goals for the campaign and for each prospect, the solicitor has to ask first for the amount set by the group.

HOW TO ASK

If you are asking a donor or volunteer from your own list, begin by finding people within the organization who have worked with the prospect. Who served on the board or a committee with this person? Who knows her from conventions, parties, or office work? What are the prospect's major areas of interest? Why did she give money in the past? Did she support Duke Ellington or Donizetti? Affordable housing or African art? Senior citizens or the sophomore class? Who asked her? How?

Write a letter thanking the prospect for his support in the past. Say you want to meet with him to discuss the goals of the organization now, and ways he can support these goals. Call to confirm that he got the letter, and ask to meet with him in person. Let him set the date, time, and place, but be prepared with some specific choices: "I'll be in your neighborhood on Friday morning for the dedication of the recycling center. May I see you at your office at 10:00 A.M.?"

Prepare a menu of choices of what the prospect might like to fund, based on his or her giving history and what your research tells you. Always include at least one choice that seems to be a real financial stretch, because you never know all about the prospect's commitment or ability to give. Take along someone the prospect knows, from the same neighborhood, congregation, workplace, or age group. Or take someone this person would like to know, such as the charismatic founder of your organization or the prize-winning doctor from your clinic.

CULTIVATION

Even if you know the prospect through work in the organization, find out more about the person. Why did he join? Why did he stay involved? What does she like best about the organization? What does she think should be improved? How? What victories is the prospect most proud of? What will be the most serious areas of need for the next ten years?

For strangers, people who are not already in the organization's "family," you need to take even more time and care. Since these prospects are new to you (and you to them), you need to develop a relationship and do more research on the spot at the same time.

Learn

The goal at every meeting is to learn all you can about this prospect's particular interests and needs. Listen, listen, listen. It is enormously helpful to have two people making the calls, so you can debrief later and make sure you both heard the same thing. With two people, one can listen while the other one talks. A partner is also invaluable for those of us prone to talk too much. Many times I have been saved by "Gee, Joan, that's very interesting, but I'd like to hear what Miss Addams has to say . . ."

Depending on the prospect's current interest in your work, personal timetable, and rapport with you, you may be able to make a match in one or two meetings, or you may need one or two years to build a relationship of trust—or more for very large gifts. Keep in touch between meetings with phone calls, letters, and clippings. Alert the prospect when your leaders will be on the radio or TV. Be sure the prospect gets a good seat at the benefit if he or she likes parties and is introduced to your top leaders, staff, and other donors.

ASK

Don't forget to ask. You do not need to ask every time you meet, but you'd better be asking at least every other time. Think of your first request as your opening bid. It is a place to start. Then as you both find out how serious the prospect is, you can refine the deal to meet her needs. Does she want her name on the building? Or would she prefer this gift to be in honor of her father? Or does she want complete confidentiality as a requirement for making the gift? Would she rather make a lead gift to kick off a campaign and motivate other givers? Or is she a "wait and see" type who pledges to give the last million if you can raise the first three million? Does she want her husband, lawyer, and accountant to approve this donation? Or can she make the transaction on her own?

What does he want to get? A seat on the board? A press conference announcing this gift? Entree to the inner circle of big givers? A private meeting with the founder? Can you deliver what he wants?

Are there any strings on the gift? If so, are they acceptable according to the organization's policies?

It may help to tell the prospect what others are giving. You can say, "Well, Miss Addams, eleven other members of the class of '82 have given $1,000 gifts." This makes it easy for her to match this gift or, if she is a competitive type, to show off and give a $5,000 gift. Even more persuasive is to remind your prospect that you personally believe in this cause so much that you have made your own major gift.

Yes!!!

The close of this gift, and the cultivation of the next gift, begins when the prospect says yes. Most people capable of making a large gift can make more than one gift. Many of our best donors know other good prospects. So the actual experience of donating a large gift should be simple, clear, and reassuring. Then it will be easy to repeat and easy to recommend to other prospects.

If you are using a printed pledge card, fill it out and ask the prospect to sign it immediately. If you are not using pledge cards, ask your prospect several questions to be sure that you understand what he or she wants to do with the money, stocks, property, or other gift. Write down the answers, hand the page to the prospect, and ask, "Is this what you want?" Ask the donor to make any changes, if possible in his or her own handwriting. If there are other people present, such as a spouse or lawyer, ask them to review your notes with the prospect's additions and to agree that it is what the prospect wants.

Thank the prospect in person immediately and ask what kind of formal recognition he or she would like. Repeat that all information will be kept strictly confidential except for the recognition approved by the donor, such as listing the gift in the annual report.

Put a handwritten thank-you note in the mail the same day. Then send an official letter confirming the agreement as you understand it from your notes and ask the prospect to confirm your understanding. Verify the spelling of all names. Also send thank-you notes to the person who made the introduction and any advisers.

If the prospect has any questions after receiving your letter, work them out as soon as possible. Use your volunteer legal and financial talents to make it easy and pleasant (cost free) for the donor. Encourage the donor to include his or her advisers to finalize the agreement.

Many successful fundraisers benefit from a split personality. On the one hand, they love risks, aim high, and believe anything is possible. On the other hand, they know nothing is more important than attention to details.

For major gifts, this means good fundraisers will ask for large amounts of money and motivate their volunteers to ask for large amounts. It also means no detail is too small for their personal attention.

Always verify that the financial department handles all financial arrangements promptly and courteously. When the financial department sends the checks for payments from annuities or pooled income trusts, the fundraiser or CEO can attach a personalized note for each donor. Be compulsive about listing all names and amounts correctly in your newsletter, campaign reports, and annual report. Push the public relations department to get news releases out to all the media serving the donor's communities and profession. In a small office, the fundraiser may also handle these financial and publicity chores. In a larger institution, the fundraiser must personally make sure the best staff handle follow-up in a way that will encourage future gifts.

No . . .

If you get a "No," call again in a year or two. If you get a "Not now," call again in six months. If you get a "Let me think about it," call again in three months. For any response that is more encouraging, ask before you leave when you may call again.

Follow-Up

After the meeting, send a thank-you note the same day, even if the prospect says no. Debrief with your partner, the staff, and the committee. Write down any suggestions for other prospects, ways to improve the material, or program ideas, and send them to the office. Strategize on what worked best and what needs to be changed before the next meeting. Most major gifts will require several meetings with the donor. Keep careful records and keep trying until you succeed.

NAMING NAMES

Some major donors prefer to remain anonymous, but most people like to see their names in your written materials, such as the annual report. For any gift, ask the donor if you may publish his or her name, and ask how he or she would like to be listed.

Today there are many more choices for listing names, so be sure you find out what your donor wants. Never simply lift a name from another charity's list because some donors will choose a different style for different organizations. For example, Martha Washington may be listed as Ms. Martha Washington in the annual report from the Mount Vernon Women's Center, but her contribution to the veteran's group could be from General and Mrs. George Washington, her contribution to the neighborhood group from George and Martha Washington, and her contribution to her elementary school from Patsy Dandridge (Mrs. George Washington).

Names are news, and a photo is worth a thousand words. Put the names and photos of your donors in the newsletter, the annual report, and anywhere else they will fit. Theaters, hospitals, art museums, and colleges put the names of donors in their lobbies. Religious congregations have allowed donors' names on specific buildings, windows, organs, and artwork. In the Renaissance, church donors actually got their own likenesses included in stained-glass windows next to the saints and the Holy Family. Today, most people settle for a brass plaque and recognition at the annual meeting.

Donors love to get their names (or those of loved ones) put up in lights. In fundraising jargon displaying names of donors is marketed as "Designated Gift and Memorial Opportunities." If your group chooses to use designated gifts, set a policy on prices, recognition, and what is or is not for sale. For example, every building owned by the American Red Cross is just called a Red Cross building, but specific rooms or equipment may be named for donors, such as the Clara Barton bloodmobile.

More and more charities are finding ways to let a donor put his or her name on a specific piece of their program. Obviously this is easiest if you have a new building, but almost anything will work. For example, at the National Cathedral in Washington, D.C., you could sponsor a Gothic pinnacle for $400,000 or pay for a single carved angel for a bargain $5,000. At the world famous Topeka Zoo you could underwrite the Lion Night Quarters for $75,000 or get the lions a scratching post for $5,000. My personal favorite is the University of Southern California's program to peddle each position on its football team. The quarterback and the center are already gone, but if you act fast, you can still get a defensive back position named for you for only $250,000.[3]

The organization wants donors' names placed where they will be seen. So if you sponsor the Gothic pinnacle your name goes up in the lobby of the cathedral, where most people will see it, not on the pinnacle, where only the pigeons would see it. High schools and colleges can create the "Hall of Fame" for alumni who have been successful and supported the school. (The Topeka Public High School complements this with the "Teachers Hall of Fame" for the faculty who helped the achievers on their way.)

In addition, many organizations use premiums for their donors, from tote bags and T-shirts for small donors to valuable jewelry and artwork for their big donors. Private time with a charismatic leader can be a great incentive for major donors if it fits the style of your leader. Some noted nonprofit CEOs are like successful politicians and love to gladhand their best donors.

The ideal form of donor recognition costs the organization little or nothing but is highly coveted by major donor prospects. Universities with popular football teams designate parking spaces near the football stadium as rewards to their biggest donors. For example, membership in the Texas A&M booster club known as the "Twelfth Man" costs from $12 per semester for students up to $25,000 for the most zealous "Aggies." The best donors are given the best parking spaces for their tailgate parties before the home games.

Choose a recognition system that is consistent with local practices. Big-city art museums in the United States literally put their donors' names in lights in an electronic display in the lobby. One art museum in Canada puts the names of its donors in small gray type on a small gray display in the back of the lobby under the stairs, because anything flashier would not be considered to be in good taste.

The ultimate recognition is to ask your best volunteer fundraisers and donors to serve on your board of directors. Then you get talent that has been in the trenches and knows the organization well. Most major donors will not want to serve on your board unless they have a deep personal interest in the cause, but some will lend their endorsement by allowing you to use their names on an honorary board.

ANONYMOUS DONORS

Not everyone wants his name in lights. The largest gift ever made by an American was from Paul Mellon to the U.S. government to create the National Gallery. He donated art worth $31 million, plus $15 million for the building and $10 million for an endowment. Mellon stipulated that the museum must *not* bear his name, so that it would be easier to get more gifts from other benefactors.[4] If a donor asks to remain anonymous, you must rigorously protect the name of that donor.

MEMORIALS

Some donors may prefer to give a gift as a memorial for a loved one. This strategy is used effectively by religious congregations, hospitals, hospices, and disease associations, whose donors appreciate any system that makes their lives easier at a very stressful time.

For example, the B.C. & Yukon Heart Foundation acknowledges memorial gifts by sending the next of kin a card bearing a picture of the foxglove plant (*Digitalis purpurea,* which is used to make a drug for heart patients) and the words "To Honour the Memory of _____ a contribution has been received by the B.C. & Yukon Heart Foundation from _____." The names are added in calligraphy. The dollar amount of the gift is never disclosed.

The next of kin also gets a smaller version of the card that he or she can send to the donor. It says, "Thank you for being so thoughtful. Your In Memorium gift to the B.C. & Yukon Heart Foundation is truly appreciated."

The Foundation itself sends a thank-you card to the donor that thanks him or her for the gift and says, "A card expressing sympathy has been sent in your name to the bereaved" and encloses another donation envelope for the donor's convenience.

THE ROLE OF THE STAFF

The staff's role is to manage the overall campaign. This means collecting names of possible prospects, supervising research to determine the best people to ask, convincing leaders to give a major gift themselves, and then training the leaders to ask for big gifts. Some volunteers are naturals at all this and love going eyeball to eyeball with a prospect.

Other solicitors have a more deliberate style and work best in steps. Instead of going right for a gift, they will ask, "Would this be a good time to discuss your gift?" If they get a "No" or a "Not now," the door is still open to ask another time. However, some leaders who can give a gift themselves and care heart and soul about the cause still have great difficulty asking for a major gift. This is where staff can help the most.

Staff can pair a person who has a great story to tell with someone who has great closing skills. Or a member of the staff can go along with the leader and ask the right question at the right time: "Joan, wasn't there something you wanted to ask Miss Addams?"

Fundraising staff can also use what organizers call the "fixed fight." If a staff person already knows that Jane Addams is going to make a big gift to her college, the staff person will take someone who needs to get a confidence boost to "ask" for that gift. Of course the request succeeds, and the next one will be easier.

If all else fails, staff can ask for a gift. This is the least desirable scenario, because then the relationship is being forged between the donor and a staff member, rather than between the donor and a leader. If the staff person gets hired away by another organization, who has the relationship with this donor? Your leader or your ex-employee?

In theory, paid fundraising staff should never ask for big gifts, certainly never alone. However, in practice, sometimes the very best leaders will simply strangle with panic, and it is in everybody's interest for the paid fundraiser to ask for the gift so the donor can make the gift he or she wants to make and the leader can be saved from cardiac arrest. Of course, the leaders will get credit for getting the gift, and they will see it is possible to ask and survive. Your hope is that praise and practice will give them more determination next time.

Professional fundraisers must have a working knowledge of the current tax laws and help you hire or recruit the best lawyers, accountants, and insurance people who are experts in their fields. Always involve your own legal counsel and the donor's tax advisers in structuring a gift, but remember that most big donors' major motivation is not getting a tax break. Donors give because they believe in your mission and want to see you make the world better.

As you can see, unlike selling memberships or gala tickets, asking for a major gift requires great diplomacy. You need to build a relationship of trust so the prospect can feel free to tell you what he or she wants. Have the courage of your convictions to articulate what the organization needs and not sell yourself short.

WHERE TO ASK

Ask where the prospect wants to be asked. Most often this will be in the prospect's office or home. Some prospects prefer to meet at their club or at a restaurant. Meals are fine for getting to know people better and sharing your stories, but they are less effective settings for closing the deal.

People with new money who are using gobs of it to buy their way into the status charities may want to be seen being courted in public. Other people, especially old money or closet rich people, may want to keep everything *sub rosa*. I know one fundraiser who wanted a gift from a wealthy workaholic from Tiburon in Marin County north of San Francisco. Since the prospect did not want his neighbors or his colleagues to know the deal was being negotiated, the fundraiser would drive from San Francisco, across the Golden Gate Bridge, and around the bay to Tiburon. Then he and the prospect would ride the first ferry for an hour to downtown San Francisco. At night the pair would ride the last ferry back to Marin County, and then the fundraiser would drive back to San Francisco. He spent three hours driving in the dark to spend two hours in private with the donor; after eight months of these meetings, the organization received a seven-figure gift.

WHERE NOT TO ASK

Never ask for money at a party. It is awkward for your prospect, embarrassing for your host, and guaranteed to make you look gauche and greedy. *Time* magazine reported that Joan Kroc, owner of the San Diego Padres baseball team, widow of the founder of McDonald's Corporation, and legendary philanthropist, was invited to a party at the home of Dr. Jonas Salk. What happened? "So many other guests accosted her with solicitations for money that she excused herself and left."[5]

If the host or hostess knows both of you, it is appropriate to ask for an introduction to a wealthy person and a glowing reference to your great work: "Mr. Tipton, I'd like you to meet Mary Smith. She's the one who has done the terrific job expanding the children's museum." Then make polite party conversation, trying to *listen* and learn as much as possible about the prospect.

The next day send your prospect a *brief* letter—one paragraph on how much you enjoyed meeting him or her and one paragraph on how you would like to have an opportunity to tell more about your project. Include one recent clipping and one brochure. Send a copy of your letter to the host or hostess with your thanks for making the introduction.

When you meet a wealthy person in a social setting, it is tempting to seize the moment and ask for a contribution right away. However, this makes you look desperate and makes the prospect feel as though you want only his or her money.

If you want to build a long-term relationship with the wealthy person, look at every contact as a step toward building a lasting partnership. This relationship needs respect on both sides. The prospect respects the seriousness of your work, and you respect the seriousness of the prospect's philanthropy. So you do not annoy a prospect at a party, and he or she does not trivialize your work. You both gain.

WHEN TO ASK

Except for parties, there is no bad time to ask for money. Door-to-door canvassers have proved that heat waves, downpours, and blizzards all increase the evening's take. The United Way in Charleston saw donations increase 10 percent after Hurricane Hugo; the United Way in the Bay Area saw gifts go up 7 percent after the 1989 earthquake. The biggest annual increase the United Ways have ever seen was 50 percent in 1942—the first year of World War II.

One fundraiser had been pursuing a certain donor for months and was always getting a polite postponement. Finally, on a winter day when it was twenty below zero, of course the prospect thought *this* was the day to meet with the fundraiser. The fundraiser had to wade two blocks through thigh-high snowdrifts to get to the house; she got a gift worth $3 million.

National and international organizations have a great advantage because they can double-team the best prospects. For example, John and Martha cultivate the prospect on Martha's Vineyard in the summer, while Bill and Amy work on him in Palm Springs in the winter.

For bigger organizations and bigger goals, major-gift solicitation goes on all year long. Since many wealthy people have more than one home and travel often, you operate on their timetable. Be ready for any opportunity for a personal meeting, and keep sending positive reports to keep your organization in the prospect's mind.

More than 50 percent of gifts of stock are made in the last quarter of the year, and 35 percent are made in December. Although you want to cultivate your best prospects all year long, if you are asking for a gift of stock, be sure you have asked for the stock by October.

For small organizations and smaller goals, it is easier to choose two months in the spring or the fall and focus your work in one very well organized campaign. The easiest way to help volunteers overcome the natural inclination to procrastinate is to compress all of your asking into one tight campaign.

Like Aristotle, most volunteers prefer working with a beginning, a middle, and an end. Before the campaign starts, the staff and leaders will have recruited the top campaign leadership, made their own gifts, researched and ranked the prospects, set a dollar goal, and recruited the troops. The first week, you train the askers; the second week, they set up their appointments; weeks three to six, they ask for gifts; week seven is for follow-up with tough cases; and week eight is wrap-up and celebration. If you end on time, it will be easier to get good recruits next year.

WHAT TO ASK FOR

The easiest gift to get is just good old cash. This can be one lump sum or a multiyear pledge. Today giant charities are asking for ten- and twenty-year pledges in order to leverage bigger gifts. Most charities ask for three- to five-year gifts. You can make it easy for the donor through electronic funds transfer or credit card payments arranged through your banks. Or the donor may prefer to get monthly or quarterly reminders (nonprofit jargon for a bill).

NONCASH CONTRIBUTIONS

Of course, you are glad to get gifts that are worth money as well as plain money itself. It may be in the self-interest of your donor to give you the ranch, the Renoir, or the Rolls-Royce. Get a professional appraisal of the property, and be sure it is also in the interest of the organization to take this kind of a gift. Ask other charities how they handle noncash gifts, and involve the donor's tax advisers in planning for the gift.

Donors may want to give property to a nonprofit to avoid paying capital gains taxes themselves or to avoid estate taxes if the property passes to their children or grandchildren. The money they save by avoiding these taxes can be invested in a "replacement policy" of life insurance, so the children or grandchildren will still see an equal or greater dollar value at the time of the donor's death. This is a win-win-win scenario: the donor, the donor's beneficiaries, and the charity all gain. The charity may want to use the property for its own programs, rent it out for earned income, or sell it for cash.

If the donor wants to give you a work of art, be sure to get an appraisal for the value of the work and an estimate of what it will cost to insure. Ever since Van Gogh paintings have been auctioned for tens of millions of dollars, some private collectors and small institutions have found they cannot afford to insure their works of art for what is considered fair market value. Work with the donor's tax advisers to negotiate the most advantageous deal for both of you.

If the donor wants to give you something like a boat or a car, consider whether it is best to use the vehicle for your program, sell it off for cash, offer it as a raffle prize, or make it a production prize for your workers.

For any noncash donation of more than $500, the donor is now required to file Form 8283, "Noncash Charitable Contributions," with the IRS. If your agency sells or trades the contribution in the first two years, it is required to file Form 8282, "Donee Information Return," with the IRS. Both of these are intended to reduce tax fraud by the rich and devious.

LOANS

Once you have a good relationship with a wealthy donor, he or she can also make you no-interest or low-interest loans. This can be a good source of venture capital in low-income communities denied credit from financial institutions. Be sure everyone knows that a loan is a loan, not a gift or a grant. Make all payments on time, or even better, pay off the loan early.

APPRECIATED STOCK

In the 1959 movie *The Young Philadelphians*, Paul Newman plays a lawyer specializing in the "new" field of tax law. On Christmas Eve, Mrs. J. Arthur Allen comes into his office looking for someone to write a codicil for her will to guarantee care for her pet chihuahua. The lawyer finds out Mrs. Allen is worth $100 million, kisses the dog, and says he will be glad to fix her will.

Mrs. Allen laments that some people do not care about

animals, and that is why she gives $5,000 every year to the Society for the Prevention of Cruelty to Animals (SPCA). The lawyer sees his opening and asks, "In cash?"

Once he learns Mrs. Allen always gives her contribution in cash, the lawyer suggests she donate appreciated stock instead. For example, if Mrs. Allen purchased stock for $1,000, and it is worth $5,000 at the time she sells it, she will owe capital gains tax on the $4,000 profit. On the other hand, if she gives the stock to the SPCA, she can deduct $5,000 from her taxable income, and she avoids paying taxes on $4,000.

As you can imagine, the multimillionaire loves this idea and decides to throw all her business to Paul Newman's law firm. This movie is more than thirty years old, and the same idea still works today. If you have a donor with appreciated property, giving it to your nonprofit organization will reduce the donor's taxes and give you the value of the appreciated stock.

CLUBS

Clubs are a strategy to urge annual donors to give more money. You buy your way into the club by giving a certain dollar amount. People who regularly give $25, $50, or $100 easily can be asked to give $500 to be a Silver Spartan or $1,000 to be a Golden Gopher.

Colleges and universities have used these clubs for many years, usually at the $500 or $1,000 level to get annual donors to think bigger. As prosperity has driven incomes up and inflation has driven the value of the dollar down, the oldest clubs are now too large to be exclusive. So organizations add on new categories at the $10,000, $100,000, or $1 million level.

The United Ways have had great success using their $10,000 club called the Alexis de Tocqueville Society. So far they have started the clubs in more than ninety cities; in 1989 their 3,500 members gave $60 million to the United Way. These clubs enable the United Way to reach major donors who are not part of the traditional corporate executive leadership already active in the United Way. The majority of donors in the society are professionals, minorities, women, and entrepreneurs.

Drawing by W. Miller © 1982
The New Yorker Magazine, Inc.

One of the most successful American nonprofits to use major-gift clubs to achieve their goals is Ducks Unlimited, the world's largest private-sector waterfowl and wetlands conservation organization. A general membership starts at $20 for one year and has to be renewed every year. If you want to make a bigger gift and never have to renew again, they offer big-money clubs starting at $10,000.

Major sponsors range from a Life Sponsor, who donates $10,000 within four years, to a Legacy Sponsor, who gives $250,000 over a lifetime. Life Sponsors get a gold Life Sponsor pin, lifelong listing in the annual report, and an engraved plaque. Legacy Sponsors get their names listed on a Legacy

Sponsor Plaque at the Ducks Unlimited National Headquarters and a replica of the plaque, a white gold pin inlaid with diamonds, and perpetual listing in the annual report.

One terrific innovation of Ducks Unlimited is their Grand Slam Life Sponsor, which combines three national programs into one recognition category. To qualify, a donor becomes a Life Sponsor in the United States, Canada, and Mexico. The cost is $10,000 within four years to Ducks Unlimited in the United States, $10,000 Canadian within five years to Ducks Unlimited Canada, and $2,000 within one year to Ducks Unlimited de Mexico. Each country has its own symbol of recognition and lists the donor in its annual report. This way the organization can market three big-money clubs at once in three countries and at the same time raise awareness of the importance of preserving wildlife habitats across national borders.

There is probably no limit to what status organizations can charge for a club. In fact, some colleges and universities have begun a club called "The First Fifteen" for the fifteen largest donors to the school. Then all they need are a few million-dollar gifts and everyone needs to jump up their giving to get in the club.

Make up some categories to fit your cause. The American Cancer Society calls its big donor club "Excalibur," based on its symbol, the Sword of Hope, and playing off the Arthurian legends of the elite knights of the Round Table. The Statue of Liberty/Ellis Island Foundation created the Torch Club for gifts of $1 million or more. One member is the Disabled American Veterans, which earmarked its gift for making the entire area accessible to the physically impaired.

PUTTING IT ALL TOGETHER

Most organizations can use a combination of gift clubs, credit card and electronic funds transfer, and naming opportunities to make it easier to get large gifts from major donors. But the professional and volunteer fundraisers still have to make the personal calls to build the relationships that will motivate the donor to give. Most big gifts are made because the donor cares deeply about the mission of the organization. The more you can share your victories and your dreams with your prospects, the more they will want to be a part by making a large gift.

THE NEED FOR BIG GIFTS

Today there is more competition for more money for more expensive needs. Although some self-help groups intentionally choose to remain small, most nonprofit groups need to grow, raise more money, and get more political power. To meet those goals, they need to be able to raise dependable big money.

Money is power, and more money gives you more power. The ability to raise and spend big money enables good organizations to solve problems as well as treat the victims. In his autobiography, *Is That It?*, Bob Geldof tells how he organized the Band Aid concerts and telethon that raised $117 million in 1985. Then he tells how the Band Aid organization went about spending the money to relieve the famine in Africa. In one effort, Band Aid did a one-to-one match with the U.S. government to build a multimillion-dollar bridge over the River Chari in Chad. Before the bridge, supplies were brought across the river by canoe.[6]

This is the metaphor for fundraising today. If you can raise more money, you can forge partnerships with other major players, both public and private. You can build the bridges that enable everyone to work better. Is your group burning out because you can afford only canoes? How many more problems can you solve if you focus first on raising big money, then on applying it to big solutions?

MAJOR GIFTS: WHAT TO ASK FOR

Ask your major-gift staff and volunteers to rate your best prospects on the size and type of gift. Start with a gift to the annual campaign or a membership on the first visit and then move on to other possibilities.

Wealthy people may have other resources to help your group. They may be able to host a party at their mansion, lend you art for your offices, or sign over stock proxies to enable your members to attend the annual meeting of a corporation.

MAJOR GIFTS: WHAT TO ASK FOR

Possible Gifts   Amount Requested

1. Money:

   Annual gift
   Membership
   Pledge
   Club
   Special gift
   Major gift
   Challenge/matching gift
   Interest-free loan
   Other

2. Noncash Assets:

   Art
   Real estate
   Vehicle
   Other

3. Stocks (List):

4. Bonds (List):

5. Life Insurance Policy:

6. Others:

CULTIVATION RECORDS
Your cultivation of each prospect needs to be intentional and recorded. Some computer software has a sort of tickler file that can remind you of birthdays, anniversaries, and religious holidays. Or you can buy a tickler file at any office supply store, and file paper reminders by days and months.

Keep a record of every time a volunteer or staff fundraiser contacts your major donor prospects. This is especially helpful when you are working with a large number of people or when your staff and volunteers turn over quickly.

A fundraiser's cultivation record for Jane Addams could look like this sample:

Name:	Jane Addams, Rockford College Class of 1882
Date	Contact and Comments
2/1	Mail annual report—flag page 8 with her name.
3/5	Visit. Ask for library books.
5/3	Mail Mother's Day appeal.
5/17	Received $10 gift from mailing.
5/18	Mail thank-you letter with invitation to graduation. Receipt sent from office.
6/11	Graduation; Addams speech to science club.
6/12	Mail thank-you for speech.
6/19	Mail photo of speech to science club with article from the school paper.
8/7	Visit. Asked for science books; left list of suggested titles.
9/6	Mail birthday card.
9/13	Mail invitation to homecoming.
10/2	Homecoming: toured library. Dinner with librarian and science students. Revised list of book titles.
11/9	Mail Thanksgiving card—"We're thankful for your support."

12/2	Received check for $1,000 for library, for science books (see list from 10/2). Thank-you note sent from me.
12/3	Receipt sent from office, with thank-you note.
12/4	Thank-you letter from the college president.
12/12	Mail Christmas card.

PROSPECTS FOR MAJOR GIFTS

In Chapter 5, each committee member was asked to list the names of ten individuals he or she could ask for $20. Do the same kind of planning for major gifts. List the names of five people you could ask for $200, three people you could ask for $2,000, and one person you could ask for $20,000. (If you are already getting gifts at this level, revise the worksheet upward; ask for prospects to give $200,000 or $2 million.)

MAJOR GIFTS WORKSHEET

Individuals I can ask for $200 or $————:
1.
2.
3.
4.
5.

Individuals I can ask for $2,000 or $————:
1.
2.
3.

Individual I can ask for $20,000 or $————:
1.

"Do your giving
while you're living,
then you're knowing
where it's going."

—*Folk wisdom*

Chapter 10

The Big Gift—Later

After you have built a broad base of annual donors and moved some of those people into giving you larger pledges and gifts, then you can consider asking for planned gifts. These used to be called "deferred gifts," but fundraisers found that prospects wanted to defer forever, so the name was changed to "planned gifts." A donor plans now to give your nonprofit organization money later, most often through a bequest in his or her will.

Bequests are the most volatile source of philanthropic dollars. From year to year, giving from bequests has gone up as much as 13 percent or down as much as 18 percent from the previous year, depending on who dies and when the estate is settled. In the big picture, bequests can account for from 3 to 13 percent of the philanthropic dollars given in the United States. The high end came in 1982 due to the $1.3 billion bequest from oil tycoon J. Paul Getty to his own museum in Malibu, California.

Most years, bequests account for about 7 percent of the philanthropic dollars, more than either corporation gifts or foundation grants, which each provide about 5 percent of the philanthropic dollars. In 1989 the amount given to charities in

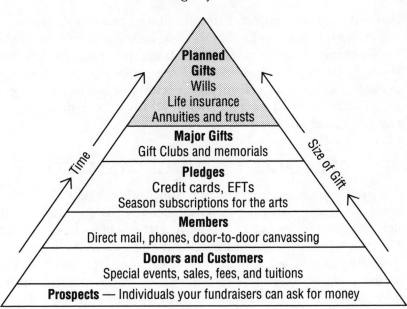

Planned Gifts
Wills
Life insurance
Annuities and trusts

Major Gifts
Gift Clubs and memorials

Pledges
Credit cards, EFTs
Season subscriptions for the arts

Members
Direct mail, phones, door-to-door canvassing

Donors and Customers
Special events, sales, fees, and tuitions

Prospects — Individuals your fundraisers can ask for money

Time

Size of Gift

bequests was $7 billion. The experts predict that funding from bequests will triple in the next decade because more charities are asking with more confidence.

How do you get in on this gold mine? You have to ask. Surveys show that 89 percent of Americans give to charity every year, and they give to between eleven and fourteen charities every year. Americans with a will remember two to five charities in their will. So of the charities they fund every year, two to five get in the will, and nine are left out. The ones that are left out are usually left out because nobody asked.

Bequests are the easiest way to get started in planned giving for any nonprofit organization. After you have begun asking for bequests, also explore using life insurance, annuities, trusts, and other instruments to allow your donors to get the satisfaction of giving.

ADVANTAGES TO THE DONOR

Planned gifts are a service to your donors. They get to give a big gift in a way that gives them credit now. They can strengthen their financial situation through reduced taxes or dependable income. And they can be motivated to do something they ought to do anyway. In some cases they will get the peace of mind that their property will be preserved for a purpose they want—for example, to serve as a historical property or a wildlife refuge. Donors can provide for their heirs or honor their spouse, parents, or grandparents.

ADVANTAGES TO THE ORGANIZATION

Asking for planned gifts forces a nonprofit organization to do *real* long-range planning, looking ahead not two or three years but three or four decades. The staff will need to hire or recruit lawyers, accountants, and investment and insurance experts to guide the organization and advise your prospects. You have the security of knowing more money will be coming in the future. Although the money takes longer to get, planned giving can add up to much, much larger dollar amounts.

You should be eager to explore any fundraising strategy that requires you to think big, think long range, and get serious about your financial management.

ASKING FOR BEQUESTS

Giving through a will is a time-honored fundraising strategy. William Shakespeare had a will. In 1616 he left his land to one daughter, £300 to another, his clothes to his sister, and his second-best bed to his wife.[1] (The Globe Theatre should have been in the will, but nobody asked.) On the other hand, one of the first restoration projects in the United States may have been at the Touro Synagogue in Newport, Rhode Island, in 1827. Completed in 1763, the synagogue was in deteriorating condition when it received a $10,000 bequest for its repair from the will of Abraham Touro, son of Isaac Touro, one of the synagogue's founders.[2] Obviously the Touro Synagogue's planned giving committee had done its job.

Statistically half of your people already have a will, and the rest know they should have a will. Your volunteers may already know about bequests for charities from their religious congregations, universities, or hospitals. They can also give and ask for bequests for your group. However, probably the scariest "ask" for a fundraiser is the first time you ask someone to remember your charity in his or her will. Despite the pioneering work of Dr. Elisabeth Kübler-Ross and the hospice movement, most of us do not like to think about death and dying, let alone talk about it.

The depth of this denial is exposed by the fact that more than half of all Americans do not have a will. Even worse, a third of all the U.S. lawyers do not have a will—and they can do their own for free! So how can we bring up this touchy subject? Somehow we need to say:

1. Yes, you are going to die.
2. No, you can't take it with you.
3. So please leave it to us.

The answer is to practice what you preach. Tell your members that they *can* take control of their own lives and they *can* control their own money. They do not have to lie down and let life run over them. So there are only two choices. They can choose to write a will and choose which of their family, friends, and favorite organizations will get their estate. Or they can choose to procrastinate and say they will write their will "soon." If their death comes before "soon," the state or province will make all of the choices.

Never underestimate people's ability to procrastinate on financial matters, even when they know they should do it, when they and their loved ones will gain from it, or even when they legally *have* to do it. Thousands of American taxpayers ask for an extension past April 15 every year to file their taxes. Eighty percent of these people will get a *refund.* They have nothing to gain, and money to lose, by procrastinating, but they do it anyway.

In the same way, your people may procrastinate on writing a will. They know they should do it, but they prefer to do it tomorrow. One of the greatest services that a fundraiser can give to a donor is urging that person to make the choice to write a will today.

PRACTICE WHAT YOU PREACH

The best way to get started on a program for bequests is to write your own will and include bequests to the organizations that matter most to you. You will never be sympathetic with your bequest prospects unless you know how hard it can be to make these choices. If you already have a will that is more than five years old, update your own will and include a bequest to the charities that matter to you.

Since every state and province has different laws, it is wise to hire a lawyer to help you prepare or update your will. Some handwritten "do-it-yourself" wills can stand up in court, but you are much smarter to ask a professional to make sure that your wishes are carried out. Books, software, and fill-in-the-blank forms can help you make a first draft, but good legal advice will guarantee your wishes will be carried out.

Also review the current materials on planned giving available at your library. Ask a veteran fundraiser, especially a planned-giving specialist, to be your mentor. Interview leaders who have chaired an endowment campaign in your community. Say "yes" whenever another charity asks if you might be interested in making a planned gift so you can see how they operate.

A LITTLE KNOWLEDGE IS DANGEROUS

With regard to bequests and other planned-giving strategies, a little knowledge can be a dangerous thing. Your own fundraising staff must have a working knowledge of current tax laws, insurance options, and investment opportunities. In addition, you can recruit legal, insurance, and investment experts from your community to help on this committee. Their self-interest is that they meet more potential customers at the same time they help the cause.

As your organization's base of renewed members and repeat donors grows, you may choose to hire a professional to work full-time to encourage those people to give your organization planned gifts. For a smaller agency one person may be able to handle research, training, and cultivation. For larger organizations, you may want to create a separate department with several professionals to handle research, publications, planning, training, and follow-up.

Planned-giving specialists have created councils for mutual support and education in about fifty large cities in the United States and Canada. Planned-giving officers from some of the largest national programs also meet in groups sponsored by similar causes, such as health care, the Jewish Federations, or United Ways. For more information on the local professional association for planned-giving officers, contact the National Committee on Planned Giving, 550 W. North St., Suite 304, Indianapolis, IN 46202.

OUTSIDE COUNSEL AND ADVICE

In addition to your own staff and volunteers, you can hire fundraising counsel with expertise in planning and managing a planned-gifts program. Several firms specialize in planned-giving literature, newsletters, training, and management of campaigns. You can get recommendations for the best firms through their satisfied customers in your community, or shop the advertisements in the fundraising periodicals and the vendors at national conventions. Professional counsel will make the planned-giving process much easier for you and your volunteers.

You can also buy special software designed to calculate the tax deductions and annual payouts of different planned-gifts options. This is one of the greatest tools to make planned giving an option for every professional. Attend demonstrations by dealers and ask planned-giving specialists which software they recommend.

Always work with the professionals retained by your donors. Be glad to have their CPA, attorney, banker, or stockbroker involved in this transaction because such professionals know more about the prospects and their current and future financial goals than you do. Also remember that these people are not court retainers; all good professionals have other customers. If you work well with them, they may recommend your charity the next time someone says, "I'd like to give/leave part of this to a good charity. What do you think?"

WHEN TO ASK FOR BEQUESTS

Most people write (or update) their will when certain events occur:

- They inherit money or property.
- They marry or divorce.
- They have a baby.
- They leave for a war zone.
- They buy a home.
- They start a business.
- They are diagnosed with a life-threatening illness.
- They acquire a great deal more money—win the lottery or make a killing in the stock market.
- They plan to take a trip out of the country.
- They have a relative who becomes a lawyer.

With the exception of weddings and babies, which generally are publicly announced and eagerly awaited events, your organization has no way of anticipating these occurrences. You can't know when someone's grandfather will die or when someone plans to fly to Tahiti. An active, diverse board and many volunteers can give you early warnings about these trigger events. For most of your prospects most of the time, you simply have to ask often and give them several opportunities to respond.

The newsletter, the annual report, and every program should always include a box to check for information about your bequest program. At least once a year, send a letter about wills. Include a "success story" about a donor that has remembered your agency in its will and what you can now do with that money. Add bequests and other deferred gifts to the "menu" you offer your prospects when you discuss ways they can support your organization. You never know when it will pay off.

For example, Christ Church in Alexandria, Virginia, has more than two thousand communicants and also draws many tourists, since it was the home church for George Washington and Robert E. Lee. The congregation's regular Sunday program includes this section titled "Stewardship":

> Christ Church is almost entirely dependent upon the discipline of annual pledging to support its ministries. The Biblical tithe is the standard of giving encouraged by the Vestry.
> Please remember the mission of the Church in all of your giving and the Christ Church, Alexandria, Virginia Foundation, Inc. in the structuring of your will and when memorials are appropriate.

This is a terrific example. First, notice they begin by asking for the annual gift. Also, the church's board knows what it wants and says what it wants (10 percent of your income). Finally, they ask you to remember the church in your will.

The church's own members will see this at least fifty-two times a year—every Sunday. The tourists will see it at least once, maybe more. As long as it is in writing, this message is easy to throw in a desk or file as a reminder or to delegate to your accountant or lawyer. If you ask often and put it in writing, your prospects can more easily respond when the time is right for them.

YOU NEVER KNOW

Let me tell you a story to illustrate the importance of asking. Democratic Congressman Richard Durbin of Illinois was trying to get onto a flight on which he had no reservation. He started with, "Any seat will be fine—just get me on this plane." The reservations clerk informed him that the only seat left was a center seat between two smokers. Rep. Durbin did not want to be sandwiched between two smokers, so he tried to use his job to get a different seat.

He said something like, "I'm a U.S. Congressman, and I do not want to sit between two smokers. Can't you move me up front to a better seat? After all, I *am* a member of Congress."

The clerk said, "Well, then, why don't *you* do something about it?"

Rep. Durbin co-sponsored the legislation that outlawed smoking on all U.S. flights of less than six hours.

I learned two lessons from this story. First, it never hurts to ask. You may get results far beyond your wildest expectations. The reservations clerk probably heard travelers and airline workers complain every day about tobacco smoke. Because she took the initiative and asked, all airline travelers are safer today. Asking gets results.

The second thing I learned is that *anyone* can make a big difference. It is tempting to think you cannot talk about wills unless you are a lawyer or a member of the clergy. But do not let your volunteers think planned giving is only for the lawyers or the clergy. Of course, involving the experts is important, but anyone can open the doors and begin the discussion.

I told this story to sales expert Barbara Pierce. The lesson she pulled from it was, "You see—you never know who you're talking to!" Retail stores teach the sales force that (except for repeat customers) you do not know until you ring up the order how much someone will spend. Every day they get a big sale from someone who does not *look* like a big spender. In the same way, fundraisers never know whom they are talking to. You can do good research on your prospects, especially people in the public eye, but you never really know their level of commitment or their ability to give. One way to find this out is to ask and keep asking.

WHOM TO ASK

The best prospects for planned gifts are the same as the best prospects for major gifts:

1. Yourself
2. The board, planned-gift committee members, and senior staff
3. Your own donors who have given for three to five years
4. New people with a commitment to your cause and the ability to make a planned gift

With your own donors, look for continuity of giving. There are stories of some regular but modest lifetime donors who leave a very large bequest. Fundraiser Kim Klein reports that Mrs.

Frank Leslie, who took over publishing *Leslie's Weekly* after her husband's death, was a moderate but steady supporter of the National Women's Suffrage Association; at her death in 1890 she shocked the association with a $2 million bequest "for furtherance of the cause of Women's Suffrage."[3] Planned-giving expert Philip Converse tells about one man who gave an organization seven gifts that totaled $17 over his lifetime; he died and left a bequest of $4.5 million.

For your own list and researching new prospects, look for people over sixty years old, single people or married couples with no children, and people who like to plan. Some planned-giving experts have focused on specific markets that have a need, such as older people who own a farm but none of whose children chose to be farmers. One expert counsels you to walk to the farthest corner of the parking lot around the newest shopping mall you can find. Look around. If you see cows, that farmer is a prospect.

Demographics is the buzzword of the nineties, and some charities are experimenting with market segmentation and hunting for the perfect list of people. This will help the largest charities that have a popular cause and the money to invest in marketing plans. However, most organizations still find their major donors and their bequest prospects one by one. Start with the people who have demonstrated they care about your cause, and then ask them to give, to give a larger gift, and to put the group in their will.

If you choose to include asking for bequests in your fundraising strategy, it must be a priority for the CEO and volunteer leaders. You need to discipline yourselves to include one or two visits every week to talk to a prospect about a bequest. Because you may not see a return for five to fifty years, it can be hard to keep yourself motivated. But the key to success is patience, persistence, and asking.

To urge their board members, senior staff, and best donors to give bequests, some charities give them more recognition. For example, the American Red Cross has the "Codicil Club" for donors who have remembered the Red Cross in their will or with another planned gift. Members of the Codicil Club get a

lapel pin to wear as recognition of their generosity and to
enable current members to become advocates for the program
when curious people ask, "What is that pin for?"

Anyone can include your group in his or her bequests.
Some people will say that they do not know anyone rich enough
to have a will, but more likely they know people who do not
plan but should. Of course, asking for bequests is much easier
when you are working with middle- and upper-income people.
More of them know about working with lawyers and making
long-range plans. As Gloria Steinem said, "Rich people do plan
for two generations hence, and poor people will plan for Saturday night,"[4] However, do not assume that simply because someone is wealthy, the person's will is made and his or her estate is
in order. Every community has a story about one of the richest
families who had to sell off everything because the patriarch
never wrote his will.

OTHER WAYS TO GIVE

Actually there are only two kinds of giving: planned giving and
unplanned giving. All fundraising strategies are designed to
make your organization more intentional about asking for
money and to make your donors more intentional about giving
their money.

The following paragraphs describe some of the other options available for planned giving. They are just a sample of
what is available.

LIFE INSURANCE

To raise money from people in their thirties, forties, and fifties
with higher incomes but fewer assets, the perfect tool is life
insurance. For a relatively modest contribution, the donor will
get credit *now* for a very large gift that will benefit the charity
later.

For example, in the plan used by the American Red Cross,
a forty-year-old woman can pay $1,199 a year for five years for a
$100,000 life insurance policy. She can deduct the payments
from her taxable income as a charitable gift. So for a total
contribution of $5,995, less than $100 a month, she leverages a

$100,000 gift and is recognized as a major donor *now*. The payment to the charity is a certainty, there is little paperwork, and the gift does not have to go through probate. The charity can borrow against the policy now, will receive annual policy dividends, and, at the time of the donor's death, will receive a substantial gift.

There are many ways that donors can use life insurance policies to benefit their favorite organizations. Check with your own insurance agent and contact the firms that specialize in selling insurance for nonprofits. These advertise in the fund-raising periodicals and will have a booth at the national conventions. Also ask a local charity that uses insurance for planned gifts to give you advice and leads on good firms.

CHARITABLE ANNUITIES AND TRUSTS

Charitable annuities are not new ideas. Clara Barton had a charitable gift annuity in 1877. She had gone to Europe in 1870 to help the victims of the Franco-Prussian War, with funding from the Boston Relief Committee. Seven years later Barton was straightening out her finances and discovered she still had $3,241 of the organization's money. (That $3,241 was worth $37,635 in 1989.) She returned the money to the committee, which in turn gave it to the Massachusetts General Hospital to invest, with the provision that the annual interest should go to Clara Barton in her lifetime. After her death, the hospital got to keep the money. Barton said this was "perfect."[5]

What is new is the number and complexity of instruments fundraisers can use to help their donors: pooled income fund agreements, charitable remainder unitrusts, charitable remainder annuity trusts, revocable charitable trusts, and charitable lead trusts. In all of these donors give cash, securities, or real estate to your organization and in return receive a tax deduction and income for themselves or another person.

This is definitely an area where a little knowledge is a dangerous thing. Get professional advice before pursuing these strategies. With more complicated tax laws, it is difficult to serve your institution and your donors well unless tax law and estate planning are already your areas of expertise.

PLANNED GIVING IN THE BIG PICTURE

Make it a goal to learn more about all of the planned-giving strategies available to your organization. Attend the planned-giving track at national conventions, and if you like the trainers, sign up for other training offered by the same firm. Recruit the best local lawyers, CPAs, trust officers, and insurance agents to organize your planned-giving efforts. Retain a good planned-giving consultant, and if your first efforts do well, consider hiring a full-time director of planned giving.

However, do not segregate the planned-giving staff and volunteers from the rest of your fundraising efforts. In smaller organizations, you have only a limited pool of prospects, so you need to offer them all the choices that are best for them. In larger charities, the work to develop a bequest may also lead to a current gift, and vice versa.

Planned gifts will take longer than other donations to pay off, and the entire agency needs to budget and plan for this. If you want to hire a planned-giving firm, do multiple mailings, and offer a few seminars every year, the program is going to be a money drain for the first five to ten years. In that case, the other fundraising staff and volunteers will need to commit to using other strategies for raising the money to cover the expenses of starting up your planned-giving program.

CONCLUSION

Experts predict that bequests to nonprofits will triple in the next decade. Life insurance, real estate, trusts, pooled income funds, and other forms of planned gifts will also become more popular ways to give a large gift to the nonprofits that donors like the best.

With the graying of America, the number of prospects for planned gifts will expand, too. By the year 2000, one in five Americans will be at least 55 years old. Successful fundraisers are planning now to establish or expand their planned giving programs to serve these donors and their agencies better.

WORKSHEET FOR PLANNED GIVING

Do I have a will?

Have I remembered my favorite charities in my will?

Whom could I ask to include my organization in his or her will?
1.
2.
3.
4.
5.

Whom do I know who could use small, deductible premium payments to purchase a large life insurance policy to benefit my organization?
1.
2.
3.
4.
5.

Whom do I know who may want to help us, and whom we can help, through a planned gift?
1.
2.
3.
4.
5.

Chapter 11

Corporate Contributions

The 1976 Olympics in Montreal ran up more than $1 billion in
debts. The 1988 Winter Olympics in Calgary ended up with a
$30 million surplus. What made the difference? In between,
businessman Peter Ueberroth ran the 1984 Olympics in Los
Angeles, made a surplus of $223 million, and taught the world
how to ask for money from corporations.

Ueberroth knew that world-class amateur sports are a mar-
keter's dream come true: a way to glue the company's image onto
values like courage, teamwork, patriotism, youth, and beauty.
Corporations could target their marketing dollars to sell more
products and improve their image. That's why Calgary could
profit when *Sports Illustrated* magazine published the bilingual
program, Kodak provided the film (after losing the bidding in
L.A. to Japanese Fuji film), Federal Express set off the fire-
works, Xerox gave the copiers, IBM the computers, and Mattel
the official Skating Star Barbie doll.

In every case, the corporations spent their money to get
what they wanted. If your nonprofit organization represents the
values or the constituency that corporations want to reach, it

could also make a deal that will benefit both your organization and the corporations.

This chapter is the first of two that explore corporate charitable giving: donations of money, goods, services, and people. For these kinds of gifts, you ask the boss or the vice president designated to handle corporate contributions. Besides the basics of corporate giving, this chapter looks at corporate sponsorships. These can be as simple as the local bank buying an advertisement in your benefit program for $100 or as significant as Texaco sponsoring fifty years of broadcasts from the Metropolitan Opera for $100 million. For the latter, you ask the boss or the vice president of advertising.

The next chapter will look at the hottest idea to come out of the eighties: cause-related marketing, a partnership between corporations and charities that makes money for both. It will also discuss business ventures, selling products, and fees for services. Last, but certainly not least, is a look at the ethics of asking for money from for-profits.

In both chapters, I will use the term *corporation* to mean any for-profit business. Because they make the highest profits and spend the most money, we typically think of corporate donors in terms of the giants such as IBM, Hewlett-Packard, General Motors, Exxon, General Electric, Merck & Company, AT&T, Dayton Hudson, Ford Motor Company, and Digital Equipment (the top ten corporate donors in 1989).[1] However, remember that 99 percent of the businesses in the United States employ fewer than five hundred workers; 80 percent of businesses employ fewer than twenty workers.[2] Even if your community has no big corporations, you can still ask for money from the local businesses, such as your grocery store, hardware store, car dealer, gas station, and restaurant.

CORPORATE CHARITY

Conservative economist Milton Friedman thinks no for-profit company should make donations to nonprofits. Instead he says for-profits should work exclusively to make profits for their shareholders, then *those* people can choose to support good charities from their dividends.

In a way, that is what happened in the late eighties. Corporate giving went up by only 6 percent from 1985 to 1988; corporate profits went up 37 percent. In the same time, individual giving went up 31 percent, so the shareholders were passing on part of their increased dividends to the charities they liked.

Fortunately, most corporations ignore Friedman's opinions. They consider corporate charity to be a smart strategy to win goodwill in their communities, and they know most people think most corporations should be giving *more* money.

ADVANTAGES TO CHARITIES

Asking for money from corporations offers many advantages. First of all, corporations are a huge source of money. In 1989 corporations as a category gave $5 billion to charities. IBM gave away $135 million, as much as the Pew Charitable Trust; General Motors donated $62 million, as much as the Andrew W. Mellon Foundation; and Exxon gave $55 million, as much as the Rockefeller Foundation.[3]

The reported dollar values of corporate gifts understate the total value of what corporations actually donate. Many of their noncash gifts, especially products, facilities, and loaned executives, are never reported as charitable contributions but are just considered "what we want to do." Also, it is not unknown for employees to do photocopying, telephoning, and other work for their favorite causes on company time without this contribution being reflected in the company's total gifts. The real value of corporate contributions is probably three to five times higher than the reported figures.

Unlike foundation support, which typically runs out after one to three years, corporations can support a good cause for decades. If you give them what they want in terms of recognition, they can support you with cash and noncash contributions year after year.

CHALLENGES

Corporations are usually more conservative givers than are individual donors. Since they are accountable to their lenders, stockholders, customers, unions, and bosses, they prefer to back a sure thing. Like banks, they more willingly give money when there is little or no risk. So most corporate gifts go to safe causes like education (38 percent of corporate giving), social services (27 percent), noncontroversial arts (14 percent), and health care (8 percent). Less than 1 percent of corporate gifts go to religious congregations.[4]

Education is the big winner because it is in the organization's own interest (the business needs smart workers) and is nonthreatening. Some companies, such as Ernst & Young, Lockheed Corporation, and Scripps Howard, gave 100 percent of their charitable gifts to educational organizations in 1988. The biggest change in recent years has been the growth of giving to elementary and secondary schools.

Corporations' conservatism works against gifts to reform movements, avant-garde art, new causes without a track record, or causes with many aggressive supporters on opposing sides of an issue, such as abortion. Also, it is common sense that most businesses will not fund any nonprofit that is, or is perceived to be, antibusiness.

ADVANTAGES TO THE CORPORATIONS

Corporations choose to spend money with nonprofits for many reasons, but in every case they give to get something they want. Some individuals at the company may share your values and vision, but do not be misled by their expressions of solidarity, no matter how genuine. For a corporation, charity is considered a "cost center," which has to compete with every other corporate department for what management considers to be scarce resources. You have to prove that, dollar for dollar, your organization is the best place for the company to put its money.

What can a for-profit company *get* from allocating dollars to a good cause?

- One benefit is goodness by association. Advertisements saying "Our company is terrific" do not work. Advertisements saying "Our company is proud to bring you affordable housing, or computers in the schools, or a free night at the art museum" make the company look good to the general public.

- The corporation can get a deduction on its income taxes for cash and noncash gifts. However, for most companies, tax savings are not the primary motivation for giving. (The same is true of individual donors.)

- The rank-and-file employees will be proud to work for a company that supports their causes. In some companies, employees can be nominated for "volunteer of the month." If Arlette is selected, she gets her picture in the company newsletter, and her charity gets $500, which then confers major-donor status on Arlette. You can bet the people in her organization know where she works and will want to know about any job openings, too.

- Supporting charities with snob appeal enables the company to show off for its best customers. It can use private showings at the sold-out museum show, champagne with the prima donna, or lectures by the Nobel Prize scientist to dazzle favored clients. World-class culture makes it easier to recruit world-class executives.

- Conversely, supporting projects for low-income people not only puts money where it is needed the most, it can also alleviate charges of elitism or lack of social conscience.

- Corporate philanthropy provides opportunities for leadership. In a recent survey of one thousand young professionals, more than 80 percent believed that companies should apply their employees' entrepreneurial talents to public service.[5]

- Company people can work with politicians and bureaucrats as peers involved in the same causes. Then when they need to contact the government for a business-related need, they can call a friend.

- It can give businesspeople a chance to sample the best nonprofits, then select their favorites for a *pro bono* job when they retire. Some retired workers are thriving in second careers, serving nonprofits they met through their company's involvement.

I saved the best two for last:

- Love. It *can* be lonely at the top. Working with a nonprofit enables even the top CEOs to meet their needs for genuine friendship and respect. The CEO of a worldwide bank on the West Coast told me he liked to volunteer as the treasurer at a seminary because it was "collegial rather than hierarchical." At his job he was always The Boss; he was obeyed, and he was feared. At the charity he was part of a team; he was needed, and he was liked.

    Romances can develop. There are many sound reasons why it is foolish to date people at your own company, but volunteering to work on the company's favorite charity gives you a chance to meet other nice people who do *not* work for your company.

- Money. Spending money in a targeted way with charities can increase sales and customers. In 1984 the American Express Company raised $1.7 million for the Statue of Liberty by offering a donation for each time customers used their credit cards. Of course, patriotic shoppers wanted to link up with a cause that was American, urgent, and easy to do. American Express increased usage of its card by 28 percent and signed up 17 percent more card customers.

The corporations' needs are your opportunities: more profits, more customers, and happier workers. Develop a strategy for how your nonprofit organization can help local corporations achieve their goals.

RESEARCH

Do your homework to find a company that is interested in funding your kind of work. Then find a person who can say yes, and make the case for funding. Like any source of funds, corporate givers need cultivation, education, encouragement, and thanks.

The giant charities employ staffs of people who do nothing but research companies, foundations, and wealthy individuals.

In big cities, ask for advice from a fundraising researcher at a university, hospital, or national charity. In smaller towns you can also get good advice from the librarian in the business section at the public library, a business professor, or a business reporter. The following paragraphs offer some other ideas to get you started.

THE GRAPEVINE

First and always best is the grapevine, one reason you want businesspeople on your board of directors. If your board is restricted to low- and middle-income people, create a "corporate advisory board" made up of business leaders to get you into the gossip loop of commerce and industry. You want to know which executives have a personal interest in your cause. Who has dyslexia? Whose daughter is a dropout? Whose son is in prison? Whose aunt has cancer? Whose uncle is an artist? Whose mother feeds the hungry? Whose father had a triple heart by-pass? The insiders can give you the tips you need to make the best match.

Begin with the business and professional people on your own board. Ask them for leads in their own companies, at their vendors, at their competition. Every business has a professional or trade association; assign your leaders to look for prospects when they go to conventions or trade shows.

Ask anyone in the company to share the employee newsletter. How do the employees feel about the company? If they have a union, what does the union leadership recommend?

OTHER ORGANIZATIONS

Who else in the community already has data on local corporations? Ask for information from the United Way, the chamber of commerce, banks, brokers, industry associations, city or state departments of tourism, economic or community development organizations, and business reporters. Best of all, ask other local charities that receive gifts from corporations whom to ask, what to say, and what not to say.

However, be very cautious about pulling prospects off lists in programs of other charities. This can result in what Joe Breiteneicher of The Philanthropic Initiative calls the "Claude Rains syndrome." Rains played the inspector in *Casablanca*

who let the real target get away while he went out to "round up
the usual suspects." A few highly visible companies get inun-
dated with requests, while other good prospects may be over-
looked.

Who makes money from your organizations? Ask all of
your organization's vendors at least once a year. Most towns have
more than one bank, travel agent, printer, computer store, and
office supply company. If your vendors are not supporting the
organization's mission with a generous contribution as well as
excellent service, shop the competition.

PUBLICATIONS

Ask someone to read, clip, and file the business press, including
the business sections of your local newspapers, the *Wall Street
Journal*, and national magazines such as *Forbes*, *Fortune*, and
Advertising Age. Be sure to get the annual issues on the *Fortune*
500 (most profitable corporations), the *Inc.* 100 (fastest-growing
public companies), and the *Forbes* 400 (highest-paid executives.)

If one industry is dominant in your town, read its trade
magazines. For example, if you want to ask oil companies in
Houston or Calgary, read *Oil Daily*, *Petroleum Intelligence
Weekly*, *Automotive News*, *Nucleonics Week*, and *Sludge*. (Never
again will you think *your* newsletter is dull!)

Go to the business section of the public library, and get to
know the librarian. He or she can show you how to use local
reference materials, especially the directories for your city, state,
or province, and the directories for specific industries, such as
agribusiness, computers, or franchises. Ask about the major
reference books such as the *Standard and Poor's Register of
Corporations, Directors, and Executives*, *The Directory of Corporate Affiliations*, the Dun and Bradstreet directories, and the
Moody's manuals.

Also ask your librarian about computer-assisted research
opportunities. Many libraries can access hundreds of data bases,
including journal and magazine articles, technical reports,
government documents, books, and dissertations. You can use
directory files to search for companies by your geographic area,
company size, or product. If you choose to start your own
business, other files can facilitate searches for patents, standards
and specifications, and export information.

For publicly held companies, read the company annual report from cover to cover. If the financial section is new to you, ask an investor, an accountant, or a broker to interpret it.

Some companies also publish an annual report of their philanthropy. Most do not, so you need to ask a company insider and the charities they already fund.

DIRECTORIES OF CORPORATE GIVING DATA

Both the Taft Group and the Public Management Institute publish helpful directories of data on corporate giving in America. You can use these for free at the Foundation Center Cooperating Collections listed in Chapter 13, some public libraries, or the research departments of friendly large charities. Or you can purchase your own based on the information in Chapter 14.

The directories make your job easier by indexing each corporation's cash and noncash giving by the location of the company's headquarters and operating locations, which will get preference over communities where the company has no employees. You can also research grants by type, such as money for a conference or an endowment, or by recipient, such as education or health care, or find allies who can give you advice. Collect data on the officers and directors and present it to your leadership to see if any of your people know any of the corporation's decision makers.

INTERNATIONAL CORPORATIONS

See the *Directory of International Corporate Giving in America* for data on giving by "firms that have a minimum of 10 percent investment by a non-U.S.-headquartered company." In 1988, foreign countries invested $329 billion in the United States, led by the United Kingdom, Japan, the Netherlands, Canada, and Germany. More and more of these companies are also becoming good prospects since smart grant making enables them to recruit and keep good workers, improve relationships with state and local governments, get a tax deduction, improve their image, and support charities they want.

The Taft *Directory* lists the five largest foreign-owned corporate donors in 1989 as: Du Pont (23 percent owned by Seagram Co. Ltd., of Canada), which contributed more than $31 million; Shell Oil (100 percent owned by Royal Dutch/Shell Group of the Netherlands/U.K.), which gave more than $19 million; BP America (100 percent owned by British Petroleum PLC, of the U.K.), which gave more than $13 million; Burroughs Wellcome Co. (parent company is Wellcome Foundation, Ltd., of the U.K.), which gave more than $8 million; and Pillsbury (100 percent owned by Grand Metropolitan PLC, of the U.K.), which gave more than $7 million.

CORPORATE FOUNDATIONS

If the company has a company foundation, it will, like other foundations, have information at the Cooperating Collection of the Foundation Center (see list in Chapter 13). At the Collection, you can also check out the Foundation Center's *National Directory of Corporate Giving*. This is the most current and complete data on 1,500 of America's leading corporations. Learn where they give cash as well as noncash contributions such as supplies, equipment, and products. All this information is cross-indexed six ways, so you can research by name of a person, name of the company, location, type of business, type of support, or subject area of funding. The directory also includes explicit lists of what each firm does *not* fund, so you will not waste your time on a sure rejection.

To research the giants, see the *Corporate Foundation Profiles*, which gives you detailed information on the grant making of the 250 top American corporations with assets of more than $1 million or annual giving of more than $100,000. This reference contains the data you want to know: where money has actually been given, background on the companies' officers and board members, and detailed financial data, all cross-indexed by location, subject field, and types of support (grants, scholarships, loans). (For order information, see Chapter 14.) The Cooperating Collection also offers more directories and how-to books on corporate fundraising.

QUESTIONS TO ASK

As you are doing your research, use the Corporate Research Worksheet. Ask committee members to add other questions they want to get answered.

CORPORATE RESEARCH WORKSHEET

Name of the company:

Address:

Phone:

Our contacts:

Executive we want to reach:

Connections to our cause: personal or professional

Projected profit for this year?   Next year?

What are the company's greatest achievements?

What are its goals?

What are its greatest needs?

Who makes up its work force?

Who are its customers?

Who is the competition?

What other charities has the company funded?

     Charity   Amount

Why did the company give there?

What did it get?

FINDING THE RIGHT PERSON

Who has the power to say yes to your request? If you can get to the president or CEO, of course the boss can say yes. Or you may want a vice president for corporate affairs, community affairs, or public affairs. Some companies have a pool of money available for good causes; any employee can ask for some.

What matters is whom you know. If you want to get an appointment with a manager, ask his or her best customer to set up the appointment. Or ask the manager's predecessor, spouse, doctor, lawyer, best friend, or mentor. It does not matter whom you use, if he or she gets you an introduction.

If all else fails, try the cold call. Make cold calls first thing in the morning on Tuesday, Wednesday, or Thursday when you are both fresh. Practice saying in one minute who you are, what you want, and what you can offer the company. Actually call a friend, practice over the phone, and record it. Redo it until your pitch is irresistible. Then prepare to be resisted. Make a goal to call ten companies a week, and assume you are doing well if three let you through to the right person and one of them wants to hear more.

Does this work? Yes, if you are persistent. In 1970, Stan Calderwood, the president of the Boston public television station (WGBH-TV) called fifty corporations to give them the opportunity to get thirty-nine hours of BBC television at the bargain price of $390,000. All fifty turned him down. On call number fifty-one he reached Herb Schmertz at Mobil Corporation (who answered his own phone), got him interested, and a few weeks later got the money to launch "Masterpiece Theatre." The partnership between Mobil and WGBH-TV is still strong after twenty years.[6] You have a lot to gain and nothing to lose from making cold calls, so try a few each week.

THE PACKAGE

Companies are different, so be sure you get current advice from employees and other local charities they fund. Generally speaking, the companies want a *short* (six-page) package from you. This will include one page on each of the following topics:

- What, exactly, you want to do and how that will advance your mission.
- How much money you want. Outline the budget for this project and state how this fits in the organization's total budget. Name names and amounts from other funders.
- Why your group can accomplish this goal. Give your credentials. Specify results, using numbers.
- Who is on your board. How much money have they given to this project? Who is the boss? Who will be working on this project?
- The specific benefits you can offer the company. How will its support be acknowledged and publicized?
- A copy of your tax-exemption Declaration Letter from the IRS. Offer to send a copy of your audited financial statement and other pertinent documents such as blueprints or research, as desired.

Some companies make it even simpler. McDonald's Corporation has a four-page application that merely requires you to fill in the blanks. Others may want more, but they will tell you. Do not overwhelm the company contact with your newsletters, annual reports, and videotapes if all the person wants is your plan, budget, and leadership. You want your organization to look cost-effective, right? Therefore, do not send twenty bucks' worth of propaganda the recipient does not want and will not read.

Send your package with a cover letter from your organization's president or the CEO. Then follow up with a phone call and ask for an appointment. Use the name of the customer, board member, or employee who can open doors for you. If possible, ask that person to send a short note alerting the company to watch out for this exciting package.

The corporation contact may be able to make a decision just from the package. Or this person may want you to come in to provide more information. Very rarely someone from the company will come out to see your project. In any case, you present your organization as a terrific opportunity for the corporation to work with a partner to meet its goals and yours.

WHAT CAN YOU ASK FOR?

American corporations may take tax deductions for up to 5 percent of their pretax net income. A few star corporations give away that much or more, such as Cummins Engine (17 percent), Adolph Coors (16 percent), Safeway Stores (15 percent), Gencorp (14 percent), Paramount Communications (13 percent), Marine Midland Banks (10 percent), Yellow Freight System of Delaware (8 percent), Pillsbury (8 percent), RJR Nabisco (8 percent), Cincinnati Bell (7 percent), and Soft Sheen Products (6 percent).[7] Most for-profits give away about 1 percent of their pretax net income in cash and noncash contributions.

Unlike most foundations, which have only money to give, corporations can give you money, goods, people, and services. Within each of these categories are many choices for you to consider. What can the corporation give that will meet your needs?

MONEY

The easiest thing to get is money. Giving money requires the least work for the company. Someone simply writes a check.

Ask for a specific amount for a specific project. Depending on your relationship with the company and what you want, you can ask for a gift of money, plain and simple, or a large challenge grant to motivate other gifts.

Many corporations will match contributions from their employees, retirees, and directors (and their spouses), and some companies match more than one to one. For example, IBM does a two-to-one match. So if you want to find a $1,000 donor, ask an IBM employee to give you $334 (less than a dollar a day) and let IBM match it to $668 to raise $1,002. Even better, if you can get individual gifts from corporate bigwigs, they can apply for multiple matches as the employee at one company and the director of another.

Besides gifts and grants, corporations can also make loans at or below current market rates. These may be called "program-related investments," or PRIs in fundraising jargon. In this way, oil companies, insurance companies, and others have invested in affordable housing and new businesses in credit-starved communities.

THINGS

Companies can give you anything from their products to their recyclable trash. In particular, any product with their name on it becomes an effective advertisement to the entire community. Ben and Jerry's ice-cream factory in Vermont gives a free ice-cream cone to each citizen who registers to vote; any merchant could copy this idea.

What does the company do that no one else can do? Du Pont makes the special paint used on railroad cars. At $150 a gallon, the paint is priced out of the budget of the National Railroad Museum in Green Bay, Wisconsin, which owns the train used by General Dwight D. Eisenhower in England during World War II. But the National Archives persuaded Du Pont to donate enough British Railways green paint to make the train shine as part of Ike's birthday centennial celebration in Abilene, Kansas, in 1990.

What does the company do best? If one company is recognized as the best in its field, ask it for products and advice. IBM in Europe, the Middle East, and Africa donated IBM hardware and software, as well as skilled employees and cash grants, to the United Nations' new Global Resource Information Data base (GRID). The total gift was worth $6.5 million and will enable the UN to literally operate on a global scale. IBM now markets computers in 132 countries and builds goodwill through its Corporate Social Responsibility (CSR) programs in all of them. For example, IBM has donated computers to help compile data for support of legal action in child abuse cases in Great Britain, to improve teaching in rural Denmark, and to evaluate new farming methods in Zimbabwe.

Think big. The Funding Information Center in San Antonio, Texas, got Valero Energy Corporation to give it an entire building, got the carpeting from La Quinta motel chain, and got skilled workers from nearby Kelly Air Force Base.

You can also use donated products as part of another fundraiser. A local store donated seventy-five teddy bears to the Lubbock General Hospital. Executive Director for Development Jacque Hastings sent out a simple mailing that depicted a child's drawing of a bear in a Santa hat and offered "For each $25 donation a teddy bear will be donated in your name to a child." In three weeks the hospital netted $3,000 and several new donors, including a number of physicians.

PEOPLE

Do you need help getting the computers up to speed? Designing a market strategy? Setting up competitive pay and benefit packages? Doing an energy audit? Starting a business? Ask a local company to lend you its best brain in that field. Assign two of your own people to learn all they can from the borrowed businessperson.

SERVICES

What services do you need that a local company could supply? In their slow times, firms can give you assistance with printing, trucking, global teleconferencing, translations, art design, data searches, or scientific analysis.

Most nonprofits lack the discretionary money for the frills like an art collection or a nice meeting space. For-profit companies may be able to offer you art on loan to improve patient or employee morale. The BorgWarner Corporation in Chicago has been very generous in hosting events for nonprofits in its penthouse meeting room overlooking Grant Park and Lake Michigan. Inner-city charities have used it to fundraise from groups of grant makers and individual givers who are reluctant to venture out to more intimidating neighborhoods.

For much more advice on noncash gifts, get *Resource Raising: The Role of Non-Cash Assistance in Corporate Philanthropy* by Alex J. Plinio of the Prudential Insurance Company of America and Joanne B. Scanlan of Independent Sector. For ordering information, see Chapter 14.

HOW TO ASK

Once you have researched the local corporations, decide where your interests and values match, and then choose what you will ask for and prepare your package. Call to double-check the exact spelling of all names and titles. Then send off your package with a cover letter saying you will call in two weeks. This gives the recipients a week to open and route the mail to the right person.

Do not wait for them to call, or you will wait forever. Call the person to whom you sent the letter and ask if you can meet in person. The company staffer may say your package is plenty, may ask for a specific addition, such as your audit, or may want to meet with you. Ask to bring another person and try to get a time in the morning.

Once you get the meeting, call at least three charities that get funding from the corporation and ask for their advice. Try to talk to two or three people in the prospect company for their suggestions, too, on the corporate culture and needs. Talk to your partner and set goals for the meeting.

It is much easier if you have a partner, so one of you can listen while the other one talks. The ideal pair is one person who has personal experience with the project and another person who can ask for the donation you want.

IMAGE

I thrill to the marrow of my bones every January 15 when TV airs the 1963 speech by Dr. Martin Luther King, Jr., in which he said, "I have a dream that my four little children will one day live in a nation where they will not be judged by the color of their skin, but by the content of their character." In a perfect world, we and our projects would be judged only on our merits, not on our appearance.

Unfortunately, we do not live in a perfect world. As organizer Saul Alinsky often said, "You have to begin with the world as it really is, to get to the world as you would like it to be."

For corporate fundraising, this means conforming to the corporate dress code. You do not want someone who can write a big check to balk because he or she is threatened by your appearance. Unless unorthodox clothing is part of your job, as it is for zoo directors who wear safari clothes year-round, look like the people whom you want to listen to you.

When Nancy Abbate began the Youth Services Program (YSP), she was a college student herself and had a pretty flamboyant style. For example, not only were her proposals on purple paper, her hair was dyed purple. Once she began asking corporations for money, she discovered that no one at American Airlines, AT&T, or Amoco had purple hair. Since her image was standing between her and her goal—getting funding for her program—she quit dying her hair. Results: She built YSP from two volunteers with no money to fifty staff running award-winning programs for three thousand youths at a cost of $1.5 million. In 1989 she won corporate support from forty-eight businesses, including the three just mentioned.

PEOPLE WHO GET PLACES, GET PLACES EARLY

Get there at least half an hour early to get cleaned up and get the feeling for the company. In large, controversial, and phobic corporations, you will need to pass through several layers of security. The worst that can happen is you will arrive early enough to read the company brochures and the *Wall Street Journal*. The best that can happen is you will get more time with the executive and make a good impression.

When you meet the executive, take a few minutes to get acquainted, but resist the temptation to just visit. After five to fifteen minutes, get to the reason you are there: you are representing a terrific program, and you are able to offer the Widget Corporation a great opportunity to support your newest (biggest, best, most effective) project. Say why you are unique, special, superior; say why you are cost-effective. Dollar for dollar, why is this the best program in town?

Engage the executive in discussion. Ask for advice, and write down any suggestions. Most of them will be good and can help you improve your funding package and the program.

Be prepared to answer questions, and be specific. Quote facts and figures, briefly, whenever you can. If you are asked a question you cannot answer, promise to get the answer and send it the next day.

As graciously and firmly as possible, say exactly what you want from the company and what you will give: "We would like you to advertise in the program for our new play to raise awareness about AIDS. Because you are the biggest chain of pharmacies in town, we would like you to have the first chance to reach this audience. The back cover is $1,000 and will give your ad the most visibility. We will also list your gift in our annual report."

Or you might say, "We would like you to underwrite the production of our new play to raise awareness about AIDS. We project our total cost will be $100,000. We will put your company's name on the marquee on 42nd Street, on all the posters and other advertising, on the playbills and the ushers' T-shirts, and on all mailings to subscribers. We have set aside one hundred seats on opening night for you to use for your own employees or customers. As the largest chain of pharmacies in town, you understand what a serious problem this is; your support will give us credibility and will position your firm as the one that is really concerned about preventive medicine."

WHAT NOT TO DO

Never criticize another nonprofit agency. Even if it is a terrible group run by your worst enemy, do not be lured into a discussion about another group. Just say, "They do A, and we do B. If you want to know more about them, call their office. Now let me tell you about our program and why we are so excited about it."

If you admire a group, say that, and then say how you are distinct from them: "You're right, that group is doing a terrific job saving the bluebird habitats. We're lucky to have such a fine organization here. Now let me tell you about the work we are doing to restore the courthouse . . ."

Do not discuss partisan politics. Remind the executive that it is illegal for a tax-exempt charity to endorse a candidate and of course your organization always follows the law. Then say, "Our research shows that a majority of citizens agreed with our stand on the need for more good jobs. So we are eager to work with all the citizens who share our goals."

ASK AND FOLLOW UP

Keep your eye on the ball. Your job is to ask for a specific dollar amount and get it. Ask at least three times for the gift you want. Leave a reply card or a pledge card with a stamped envelope.

You may also ask for the names of other companies that may be interested in this sort of project. In most communities there are a handful of companies that provide leadership in any project, so if you get one leader, he or she can also introduce you to other savvy funders.

Before you leave confirm a date when you will know the

decision. Some gifts will be decided while you are in the office; others will go to the committee to decide if it can go on the agenda of the meeting six months from now. Either way, ask what you should do until you hear.

Before you leave the building, put your thank-you note in the mailbox. This means that the day before the meeting you have written a short note saying, "Thank you for meeting with us." This can be printed off the computer or handwritten if your handwriting is legible. Add a postscript if you want, and then drop it in the mailbox in the lobby so your contact will get it the next day for sure.

Some people are now using their fax machines for thank-you notes, saying something like, "I just couldn't wait to tell you how much I appreciate your taking the time to meet with us today." This is much more impersonal and can be read by anyone near the fax. Also, remember the wisdom of *Thoroughly Modern Millie*: rich people can nickel and dime you to death. An executive at a multibillion-dollar company once told me, with a straight face, that he resented other people faxing their thank-you notes to him, because they were using *his* paper instead of their paper. Better to spend your own thirty cents and look distinctive than to spend his penny and get a penny-pincher riled up.

When your organization gets the company's check, send another personal thank-you note the same day. The office must send an official receipt with all the information needed for the company's tax records, including the organization's federal tax identification number, and the signature of an officer. Since the amount the company may deduct on its federal taxes is determined in part by what the money is spent on, keep meticulous records of every expenditure made with corporate funds, and send the totals with the final report to the company. If this is your first contribution from the company, ask for the name of someone in its accounting department who can brief your bookkeeper on exactly what the company wants.

Deliver everything you promised and more. Send multiple copies or photocopies every time the company's name appears in print in your literature. Put the company on the newsletter mailing list and invite representatives to your special events, too. Go to the company's annual meeting and tell all the stockholders what a terrific company it is.

Best of all, measure and report the results you got from the company's gift. Try to meet again in person at least once just to ask for advice. Then go back and ask for a larger gift next year.

CONCLUSION

Good nonprofit organizations make it easier for corporations to compete for top executive talent, retain the best employees, and market their products to the public they want to reach. Successful fundraisers know they have a lot to offer, and a lot to gain, by raising money from the business community.

"You gain strength, courage, and
confidence by every experience in
which you really stop to look fear in
the face."

—Eleanor Roosevelt

Chapter 12

Business Partners and Business Ventures

In 1989 American corporations gave $5 billion in philanthropy.
In the same year they spent $300 billion on marketing. More
and more, nonprofits are asking for money from the marketing
and advertising departments as often as from the community
affairs department. This chapter will discuss how your organization can use this strategy to raise money and how to do it in a
way that is right for the values of your group. Then it will cover
how to use your own business ventures to make money, especially selling products or charging fees for your services.

CAUSE-RELATED MARKETING

Combining marketing and philanthropy to form cause-related
marketing is a fundraising idea from the eighties that is here to
stay. It is a marriage of convenience that makes money for both
the nonprofit and the for-profit. In the simplest form of this
strategy, the for-profit advertises that it will contribute a specific
amount or a percentage of each sale of its products in a certain
time period to the nonprofit. The corporation gets to connect
itself to a good cause and motivate consumers to spend money.

AMERICAN EXPRESS:
CAUSE-RELATED MARKETING PIONEER

The American Express Company was the outstanding pioneer in developing this concept. When Ronald Reagan cut funds for social programs, urging Americans to "return to self-reliance," what he did was unleash thousands of fundraisers, all knocking on the same corporate and foundation doors. Although many for-profit companies wanted to support good nonprofits, there were serious limits to what "checkbook philanthropy" could do to replace the lost government funding.

American Express assigned its marketing department to devise a way to raise more money for the nonprofits and at the same time make more money for the company. As Warner Canto, Jr., Senior Vice President for Worldwide Marketing, Development, and Communications, said, "Why not admit without embarrassment that there is nothing wrong—and everything right—with doing well for American Express by doing good in the communities where we do business?"

Since the program was launched in 1981, American Express's cause-related marketing has generated more than $35 million in donations and advertising support for eighty-eight causes in the United States and seventeen other countries. They are most famous for raising $1.7 million for the Statue of Liberty restoration, the campaign that increased usage of American Express cards by 28 percent and increased customers by 17 percent. "Project Hometown America" raised more than $3 million for 205 grass-roots programs throughout America in 1985.[1]

Charities selected for a cause-related marketing promotion get more than money from the corporation because of the effectiveness of the advertising that is aimed at consumers. Heightened public awareness of a good cause produces more individual and corporate gifts. Performing arts groups see ticket sales skyrocket during a promotion. Employee and volunteer morale goes up because the print and broadcast ads highlight the value of their cause. For example, the Lincoln Park Zoo in Chicago featured its blue rhino in ads to urge American Express cardholders to "Charge Wildly for the Zoo." As one of the few free zoos in America, it benefited not only from the $152,000 raised through the promotion but also from all the new members and customers produced by the advertising.

OUTREACH

For nonprofits, cause-related marketing is an ideal way to reach millions of consumers who may not be givers to charities. Forty percent of Americans never respond to mail; probably more hate the intrusion of phone calls and door-to-door canvassers. But almost everybody buys food and household supplies. Corporate tie-ins enable millions of people to learn about your cause and give in an easy way. A lot of small donations can add up to a large dollar gift for the charity.

One good example is the partnership between Nabisco Foods, local retailers, and the American Red Cross. In March, Red Cross Month, Nabisco ran special advertisements to urge shoppers to buy its products and support the work of the Red Cross. The 2,700 local Red Cross chapters encouraged their millions of members, donors, and friends to purchase Nabisco products and urged local retailers to feature Nabisco products during the promotion. Nabisco paid a $500,000 sponsorship fee to the national Red Cross Disaster Relief Fund and established an additional incentive fund to reward local chapters. Using a formula based on increased sales, Nabisco also donated money from the incentive fund to local retailers, who in turn donated it to their local Red Cross.

As John Linderman, the Director of Trade Marketing for Nabisco Foods, explained, "Cause-related marketing improves Nabisco's impact in the local markets. We get into more stores, and our products are bought by more customers. It also gives the local stores a way to stand out, to stand for more than just a place to shop for food. Internally, this kind of promotion also makes the Nabisco sales force feel proud of the support they can give to the Red Cross that teaches kids to swim, helps in local emergencies such as house fires, and helps around the world in times of war."

Nabisco products are popular with millions of consumers anyway, so the advertisement provides an easy way for shoppers to support a good cause. What a great opportunity to reach

A portion of the 1991 Nabisco Company advertisement

The American Red Cross name and emblem are used with the permission of the American Red Cross and do not imply an endorsement of these products

millions of possible donors who may never respond to your letters, phone calls, or door-to-door canvassers.

Nabisco Foods Company paid a sponsorship fee of $500,000 as part of this 1991 promotion benefitting the American Red Cross Disaster Relief Fund. Steve Delfin, Officer for Corporate Development of the Red Cross explained, "Cause-related marketing provides a new source of money and visibility for our work today. Plus it positions us with senior marketing personnel, a talent pool for many of tomorrow's CEOs."

HIGH VISIBILITY

A visual, urgent, well-publicized cause is the easiest to market. If you have a really hot issue covered by TV, a cause-related marketing effort can give your group a way to reach millions of people while the images of need are still in their heads. In 1989 Burger King used cause-related marketing for the American Red Cross's relief work for victims of Hurricane Hugo and the San Francisco earthquake. From October to November, Burger King gave twenty-five cents for every "special double" burger sold, raising a record $5.7 million. This represents nearly twenty-five million hamburgers.

Of course, very few nonprofit organizations can have their needs presented on worldwide television at the start of the World Series, then have their neighborhoods toured by the President and the Vice President of the United States for three solid days of lead stories on every news show. However, many organizations can find partnerships with for-profit businesses that will benefit both partners.

The Red Cross is the kind of nonprofit organization that corporations like because:

1. It has a long history of productive partnerships with corporations. A Red Cross magazine from 1918 shows a Wrigley Gum advertisement promoting the Red Cross War Relief Fund.
2. It has a very high visibility. The Red Cross logo is— surprise, surprise—a red cross on a white background.

What *is* surprising is its logo is the number one most easily recognized logo in the world, scoring even higher than Coca-Cola, McDonald's, or Playboy. Awareness of the importance of Red Cross work skyrockets in times of disaster (Hurricane Hugo) or war (Desert Storm).

3. It has a universal appeal.
4. It has an immense, extremely committed corps of volunteers, including many of the local retailers who national marketers want to reach.

If your organization is both recognized and respected by corporate decision-makers, then cause-related marketing can also be a good fundraising strategy for you.

MAKING A DEAL

Ask your fundraisers to collect samples of cause-related marketing from stores, television, magazines, and newspapers. Discuss these samples and brainstorm on possible partners for your organization.

What does your group have to offer? Think about the size of your base, especially members, donors, and volunteers. Can you measure and show the purchasing power of your donors, the visual appeal of your constituents, or the urgency and popularity of your cause? What does the corporation want in terms of markets, credibility, selling more products, or improving its image? Where is the match?

Steve Delfin of the Red Cross cautions, "Charities must ask 'What do we bring to the table that will help this company sell more product?' We may love our organization because of the wonderful work it does, but our business partners love our organization because we make their sales figures look wonderful."

Review the last chapter's ideas for finding a corporation to ask for money. Focus on meeting with the manager of marketing or advertising. Once you have found a corporation that likes your presentation, you need to be politely persistent. It can take months for all the right people to approve the deal, from the marketing manager to the brand manager, plus approval from both the subsidiary and the parent companies, plus approval from the lawyers at every level. So allow plenty of time and assign your most determined and diplomatic fundraiser to negotiate the deal.

To close the deal, create a deadline by connecting your promotion to a date linked to your cause, such as February for Heart Month or Black History Month and March for Science Month or Women's History Month. Or simply give the company a finite "window of opportunity." If it has not signed an agreement by your deadline, cancel the negotiations and pitch the competition.

Cause-related marketing works best for organizations that are highly visible and appealing. More controversial causes, partisan causes, or causes without visual appeal are much harder to sell. Thus, cause-related marketing will not be an option for every organization or every corporation, but it is here to stay. It is worth investigating if you think it could be a good strategy for your organization.

MARKETING YOUR OWN ORGANIZATION

The man who has revolutionized the way nonprofits look at marketing is Dr. Richard Steckel. He is famous for taking over the Children's Museum of Denver and transforming it from an impoverished, grant-dependent museum operating out of an abandoned dairy to a self-sufficient museum with its own multimillion-dollar building. The museum developed a system to negotiate partnerships with many for-profit businesses that would pay to be connected with the wonder, innocence, and excitement of a children's museum. Most nonprofits can copy these ideas to find business partners, create desirable products, and negotiate advantageous deals.

A few of Steckel's successes include selling a children's activity book about money to a bank ($10,000); organizing a "toy trade" for a department store and a fast-food chain ($4,900); and leasing traveling hands-on children's exhibits to shopping malls and other museums ($65 per day per exhibit). His system makes it much easier for a corporation to become a partner because it involves buying a specific, ready-made product. There is virtually no risk to the marketing people; in contrast, the staff in the charitable-giving department need to go out on a limb and actually fund the *work* your organization does to achieve its mission.

For more on these ideas for marketing products or services to for-profits, get Steckel's book *Filthy Rich & Other Nonprofit Fantasies* and the Children's Museum of Denver book *Nonprofit Piggy Goes to Market*. Both are listed in Chapter 14.

ADVERTISING SPONSORSHIPS

Another way for-profit companies can support nonprofits is through intentionally advertising in or on certain media or supporting certain projects in order to connect with their constituents. In advertising jargon, the goal is to target a certain market, which means the company is going to spend money to reach a specific group of consumers.

This has worked best for companies that support artistic projects aimed at upscale audiences. For example, Mobil Corporation pays for "Masterpiece Theatre" and "Mystery!" on American public television. Both are classy British TV shows that attract well-educated, affluent people. Mobil's 1982 survey of upscale viewers revealed that 31 percent said they bought Mobil gasoline most often, compared to 16 percent for Exxon, 15 percent for Gulf, and 10 percent for Texaco. When Mobil surveyed new stockholders, most gave investment goals as the reasons they bought the stock; however, 7 percent said they bought the stock because Mobil sponsored quality television programs.

What company would like to be connected to your project or your audience? What company sells a product that will connect in the consumers' minds? For example, in 1985 the Metropolitan Museum of Art produced an exhibition entitled "Man and the Horse." The museum's fundraiser, Emily K. Rafferty, asked Ralph Lauren to underwrite the exhibit, since his Polo brand logo is a polo pony and his clothes are marketed to people in the horsey set. Results: the museum received $350,000; Ralph Lauren got the Polo name on the invitations to the swanky Costume Institute benefit. As Rafferty points out, corporate sponsorships are not a one-shot deal but often the beginning of an ongoing relationship. Corporations that sponsor exhibitions often support other museum projects and activities, or at the very least remain active as corporate members.

ADVANTAGES

This kind of marketing partnership will continue to grow as more companies want to reach certain markets in a believable way. Many people pride themselves on their sales resistance; they will never believe any advertising. The 77 million babyboomers (born 1946 to 1964) have spent forty-five years watching TV commercials and know they are phony. With the enormous growth of cable channels and VCRs, couch potatoes can watch TV all weekend and never see a commercial. Clever companies need to find new outlets to reach the audiences they want. Supporting worthwhile nonprofits is one way to reach people that traditional advertising dollars will not reach.

Sponsoring nonprofit programming is not only good work, it is a good bargain. For example, Pepsi paid $750,000 to be a co-sponsor of the 1985 Band Aid concert; it received sixteen hours of impressions. For the same $750,000, Pepsi could have bought one forty-five-second spot during the Super Bowl.[2]

Herb Schmertz, the Mobil vice president, explained in his book *Good-Bye to the Low Profile,* "The consumers who are reached by affinity-of-purpose marketing are not always motivated by lower prices, convenience, or gimmicks like trading stamps. As we've already seen, they're increasingly resistant to advertising. But very often, they can be reached through an intangible value such as social responsibility."

STRATEGY

For nonprofits, the corporations' need for new markets is another reason to begin your fundraising strategy by building a broad base of support from individuals. Then continue to build the base by analyzing who joins and why, and deepen each donor's involvement by asking for larger gifts. If you have no members, or no members with purchasing power, your organization will not seem like a good partner for advertising. On the other hand, if you have done the work to build a large membership of people committed to certain values, and some of these people also have the means to spend more money, you can make a match with a for-profit that will benefit both the company and your organization.

Advertising expenditures are not limited to million-dollar high-brow projects. Creative fundraisers can ask for advertising dollars for almost any project. For grass roots groups, simply look at which local merchants do the most advertising. Who takes the largest display ads in the local newspaper, the Yellow Pages, the high school yearbook, the theater programs, the backs of church programs, and politicians' ad books? Use all of these for leads, as well as the suggestions in the last chapter.

For example, a high school in Abilene, Texas, wanted to send its band to march in the Rose Bowl parade in Pasadena, California. They knew they could never sell enough candy bars to send the band out of state. So they decided to ask for money from local retailers, targeting the merchants with a musical advertisement. For a contribution, the band would play the merchant's jingle during time-outs and halftime. While the band played, "You deserve a break today, so get up and get away, to McDonaaaaaaald's!" the local franchise flashed an advertisement up on the scoreboard.

It was a good partnership. The retailers got music to go with their visual advertising, they reached an audience they wanted to attract, and they supported a good cause. The band made more money outside its regular donors (families, friends, and candy customers) and learned to play songs the students actually already knew.

Once you build a good relationship with a corporation through its advertising sponsorship, you can also ask the company for grants. For example, in 1983 Texaco not only paid to sponsor the radio and TV broadcasts of the Metropolitan Opera, it also made a leadership gift of $5.5 million toward the Met's $100 million centennial campaign.

ETHICS

The last step of your fundraising strategy is to plan where you will *not* ask for money. You can be intentional about what sources of money you want and which sources you do not want. Your organization must have a written policy on fundraising ethics that has been approved by the board of directors and distributed to every fundraising employee, volunteer, and consultant. A written policy on fundraising makes it easier to review your fundraising employees and train your volunteers.

There are strings attached to all sources of money. One advantage of working with for-profits is they can be explicit about the strings they attach to the money. In the same way, your nonprofit organization can be explicit about the rules it has for accepting corporate contributions or choosing to participate in a marketing partnership.

You need to be careful about both real strings and perceived strings. For example, in 1989 the board of directors at APRN, the public radio network in Alaska, rejected a $32,000 contribution from Exxon because they believed it would appear to some people that their news reports on the Exxon Valdez oil spill could be compromised. APRN's written policy on underwriting specifies that it may not accept money that even "creates the appearance of a conflict of interest." Although Exxon attached no strings to the money, the suspicions raised from accepting the contribution could have cost the network's news department some of its credibility.

GET IT IN WRITING: YOUR POLICY

A written policy connected to your mission makes it easier to resist temptations. If your organization is well respected, for-profit corporations will want to connect to your positive image. Or your members may be the market they want. For example, in Chicago, Bethel New Life sponsored Umoja Fair to raise money to reduce infant mortality in its community, which is 99 percent African American. (*Umoja* is Swahili for "unity.") Bethel had brought the infant mortality rate in the West Garfield neighborhood down from thirty-three per thousand to seventeen per thousand in four years by promoting better health habits for pregnant women, including abstaining from alcohol and drugs.

A beer company that wanted to get a bigger share of the African-American market offered to underwrite expenses of the fair. Of course, this was a tempting offer, since it was a lot of money for no work; all the brewery wanted was the company name on the printed materials and its giant inflatable beer can at the fair. But Bethel New Life's board of directors turned down the beer money, since alcohol consumption is one cause of infant mortality. The board members knew their organization ethically could not tell pregnant women that drinking was wrong and, at the same time, accept money from a beer company.

Setting specific limits on the specific companies or the kind of companies that are not acceptable to your values need not put a chill on your overall fundraising. Show your leadership that your fundraising strategies, including raising money from good business partners, are just as important and ethical as your program strategies. If you have bold goals and high standards, you can win big victories and raise big money, too. For example, the year that Bethel New Life voted to reject the money from the beer company, its budget *grew* 35 percent to $4.9 million, including contributions from for-profit businesses such as Allstate Insurance, Amoco, the *Chicago Tribune*, Illinois Bell, Sears, and Walgreen's.

GET IT IN WRITING: THEIR POLICY

Written policies are a two-way street. Whenever you are negotiating with any funder, ask the company to put in writing *exactly* what it wants from your agency. Then you can be sure that its terms are acceptable to your leadership, and you can ethically conform to what the donor wants.

A written agreement can also eliminate last-minute surprises and embarrassment for either party. For example, in 1990 IBM canceled its advertising for a Professional Golf Association (PGA) tournament three weeks before the event, when the company learned the tournament would be played at an Alabama golf club that excluded blacks. "Supporting even indirectly activities which are exclusionary is against IBM's practices and policies," said Gina Chew-Holman, IBM spokeswoman.[3]

ETHICS IN CAUSE-RELATED MARKETING

The growth of cause-related marketing in the past ten years has provoked a great debate on the ethics of using this method of fundraising. Some fundraisers believe that charities should not get involved in promotions with the advertising or marketing people but should just stick with asking for donations from the corporate-giving people. The thinking is that nonprofits should accept money that is given only from purely charitable motives, not to help the corporation's profit motives.

However, it is hopelessly naive to expect corporate gifts to come from pure motives. Do our friends and family donate only from pure motives? Individual donors give because they want status, power, and ego reinforcement as well as beauty, truth, and justice. Why should corporations be expected to be less self-interested than the individuals who give nonprofits 90 percent of their budgets?

The corporation has a self-interest, and so does your organization. Put them both in writing, and if the deal and your values agree, then get a written contract and proceed with enthusiasm. If you cannot negotiate a contract that is right for both parties, consider a different strategy to raise your money.

RESEARCH

An organization can write into the contract specific limitations to protect its reputation if circumstances change before the campaign. For example, in 1989, Continental Airlines wanted to link up with the March of Dimes. It would have been a good deal except that before the campaign began, the airline's CEO, Frank Lorenzo, became involved in a lengthy and very bitter strike. The March of Dimes inadvertently found itself linked to one of the most despised bosses in America.

As Benjamin Disraeli said, "There is no education like adversity." Now the March of Dimes has a *very* thorough system for clearing corporate partners. Jamie McCreary, the current March of Dimes director of national promotions, says they check a possible corporate partner with

1. the AFL-CIO
2. the Federal Trade Commission
3. the Environmental Protection Agency

4. *The Directory of Corporate Affiliations*
   Who owns them?
   Whom do they own?
5. Dun & Bradstreet
6. the Better Business Bureau
7. the corporation's annual report

Internally, the promotions department also checks any possible corporate partners with the legal, community services, science, and communications departments, regional offices, and the field staff.

This may be more research than your organization wants to do, especially if you are working with a local company you already know and trust. However, every group can do simple research in its own community. First, check out the corporation with all of the players, not just the marketing department. Talk to the unions, the business reporters who cover the company, and the competition.

Second, be sure the marketing dollars are a small part of your organization's budget. The core budget should come from dependable, renewable individual donors. Then you have the freedom to walk away from any relationship that is not right for your group.

Third, choose partners that are logically connected to your mission. For example, Gaines dog food company raised money for the American Humane Association. Johnson & Johnson, "the first name in first aid," raised money for the American Red Cross. Since 1969, Sears has donated paint to preserve and protect the Great American homes of the "Who's Who" of history. Thousands of tourists see Buffalo Bill Cody's ranch in Nebraska, John Paul Jones's house in New Hampshire, and Helen Keller's home in Alabama spruced up with the same Sears paint they can buy for their own homes. Since 1989 Sears also has been the sole sponsor of the National Trust for Historic Preservation's contest to recognize the best restoration efforts by ordinary Americans. The closer the connection is, the better for both partners.

You need clear, explicit principles about money, as you do about the rest of your mission. You do not want to let your leadership demean fundraising itself or miss the opportunity to work with local businesses who care about your mission. Money is the oxygen that keeps your organization alive. As members of a worthwhile organization doing important work, your fundraisers want to find all the allies who share your goals and your values—including the best for-profit companies.

STARTING YOUR OWN BUSINESS

For middle- and upper-class communities and institutions, earned-income enterprises are becoming more and more popular and profitable. They can range from selling quality products such as UNICEF cards or Girl Scout cookies to operating an entire store. Universities and libraries run bookstores, hospitals and museums run gift shops, international relief organizations sell crafts from around the world, historical houses license reproductions of their furniture, hospitals operate pharmacies, and zoos organize photographic safaris—all to make money for their missions. In addition to these in-house ventures, today nonprofits are running bigger ventures, often in partnership with a for-profit. Thus, a museum may work with a developer to build condominiums in the airspace above the museum, or universities may work with drug companies to patent their research.

Using sales to make money for a nonprofit is not a new idea. Medieval churches made money by selling ales brewed in the church house and by renting out vestments to other churches for funerals and festivals. In Cornwall, England, the parish accounts from 1526 showed that gypsies stayed in the Stratton church house several times, and the "keepers of the bear" paid one pence rent for it.[4] Today churches near popular sports stadiums, such as Fenway Park in Boston and Wrigley Field in Chicago, can make money selling parking to sports fans.

SELLING PRODUCTS AND SERVICES

Selling products and services is one of the easiest ways for nonprofits to earn income. Most Americans already have experience as nonprofit salespeople selling Girl Scout cookies, band candy, T-shirts, bumper stickers, light bulbs, or pizzas in their youth. Like other fundraising strategies, creative groups find a way to connect product sales to their mission.

Probably the most familiar example is Girl Scout cookies. Girl Scouts began selling homemade cookies in the 1920s and went to commercial bakeries in 1938. In 1989 the 333 American Girl Scout Councils organized cookie sales to make money and teach good skills and values. One million girls sold 165 million boxes of cookies, priced from $2 to $3, grossing more than $300 million for the Girl Scout programs.

Even enterprising Scouts are finding corporate partners for their sales. Jorie Miller of Brownie Troop 1207 in Burr Ridge, Illinois, sent her neighbor David Hinson a picture and a letter about Girl Scout cookies. As a cookie connoisseur Hinson bought a box of Thin Mints for himself; as CEO of Midway Airlines he bought 2,000 boxes of Trefoils for his lucky passengers. Successful fundraiser Jorie Miller is seven years old.[5]

The Scouts use the cookie sales as more than a money maker; selling cookies is considered a program activity to teach girls goal setting, decision making, and responsibility. Some troops learn telemarketing and advertising skills. For most of the girls it is their first exposure to the business world—an important experience, since the majority of American women will work outside the home. Thus, the scouts have fun and learn useful skills at the same time they are making money for their troop. If you want to add sales to your fundraising strategy, see if you can also use the activity to advance your mission.

ADVANTAGES OF SELLING PRODUCTS

The main advantage of selling is that your customers are going to get something they want anyway. Ideally your product will be connected to the work you do, so you can discuss your issues at the same time you make sales. For example, environmental groups sell trees, biodegradable diapers, and cloth lunch bags to make money for their causes.

You can connect the sales to your mission. For example, the UNICEF 1990 holiday card catalog advertises:

One box of UNICEF cards can

- buy 107 chloroquine tablets to control malaria
- pay for inland transport of enough high-protein food to feed two malnourished children for a month
- buy enough vaccine to immunize 9 children against polio

Measure and talk about the results your organization gets. UNICEF tells about one successful program on every page of its catalog. For example, the 1990 catalog reported, "Unsafe water contributes to diarrhea-related illnesses—the major cause of mortality in infants and children under five. In the last year alone, over 100,000 new water systems were completed with UNICEF assistance."[6]

People like to do sales. It is an easy, quick, agreeable way to ask for small amounts of money. Since there are many different jobs, there are many different opportunities for different people. The outgoing self-starters can handle the selling; the shy, well-organized people can handle the order forms and bookkeeping.

A business can start small and grow a lot. Almost any group can hold a bake sale or a rummage sale and bring in $500 to $1,000 in a weekend. The Junior Leagues of America made $2.5 million from their cookbooks and $5 million from their thrift shops in 1989.

Nonprofit businesses can also appeal to their customers' good intentions. Buying products from nonprofits can be an act of socially responsible consumerism. Why buy a T-shirt with rude remarks or cartoon characters when you could look just as good and benefit a local charity at the same time buying the charity's T-shirt? As long as you plan to splurge on expensive furniture, why not buy one of the outstanding licensed reproductions from the National Trust for Historic Preservation and benefit the historic properties it manages?

CHALLENGES

There are always some people who will not want your product although they think your group and its work are just wonderful. For example, dieters, diabetics, and health nuts may not buy Girl Scout cookies, although they probably want girls to learn Girl Scout values such as loyalty, courtesy, and cleanliness in thought, word, and deed.

So every time you sell merchandise or send out a catalog, also include a written request for memberships, donations, and bequests. Even people who do not want your product may want the mission and will contribute if you give them the option.

TAXES

If your nonprofit organization sells products or runs a business, will it have to pay taxes on the profits? Maybe.

The Internal Revenue Service (IRS) is getting tougher on nonprofits that run businesses, and associations of small businesses are going to keep up the pressure to cut down on what they consider unfair competition from nonprofits. Because the laws and court rulings on these questions are changing quickly, you need to get good up-to-date legal advice.

Start by reading the IRS Publication 598, *Tax on Unrelated Business Income of Exempt Organizations* (free; 800/424-FORM) or the section on unrelated business rules in Bruce Hopkin's *The Law of Fundraising* (ordering information in Chapter 14). Then hire or recruit a lawyer with experience in this area of the law. If your proposed business will owe any local, state, or federal taxes, of course the business manager must pay all taxes on time. Do not dismiss the possibility of a money-making business just because it may have to pay taxes. If necessary, consider taxes a cost of doing business and add them to the expenses in your plan.

LOW-INCOME COMMUNITY VENTURES

In the 1980s, there was a flurry of studies promoting the idea of for-profit enterprises run by nonprofit agencies to promote social goals and produce earned income in low-income communities. Many of these enterprises were started, and some achieved their social goals. Almost none produced a net profit for the parent agency.

Profitable enterprises depend more than anything else on a single-minded profit-motivated entrepreneur; few low-income community ventures could find or keep this type of person. Most community businesses were undercapitalized up front, underestimated the real cost of operating in a low-income community, and lacked the systems to manage a business. Also, nonprofit leaders were naive about the change a venture could make. They learned that a business, by itself, will not turn around the lives of low-income people. After their communities have undergone twenty-five years of disinvestment not even the hardest working people can escape poverty by running a laundromat.

So what is the role of earned-income ventures for nonprofits today? In low-income neighborhoods, business ventures can still be part of an agency's overall strategy for improving a community. Ventures serve useful social goals such as getting people off welfare, teaching work skills, giving incentives to stay in or go back to school, and providing better goods and services at fair prices. They can add another source of income, which may be vital in times of uncertain cash flow. It is not uncommon for community agencies to pay the phone bill with cash from the recycling center while they wait for some state office to approve $50,000 in vouchers that are long overdue.

Today, most realistic agencies working in the toughest neighborhoods acknowledge community ventures will be money drains rather than money makers. For low-income communities, earned-income ventures are run to meet social goals, and the organizations raise money from other sources to cover the costs.

FEES AND TUITIONS

Fees and tuitions account for about 40 to 45 percent of the total budgets of nonprofits other than religious congregations. With government cutbacks in the 1980s, every organization had to look at initiating fees for service or increasing the fees they already had. Instead of selling a product, you sell the work your organization does by setting fees. Most schools call their fees "tuitions."

Fees are good for a nonprofit because the people who want what you do are the ones who pay for it. If you believe in the value of your work and price it so that you will make a profit, fees and tuitions can help support your group.

Some organizations are reluctant to set fees for fear of discovering that their clients do not want the services enough to pay for them. If your clients do not want what you do, why are you doing it? Even worse, why should the taxpayers or grant makers pay for services local people do not want?

If you are providing a quality service, fees allow your organization to grow as the market for your services grows. For example, in 1978 Bill Draves was the only staff person for the Free University Network. With a budget of $20,000, the Free U Network provided technical assistance and organized a national conference for noncredit adult education courses. Half of the budget came from foundation grants because, as Draves says, "I thought that was where the money was."

Today the organization is called the Learning Resources Network (LERN). It has a million-dollar budget raised entirely from fees for its technical assistance, its national conference, and sales of its publications. LERN receives no foundation grants. The organization now serves 5,000 adult education programs in the United States, Canada, and Australia.

FEES FOR LOW-INCOME MARKETS

The obvious difficulty with fees or tuitions is that some people will not be able to pay. Your organization can choose from several strategies to solve this problem.

You can charge more for some services to subsidize other services. Measure the popularity of everything you do and charge more where you can. For example, in 1978 Bill Draves was opposed to charging fees for adult education classes because he wanted low-income people to be able to take classes in survival skills such as home canning and auto repair. However, an analysis revealed that the most popular adult education courses in Kansas were "Rodeo History" and "French Hair Braiding," neither of which could be considered survival skills. Then he realized he could charge the rodeo fans and beauty queens more for their courses and use those profits to subsidize the classes for low-income people.

LERN uses the same policy today. It makes enough of a surplus on its most popular services to give free scholarships to programs offering classes for low-income people. This helps programs that teach English as a Second Language (ESL) and ESL Keyboarding, which teaches immigrants how to use the English-language keyboard so they can get jobs. As Draves says, "We *should* be doing some things for people who can't pay." (For more on LERN, call 913/539-LERN.)

Consider other strategies for setting fees. Some counseling programs charge fees based on a sliding scale keyed to income. Everyone pays something so they are more likely to continue and benefit from the counseling, but the people with little or no income pay very little, while the people with high incomes pay much more.

Some groups provide sweat-equity opportunities so people can earn the fee. Habitat for Humanity helps low-income people earn a down payment for a home by working a specified number of hours building their own home and then volunteering a certain number of hours to help another family build a home.

Most people can and will pay when asked. If you want your agency to be perceived as a permanent, powerful organization literally accountable to the people it serves, always ask those people to pay a fee for the services they use.

CONCLUSION

There are many advantages to working with a business partner or running your own business. Your organization can reach beyond its current membership to everybody who shops. The talents that make a business profitable—good management, taking risks, and thinking big—are the same talents you need to be a successful fundraiser. Best of all, you get the chance to meet the people who think that profit is *good.* Working with the top marketing and advertising people in your community will help your fundraisers learn to "sell" your own cause with integrity, creativity, and profitability.

"What are you willing to pay in order
to live in the kind of society that you
want to live in?"
—*Andrea Kydd*
  Director, Health Program
  The Nathan Cummings Foundation

Chapter 13

Grant Makers

Foundations, United Ways, Religious
Denominations, and Civic Organizations

Fundraisers have many opportunities to ask for grants. A grant
is simply a donation, usually relatively large, from an institution rather than an individual person. Grants range in size from
hundreds of dollars to millions. Unlike a loan, a grant does not
need to be paid back.

This chapter will look at four different kinds of grant
makers and give you some general advice on how to research
them and ask for grants. In every case, get more current detailed
advice from a local group they fund now.

Foundations are the easiest grant makers to research. All
foundations get a tax break from the U.S. government and in
exchange have to file a detailed report on their activities to the
IRS every year. All the foundations' financial data from the
IRS, including specific names and amounts, are made available
to fundraisers in the Foundation Center's publications and data
bases.

Foundations represent an immense amount of money. In
the United States, more than thirty thousand foundations gave
away $7 billion to millions of charities in 1989. In Canada in

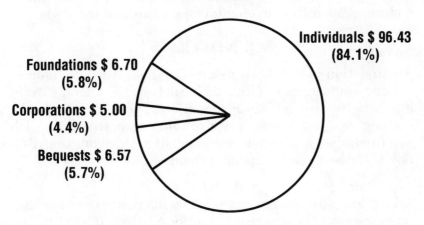

Giving 1989: $ 114.70 Billion
Sources

Individuals $ 96.43
(84.1%)

Foundations $ 6.70
(5.8%)

Corporations $ 5.00
(4.4%)

Bequests $ 6.57
(5.7%)

Source: *Giving USA 1990*. Reprinted with permission from the
AAFRC Trust for Philanthropy

1988, 848 foundations gave away $269 million in grants larger
than $2,500.[1]

Charities also received $2.3 billion in 1989 from the 2,300
United Ways in the United States. United Ways fund primarily
noncontroversial health and human services agencies. It is difficult for a new group to get into the United Way allocations, but
it is worth the effort because this organization is a dependable,
renewable source of money once your group is in.

Religious denominations are the hardest to research because they are accountable to their own governing bodies and
not to the U.S. government. But it is well worth the work because religious grant makers as a group gave more than $19
billion in 1989, more than foundations and corporations combined. Unlike foundations and the United Ways, they are not
limited as to the kinds of nonprofits they can fund.

Every community has an array of civic and social clubs that
raise money and give some of it away in grants to other good
charities. These can range from very small grants ($50) from
student groups to medium-sized grants from the VFW, the

Junior League, the Lions Club, and fraternities and sororities, to the giants like Rotary International, which has made grants totaling $230 million to erradicate polio around the world.

FOUNDATIONS

A foundation is simply an institution that gives away money. Because foundations receive a tax break from the federal government, they have to give away money every year. Unfortunately, nothing says they have to give it to your organization. Your job as a fundraiser is to convince a foundation that your organization is the best place to spend its money.

ADVANTAGES

Asking for foundation money provides many advantages to your organization. The best thing that foundations offer is the requirement that you write a proposal. This is a written request for money that helps you to think through a new project from beginning to end. Even if you do not receive a grant, the process of planning the project, making the budget, and devising a way to measure the results is worth the effort.

Foundations are the venture capitalists of the nonprofit world. Some will fund the sizzle before there is a steak. Although the money usually runs out after one, two, or three years, it can buy your organization the time it needs to establish a funding base in its own constituency and create a track record.

The number of foundations is growing. In the 1980s, 1,095 new foundations were established with assets of $1 million or more; in the 1970s, 790 large foundations were established.[2] Community foundations are being created across the United States, and new public foundations are raising money for special populations, such as the forty-one American foundations that fund programs for women and girls.

Foundations can give big money. The largest reported grants in 1989 were $30 million from the Arnold and Mabel Beckman Foundation to the California Institute of Technology, $14 million from the W. K. Kellogg Foundation to Michigan's Industrial Technology Institute, and $12.8 million from the Henry J. Kaiser Family Foundation to the New England Medical Center.[3] With higher goals and more persuasive fundraisers, the number of large grants is increasing. In 1989, there were 41 foundation grants of $5 million or more, up from 28 in 1988; there were 60 grants of $2.5 million or more.[4]

Some foundations can also give you loans or venture capital known as "program-related investments"—PRIs in fundraising jargon. This funding can be very helpful for groups working in low-income communities that are denied credit by conventional lenders.

The largest foundations have savvy staff who can serve as a helpful sounding board for new ideas. Foundation staff can put you in touch with people you should know; national foundation staff are especially good at getting the leaders of a certain field together.

CHALLENGES

Foundation grant making is notoriously "trendy," going from cause to cause. You can get no money if your cause is considered passé. Even worse, you can get too much money if you ask the year your cause is hot, then get cut off the following year when it is not.

Unlike government, corporate, and United Way funding, which can be renewed year after year for decades, foundation funding usually runs out after one, two, or three years. On the one hand, foundations are always looking for new programs to fund. On the other hand, you can invest a lot of time and effort (and sometimes money) cultivating a relationship and mastering applications and reporting requirements, only to see the grant run out so that you have to start all over on another source of funds.

Grant makers like to fund a specific piece of your overall work, since it is easier to understand and easier to take credit for a single program. There is also less risk of funding a failure. Never expect a foundation to pay for your organization's everyday operating expenses; that money needs to come from renewable sources like dues and donations.

Forty percent of the foundation money is controlled from New York City, which of course favors organizations that New Yorkers think are important. If your organization is in New

York City's Manhattan, you could find 2,967 foundations controlling $24 billion in assets. If your organization is in Manhattan, Kansas, you could find four foundations controlling a total of $75,000 in assets. Rural organizations are at a serious disadvantage in raising money from foundations, with the exception of a handful of foundations that are based in rural communities themselves.

Most foundation money goes to human services (26 percent), health care (22 percent), education (17 percent), and culture (14 percent.) There has been great growth in giving to organizations for children and youth, science, international support for protection of global ecosystems, and grants for research on AIDS.

Despite some growth, most organizations for minorities and women still get a tiny sliver of the foundation pie. For example, foundation funding for African-American organizations tripled in the eighties but is still less than 5 percent of the total. Hispanic, Asian-American, and Native American groups got even less. Programs for women and girls received 5 percent of foundation grants. Religious congregations get 2 percent of foundation grants.[5]

WHO MAY ASK

In the United States, foundations legally may give grants only to nonprofits that are tax-exempt under section 501(c)(3) of the Internal Revenue Service tax codes. Every nonprofit is incorporated in its state, then applies to the IRS to be exempt from paying federal corporate income taxes. The federal government first imposed a tax on "all corporates organized for profit" in 1894; at the same time, it specifically exempted charitable institutions.

Twenty-eight tax categories are exempt from paying corporate income taxes. These include 501(c)(4) for civic leagues, 501(c)(5) for labor unions, 501(c)(6) for chambers of commerce, and 501(c)(7) for social clubs. Only organizations in the 501(c)(3) tax code are both exempt from paying corporate income taxes and able to give their donors the right to deduct the value of contributions from their taxable income. The 501(c)(3) is often shortened in fundraising jargon to simply "C3." In 1990, 450,000 charities had 501(c)(3) status.

American lawmakers want taxpayers to support good causes, so the IRS gives tax-exempt status to groups they want to promote. These include "religious, educational, charitable, scientific, literary, testing for public safety, to foster national or international amateur sports competition, or prevention of cruelty to children or animals organizations."[6] These all fall into the 501(c)(3) tax code, and gifts made to them are deductible from individuals' taxable income.

Most foundations will give grants only to 501(c)(3) organizations, but there are a couple of loopholes. For example, a volunteer fire department is legally a 501(c)(4) organization, but foundations and individuals may still give deductible funds to the volunteer fire department's work for "exclusively public purposes." Some nonprofits that are not C3s, such as chambers of commerce, may legally create a special charitable fund exclusively to do 501(c)(3) types of activities. In that case a foundation may make a grant to the chamber's charitable fund and deduct the grant. For more information on tax codes, get Publication 557 free from the IRS. For more information on creating a new tax-exempt 501(c)(3) nonprofit organization and protecting the tax-exempt status of an existing charity, read chapters 1 through 9 of *The Successful Volunteer Organization*. Both publications are listed in Chapter 14.

Foundations may also give grants to governmental bodies, such as a park district for a new swimming pool, a library to computerize the collection, or a school district for a better building. More and more towns and counties have a foundation fundraiser in the office of economic development.

THE IRS TELLS ALL

It is easy to research foundations because every American foundation has to file a Form 990PF every year with the Internal Revenue Service, just as an individual taxpayer has to file a Form 1040 or a charity has to file a Form 990. The 990PFs are a gold mine of information, because they actually name names of the trustees, the staff, and the charities that got grants.

All of the data from the 990PFs and other foundation materials are collected as a public service (and a very successful example of earned income) by the Foundation Center in New York City. This organization compiles the data in publications and data bases for easy access.

RESOURCES FROM THE FOUNDATION CENTER

At your own public library you can probably find *The Foundation Directory*, which will introduce you to the 7,600 largest American foundations. Ask the reference librarian for other information on local foundations, corporations, philanthropists, and scholarships.

If foundations are brand-new to you, get *The Foundation Center's User-Friendly Guide*, listed in Chapter 14. It is the easiest and clearest explanation of how to ask for foundation funding.

Cooperating Collections

The Foundation Center operates four free libraries in New York, Washington, D.C., Cleveland, and San Francisco and supports Cooperating Collections in every state, Puerto Rico, and the Virgin Islands. See the list at the end of this chapter.

Phone first to ask when the collection will offer an orientation. Take a partner and learn about foundation and corporate fundraising. Most of the Cooperating Collections sell the Foundation Center publications as well as state and city directories such as the *Directory of Kansas Foundations* (James H. Rhodes, editor) or *Directory of Texas Foundations* (Candace Chumney, editor). At the Cooperating Collections you can also look at copies of the 990PFs for the foundations in your state and often neighboring states; at the four national collections you can see the 990PFs for national foundations.

Most of the Cooperating Collections are staffed by professional librarians; others have expert volunteers to help you. They will *not* do the work for you, but they will teach you how to work most efficiently. The Cooperating Collections are by far the best sources of information on foundation and corporate giving. Your own local library may have more information on local philanthropists and scholarships.

COMPUTER ACCESS

Many public and academic libraries can also access the Foundation Center's information via their computers. This may be in a specialized computer-assisted reference center (CARC) or through the business section. Libraries can use a service called EasyNet to access the Foundation Center data. Other ways you can use EasyNet are through a local business that uses the IBM Information Network or through an individual investor who subscribes to the GE Network for Information Exchange (GEnie). The library will charge you a fee for the amount of time you access the service; a friendly business or investor may be willing to donate the access if you ask.

EasyNet and other similar services are available through twenty-five computer distribution channels in sixteen countries, including Australia, Canada, Great Britain, India, Ireland, Israel, and even back in the U.S.S.R. These are all user-friendly services that allow anyone to use simple English-language commands to retrieve the data from the Foundation Center data bases.

For more knowledgeable computer users, foundation data can be retrieved through a company called Dialog Information Services. Your organization can subscribe to Dialog, or you may access the files through the computer-assisted reference center at your public library or through a friendly nonprofit or for-profit that uses Dialog. In this case you need to learn special codes and commands, but you can retrieve more current information more quickly.

The big advantage of using the computerized services is that the computer does all the searching for you, and it will organize and print the data in whatever format is most useful for you. The cost in 1990 was $60 an hour. If your organization does a lot of foundation research, the computer searches will pay for themselves in saved time and labor costs. Since the five hundred largest foundations reported forty-five thousand grants in 1989, the field has outgrown the ability of even the most zealous volunteer to retrieve on paper. For more advice, check with the online support staff at the Foundation Center in New York at 212/620-4230.

Foundation Center Publications

Several basic reference books are published by the Foundation Center:

- *The Foundation Directory*, with information on more than 7,600 of the largest foundations that give out nearly $7 billion. The same information is also retrievable on a computer through Dialog File 26.
- *Source Books Profiles* give you much more detail on the top one thousand foundations.
- *National Directory of Corporate Giving* has data on more than 1,200 corporate foundations and 500 direct-giving programs that gave away more than $4 billion in cash and in-kind gifts in 1988. All of these listings are cross-indexed by location (for example, Alaska), type of charity (elementary school), type of constituency (youth), type of fundraising need (endowment), and amount of grants given ($20,000).
- *National Data Book of Foundations* gives information on more than thirty thousand U.S. foundations. This is the best guide to local funding, since many of these are quite small family foundations and all are listed by state. Brief information on twenty thousand of these foundations is also retrievable by computer via Dialog File 26. The ten thousand smallest foundations will be found only in the *National Data Book of Foundations*, so be sure to use it for smaller local family foundations or to research local major donor prospects.

You may also use the Foundation Center guides that are tailored for a specific cause, such as aging, AIDS, alcohol and drug abuse, arts, health care, higher education, or historic preservation.

All of these books and data bases give you the guidelines on where the foundations say they will or will not make grants. The reality check is another book and database that tells where the foundations really *made* their grants. This is *The Founda-*

tion Grants Index, which lists forty-six thousand grants of $5,000 or more made by 472 of the largest foundations. This information is also retrievable via computer on Dialog File 27.

Although this data comes from less than 2 percent of the foundations in the country, it represents about 44 percent of all grants from private and community foundations. *The Foundation Grants Index* or Dialog File 27 will name the dollar amounts for grants that were given to charities in your state.

If you see that a good local nonprofit has received a grant from a foundation you want to ask, get more information from the fundraiser who got the grant. Always add current advice from real people to the data in the books. Ask whom to approach at the foundation and whom to avoid. What does the foundation like and what do they dislike? What are recent changes?

The Foundation Center also publishes excellent how-to books to get you started on deciding whether foundations are a good fundraising strategy for you to pursue, planning programs, writing proposals, and researching foundations. See Chapter 14 or call 800/424-4230 to order the Center's publications catalog.

Caution

The Foundation Center has presented fundraisers with an embarrassment of riches. So much data is available on foundations that you can easily get overwhelmed or, even worse, distracted from your original mission by the lure of easy money. Always begin with your own organization's mission, goals, and values. With your leadership, decide what you want to do and how you want to do it. Be sure that your everyday operating expenses are already covered by a dependable fundraising base of dues and donations.

Then if you want to explore foundations, choose a specific program, and research foundation funding for that. Remember, independence comes from diversity in fundraising. Never depend on foundation grants, and never budget the money till the check is in your hand.

TYPES OF FOUNDATIONS

You can get more information at the Cooperating Collection, but basically there are five kinds of foundations: private, community, corporate, public, and operating foundations.

Private Foundations

The Foundation Center defines a private foundation as a nongovernmental, nonprofit organization having a principal fund of its own, managed by its own trustees and directors, and established to maintain or aid charitable, educational, religious, or other activities serving the public good, primarily by making grants to other nonprofit organizations. Most of the biggest foundations are private foundations, such as the Ford Foundation, which made $212 million in grants in 1989: the John D. and Catherine R. MacArthur Foundation, which gave $165 million; and the W. K. Kellogg Foundation, which gave $102 million.

If you are asking individuals for major gifts, some of them may choose to give to you from their family's foundation. Foundations were invented in 1917, the same year the federal government began levying an income tax. Wealthy families found that one way to avoid paying taxes was to create a foundation. Then the money could be squirreled away tax-free in a foundation, but the family could still control how it was spent.

Community Foundations

You can think of community foundations as sort of foundation co-ops. Many donors pool their trust funds in a community foundation and gain economies from a shared staff. Funds may be earmarked for a specific interest in the community. In 1989 there were more than 250 community foundations that gave more than $430 million in grants.

Community foundations are now the fastest-growing sort of foundation in the United States, because they give a donor all the advantages and prestige of being a foundation without the headaches of running one's own foundation full-time. Also, their donors can get the blessings of anonymity if they want. The most generous community foundations in terms of grants paid in 1989 were the New York Community Trust ($50 mil-

lion), the Cleveland Foundation ($28 million), the Chicago
Community Trust ($26 million), the Communities Foundation
of Texas ($22 million), and the Marin Community Foundation
($22 million).[7] Even smaller communities such as Elk River,
Minnesota (population 6,785), and low-income communities
like East Chicago, Indiana, are creating community foundations.

For fundraisers, community foundations are a good source
of money because they are, by definition, committed to the well-
being of the particular community. They can be the first source
of money for new issues. For example, when nine volunteers
started Horizon Hospice in Chicago in 1978, there was no
rubric in the directories for "hospice" because only a handful
were in operation in North America. The Chicago Community
Trust gave Horizon Hospice its first grant of $35,000 to hire staff
and open an office.

Corporate Foundations
In addition to their direct-giving programs, 1,300 American
companies also have foundations to make grants to the causes
they want to support. The largest company-sponsored foundations in 1989 were AT&T, which gave $30 million in grants;
General Motors, which gave $25 million; Amoco, which gave
$22 million; Ford, which gave $20 million; and Exxon, which
gave $19 million.[8]

Public Foundations
A public foundation raises money, then gives it away, so this
type of foundation is both a donor and donee. This role gives
public foundations the advantages of being included in the
inner circles of foundations, like the Council on Foundations.
Most of these target their grants for specific constituencies, such
as the Black United Funds (BUFs).

Another example of public foundations is the fifteen local
"alternative foundations" that raise money and make grants to
fund progressive grass roots organizing. These include the
Haymarket People's Fund in Boston, the Chinook Fund in
Denver, and the Vanguard Public Foundation in Los Angeles.
Unlike traditional community foundations, the alternative

funds include low- and middle-income community leaders in the grant making process and raise money from all economic classes.

Operating Foundations

Although operating foundations are called "foundations," you cannot ask most of them for money, because they do not make grants to other nonprofit groups. The most common examples are foundations run by hospitals as a way to raise money and maintain an endowment for the hospital foundation. These spend money only on expenses incurred by their own hospitals, usually for indigent care not covered by government funds or private insurance.

One exception is the J. Paul Getty Trust, an operating foundation that is the number two foundation in terms of assets in 1989. It gave $137 million to its own programs, especially the Getty Museum in Malibu, California, and also gave $13 million to outside programs.

On the other hand, some foundations are grant makers but call themselves something other than "foundations." Examples include the Lilly Endowment ($92 million in grants in 1989), the Carnegie Corporation of New York ($39 million), and the Robert R. McCormick Charitable Trust ($20 million).

HOW TO ASK FOR FOUNDATION GRANTS

To ask for a grant from a foundation, begin with whom you know. If any of your board members or volunteers already know the staff or trustees of a foundation, begin with those donors. Research their foundation through the Foundation Center publications or data bases and the groups they have funded. Send a one- or two-page letter outlining the program you want the foundation to fund, then call to discuss it further.

If you do not have any prospects from your own leadership, ask the fundraisers from similar organizations to recommend foundations that might fund your organization. Then research those and begin a dialogue.

If you have no leads at all, attend an orientation at a Cooperating Collection to learn how to use Foundation Center data to make a *short* list of foundations that might be interested in funding your kind of organization in your community. Begin with a list of ten or fewer. Never assume that more is better and send off your proposal to every foundation in Michigan or every foundation that ever gave to substance abuse. You will spend a lot of time and money for little or no return.

Instead, begin with an intentional plan to get a grant for a good program from one to five foundations the first year. After you have received some grants and developed a good relationship with local foundations, ask them to recommend other local foundations and the best people at the larger national foundations.

What to Ask For

The best grant to ask for is a matching grant, where the foundation gives you money to match what you raise. Then you have another motivator for your individual fundraising campaign. The grant does not need to be a one-to-one match; for low-income communities, you may need a five-to-one or ten-to-one match. However, it will be another incentive for your fundraisers to ask their prospects *now*. For the foundation itself, a matching grant reduces the risk of making a bad grant.

Otherwise, match your needs and the foundations' giving guidelines. Most foundations will prefer to fund a specific piece of your program. A few will offer a range of funding from endowments to capital campaigns to scholarship funds. Some foundations will also make loans and program-related investments (PRIs). Especially in low-income communities that are denied capital from conventional lenders, foundation loans and investments can provide the venture capital needed for bigger projects.

If your group is brand-new, controversial, or both, a foundation may be the only lender you can find (besides your own donors). For example, when the Roslyn Group for Arts and Letters wanted to present the massive Judy Chicago sculpture called "The Dinner Party" in Chicago in 1980, we were just a small literary salon with no treasury. So we asked the Playboy Foundation for a loan of $850 to buy a movie about the making of the sculpture, and then showed the movie at meetings and parties to raise money and recruit volunteers.

After six months the loan was repaid. Film parties alone raised $7,800 (a nine-to-one return on the loan) and helped recruit thirteen hundred volunteers. Overall, more than seventy thousand people paid to see the exhibit and shopped at the store. After all the bills were paid, the Roslyn Group contributed the surplus of $27,000 to the Chicago Foundation for Women, meaning the Playboy Foundation's original loan was multiplied thirty-two times.

Proposals

Most foundations want you to ask for money in a written document called a proposal. This is similar to a business plan for a for-profit business: it must persuade the foundation that your organization is a good investment. Tell the foundation what you want to do, why this program is needed, how you will do it, how much it will cost, and how much money you want from the foundation.

Set measurable goals and specify how you will measure the results. Include a detailed budget to say exactly how much you want from the foundation, how much your organization will donate, and how this fits into the total budget of the organization. If there are other funders, name them, and include projections for how the programs will be funded after the grant runs out.

Attach a copy of your IRS Determination Letter to prove your organization has 501(c)(3) tax status and a copy of your audited financial statement to show your organization is well managed. Also attach a list of your board of directors, with credentials, such as "president of the school board," "CEO of Widgets, Inc.," or "person living with cancer." Use one or two copies of positive news stories and letters of praise for your work. If part of the grant will go to pay for professionals already on your staff, include their current résumés.

For more details on how to write a proposal, use the Foundation Center books at the Cooperating Collection, or order the Grantsmanship Center's classic, *Program Planning & Proposal Writing*, which is listed in Chapter 14.

If you can write a term paper, you can write a proposal.

Keep it as simple as possible. Spell out every single acronym and explain or eliminate all jargon. You may know that DRG means "Diagnostic Related Group" and that it is a way for the federal government to restrict health care payments, but there is no reason to expect that the average Joe working for a foundation should know that. Test your proposal on your mother or a teenager; substitute simple English for any word or concept that person does not know. Then double-check the proposal, especially the arithmetic, and triple-check the name of the person at the foundation.

Send your proposal off with a very short and very positive cover letter. Since most proposals begin with a statement of the need for the program seeking funds, your proposal begins by describing the problem. Marketing whiz Richard Steckel calls proposals a "competition of woes." When you lead off with your "needs statement," of course you have to say the South Side has more drugs, more crimes, more empty houses, more dropouts, and more problems than the east, west, or north side. Fundraising this way can demoralize the most determined optimist.

So in your cover letter and any meetings with the foundation staff, you need to be very positive and paint a picture of determination to succeed. Emphasize how your organization can get results and how, dollar for dollar, you are the best investment in your field. Give the foundation hope that its grant will stop the drugs, fill the houses, and keep the kids in school.

Person to Person

The foundations with most of the money employ staff to screen the grants and interview the applicants. Foundation staff may be able to recommend a decision just from your proposal and reputation, or they may want to meet with your people. In that case, use the strategy you used to ask for corporate money. Take a team, get there early, listen hard, never argue, never lie, know what you want, say what you want, and send a thank-you note the same day.

In rare cases, foundations have staff who can make a site visit to see your organization and the work it does. Put your best

foot forward, but do not make any major changes simply because the foundation folks are coming to visit. If they do not
like the program the way you run it, there are plenty of other
places to ask for money. Especially for low-income organizations, usually a trip to the neighborhood is the most persuasive
part of asking for a grant, since the grant maker will get a much
better appreciation of your work.

Smaller family foundations may not have paid staff, so you
may need to follow up your proposal with a phone call to a
trustee. Ideally this will come from someone the trustee knows,
either a community leader or someone from your board. Simply
verify that the foundation received your proposal, ask if the
trustee wants anything else, and offer to answer any questions.
If the foundation is not staffed, it is not likely that someone will
meet with you in person or make a site visit.

AFTER THE GRANT

The same day you are notified your organization will receive a
grant, send a thank-you note. Be sure your bookkeeper or treasurer knows what kind of financial records are needed on the
grant; be sure the fundraiser knows what kind of reports are
needed when. Always send the foundation more than requested
about its grant. Mail before-and-after photos, letters from people
helped, any kind of measurable data from an objective third
party (police statistics showing crime is down, school statistics
showing attendance is up, hospital statistics showing less use of
the emergency room by victims of domestic violence). Invite
foundation staff to your special events; notify them when your
leaders will be on radio or television; try to meet in person at
least once to report on progress.

If the foundation turns you down, ask for advice to improve
your planning and proposal next time. Also ask if the foundation can recommend other grant makers.

As with any other major donor, you want to be building a
good long-term relationship with the grant maker. Although
most grants run out in one, two, or three years, the foundation
world is small. Foundation staff know each other and can recommend you to other good funders when the first grant runs
out.

RELIGIOUS GRANT MAKERS

Although religious grant makers give much more money than either foundations or corporations, they are more difficult to research. Unlike foundations, they are not required to file a 990PF with the IRS, and unlike corporations, they are not accountable to stockholders. So you need to ask each member of your board to do the work to research his or her own denomination through internal documents and current grantees.

In 1989 religious congregations gave an estimated 38 percent of their money, or $19 billion, to support other charities. This was in addition to $35 billion for their own local, national, and international work. The largest single religious grant maker is the United States Catholic Conference's Campaign for Human Development, which gave away $7 million in 1989.

Asking for money from religious grant makers is complicated, because every denomination operates differently. The common factor is that each one operates at the local level through the church, synagogue, mosque, or temple. This level is the easiest for a member of that congregation to approach.

Local congregations can also give you a lot more than money. Most have a building with a kitchen and nursery. Many host musical and theatrical performances. Best of all, they are the best source for volunteers with fundraising skills, since religious congregations get less than 2 percent of foundation or corporate funding. For experienced volunteers who know how to raise big money from individuals, look to your local congregations.

After the local congregation, the next level up is known generically as a judicatory and may be called a diocese, synod, conference, or another term. At the top level are the national programs, which fund both in the United States and internationally. For the regional and national grant makers, ask your local congregation for advice, and ask other groups that receive funding from the denomination. Like foundation grants, most grants from the national level of denominations run out after one to three years. Support from a local congregation is more likely to be renewable year after year.

Religious grant makers give their grants to achieve their goals for peace and justice. They do not need to limit their money only to 501(c)(3) organizations but can give to any group that can do work they want, like feeding the hungry, housing the homeless, or visiting the prisoners. However, each denomination is explicit in asking that "the project activity for which funding is requested must conform to the moral teachings"[9] of the denomination.

To find out more about religious grant makers, ask your own leaders to ask in their own denomination for the rules and applications for each funding level. Then ask your leader to recruit an important layperson and a member of the clergy to work with him or her to investigate whether religious funding would be a good part of your strategy. For more information, get the current edition of *The Church Funding Resource Guide*, listed in Chapter 14.

UNITED WAY

As mentioned earlier, there are more than 2,300 United Ways in the United States, each of which allocates money to local health and human services agencies. Some also make grants for special projects. In 1989 the United Ways raised and allocated a record $2.98 billion to more than forty thousand health and human services agencies. This makes the United Way by far the largest grant maker in the United States. In total, the United Ways give more money than the largest foundation, the Ford Foundation, which gave $184 million, or the largest corporate donor, IBM, which gave $135 million in 1989. The Chicago United Way alone raised $100 million in 1989; Los Angeles raised $96 million; New York City raised $76 million. Most United Way funds go to traditional agencies such as the American Red Cross, Catholic Charities, the Salvation Army, Girl Scouts and Boy Scouts, the Urban League, the YMCA, and the YWCA.

United Ways collect money through workplace solicitation (64 percent), corporate gifts (26 percent), and a growing campaign for major gifts from individuals. They also get grants from private foundations, such as a grant from the W. K. Kellogg Foundation to increase minority participation, and they broker big grants, such as a $500,000 seed grant from the Ford Foundation, which leveraged $17 million in five cities for affordable housing.

In addition to their cash allocations, the United Way collects in-kind contributions from corporations that get a tax break for giving products to nonprofits. Since 1983, the Gifts in Kind America has brokered more than $250,000 worth of products from more than 500 companies for more than 50,000 charities. Fifteen hundred local United Ways are involved in Gifts in Kind America; contact your local United Way for more information.

Of the 64 percent of United Way money that comes from workers through payroll deductions, 51 percent is from employees of corporations and small businesses, and 13 percent from nonprofit and government workers. More than 43 percent of all working Americans over age eighteen gave to the United Way in 1989.

United Ways are also getting more aggressive about asking for major gifts from wealthy individuals. They have created a major gift club called the Alexis de Tocqueville Society; membership costs $10,000 or more. In 1989, 3,523 members in ninety cities gave $59.9 million. In the past five years, the Tocqueville Society's profits have increased 400 percent.

For the really big gifts, the United Ways have copied insurance salespeople and created the Million Dollar Roundtable. Some million-dollar donors include Leslie Wexner, chairman of The Limited Inc. in Columbus; Jenny and Sid Craig, founders of the Jenny Craig Weight Loss Centers in San Diego; and Bill Gates, chairman of Microsoft Corporation in Seattle. United Ways are also joining other big charities in working harder at asking for planned gifts and building up their own endowments.

HISTORY

The system of running one campaign to raise money for several charities at the same time was first tried in Denver in 1888. In the depth of the depression, Community Chests raised more than $100 million to help the hungry and homeless.

The United Way name was invented in Detroit in 1949 and is now used across the United States. However, "Community Chest" still lives on in a few communities and in Monopoly games.

The United Way concept of one fundraising campaign to raise money for multiple charities has spread to twenty-four other countries, including the United Way/Centraide Canada, which raised Can $200 million in 121 communities in 1989. In nortwest England, United Way raised £500,000.

ADVANTAGES

United Ways can raise money with very low overhead because most of the work is done by volunteers and most of the money is collected through corporate payroll deduction. The United Way claims that only 10.5 percent of all funds raised are used for administrative expenses.[10]

The United Ways demand high standards for the charities they fund. United Ways require that each group be run by volunteers and submit to an annual independent financial audit; provide services at reasonable costs; and maintain a policy of nondiscrimination.

Eighty million Americans gave to the United Way in 1989, most at their jobs through payroll deduction. The United Ways are probably the most widespread training ground for giving and asking for money. Since payroll deduction makes it easy to give larger gifts, they also help every charity by setting the standard of asking for larger gifts.

The United Way is usually the broadest based and most tightly organized structure working with nonprofits in any community. In some communities, it is the only forum where corporate executives come in contact with minority leaders from low-income neighborhoods.

CHALLENGES

For corporate donors, it is hard to get recognition or "credit" for making a donation to the United Way, since it just disappears into a giant pot of money. Some corporations have chosen to use their corporate giving more intentionally to achieve specific marketing goals, so those companies prefer to do their own charitable giving outside the United Way. Other corporations earmark their gift to guarantee that it is spent on what they want. For example, in 1989 the Mellon Bank in Pittsburgh designated that $100,000 of its total gift of $500,000 be spent to create affordable housing.

For charities, the United Way is a very exclusive club. Since 1983 the 2,300 United Ways have accepted only 6,245 new agencies, an average of less than one-half per year per local United Way.

United Way has a written policy against coercion. Nevertheless, employees, especially at the lower levels, often feel coerced to give. Since workplace solicitation uses the structure that is already in place, and since it always works from the top of the pyramid down, it is inevitable that each boss, supervisor, or foreman asks his or her subordinates. The employees rarely feel this is a totally voluntary choice. Hopefully, as more United Ways allow more donor options, all employees will feel as enthusiastic about their gifts to the United Way as they do about their gifts to other worthwhile causes.

HOW TO ASK FOR UNITED WAY FUNDS

United Way boards are dominated by business leaders, so you pursue United Way funding the same way you pursue corporate funding—what matters is whom you know. Contact your local United Way and ask for information on its application procedures. Each of the locals will be a little different, but most are limited to funding only noncontroversial health and human services agencies.

Find out who serves on the board and on the committee that admits new agencies. Then get your heavy hitters to lobby to get your group in.

Usually, only two or three new agencies will be accepted, so continue your other fundraising while you apply. If your agency is accepted, you must conform to the rules of the United Way. Most United Ways forbid you to do your own fundraising during their campaign in the fall. Most also put other restrictions on when and how you can ask for money, and they ask that your own employees give to the United Way.

The advantage of being a United Way agency is that it gives

you credibility and legitimacy in the community, it gives you the opportunity (use it) to serve on United Way committees with the movers and shakers in your town, and it is a dependable source of money once you have been accepted. In very rare cases, the United Way does not make its goal and has to cut allocations, but most United Ways have seen a steady growth of income at around 7 percent every year.

If your agency is not accepted by the local United Way, consider organizing a donor option campaign or joining a local alternative fund, as described in Chapter 6.

CIVIC ORGANIZATIONS

Many civic and social organizations raise money for worthwhile causes in the United States and around the world. The biggest and boldest is the Rotary International, which has raised more than $230 million in one hundred sixty countries to immunize against polio more than 500 million children. In Zambia alone, the number of reported cases of polio has dropped from seven hundred to seventy because of Rotary's fundraising.

The Junior Leagues of America, Canada, Mexico, and England raised $20 million in 1989 through special events, cookbooks, thrift shops, and grants. They not only give most of this money back to their communities but also train volunteers, who go on to leadership roles in other organizations. Their most notable alumni are former First Lady Nancy Reagan and Supreme Court Justice Sandra Day O'Connor.

In smaller towns and rural communities, organizations like the VFW, the Knights of Columbus, and ethnic clubs may be able to give you small grants for your cause. In minority communities, fraternities and sororities are often the place to look for small grants and leadership talent.

In any case, the easiest way to get a grant from a civic organization is to ask a member of the organization to advocate for your group. He or she will know the official and the unofficial application procedures. A woman in Brainerd, Minnesota, told me she was saved when an organization insider told her to ask again after her request was rejected the first time. The insider said the committee always turned down everyone the first time as a test to see who was serious; everyone who came back the second month got a grant. If the fundraiser had not had the tip and the encouragement from the insider, she might have lost the chance for an easy grant.

Civic organization grants are usually smaller amounts, but they give your group legitimacy in the community. With careful cultivation, you may be able to get the grants year after year and hopefully involve some of the organization's volunteers in your group, too.

CONCLUSION

Successful fundraisers can use foundation grants as the seed money for new projects and then replace that money with renewable income from dues, donations, fees, and sales. You know your organization cannot depend on foundation grants to pay your everyday core budget. Operating expenses have to come from the people who need and want what you do.

On the other hand, many United Ways, religious congregations, and civic clubs are willing to support their favorite nonprofit groups year after year. Once your organization has been approved, these grants should be a dependable source of funding. Keep local grant makers involved as members and guests at your events and informed through your mailings and personal contacts. Working together, you will all be able to achieve more for your community.

THE FOUNDATION CENTER COOPERATING COLLECTIONS NETWORK
Free Funding Information Centers

The Foundation Center is an independent national service organization established by foundations to provide an authoritative source of information on private philanthropic giving. The New York, Washington, DC, Cleveland and San Francisco reference collections operated by the Foundation Center offer a wide variety of services and comprehensive collections of information on foundations and grants. Cooperating Collections are libraries, community foundations and other nonprofit agencies that provide a core collection of Foundation Center publications and a variety of supplementary materials and services in areas useful to grantseekers. The core collection consists of:

Foundation Directory   **Foundation Grants to Individuals**
Foundation Fundamentals   **Literature of the Nonprofit Sector**
Foundation Grants Index   **National Data Book of Foundations**

National Directory of Corporate Giving
Source Book Profiles
User-Friendly Guide

Many of the network members have sets of private foundation information returns (IRS 990-PF) for their state or region which are available for public use. A complete set of U.S. foundation returns can be found at the New York and Washington, DC offices of the Foundation Center. The Cleveland and San Francisco offices contain IRS 990-PF returns for the midwestern and western states, respectively. Those Cooperating Collections marked with a bullet (•) have sets of private foundation information returns for their state or region.

Because the collections vary in their hours, materials and services, IT IS RECOMMENDED THAT YOU CALL EACH COLLECTION IN ADVANCE. To check on new locations or more current information, call 1-800-424-9836.

Reference Collections Operated by The Foundation Center

The Foundation Center
8th Floor
79 Fifth Avenue
New York, NY 10003
212-620-4230

The Foundation Center
Room 312
312 Sutter Street
San Francisco, CA 94108
415-397-0902

The Foundation Center
1001 Connecticut Avenue, NW
Washington, DC 20036
202-331-1400

The Foundation Center
Kent H. Smith Library
1442 Hanna Building
Cleveland, OH 44115
216-861-1933

ALABAMA

● Birmingham Public Library
Government Documents
2100 Park Place
Birmingham 35203
205-226-3600

Huntsville Public Library
915 Monroe St.
Huntsville 35801
205-532-5940

University of South Alabama
Library Reference Dept.
Mobile 36688
205-460-7025

● Auburn University at
Montgomery Library
7300 University Drive
Montgomery 36117-3596
205-244-3653

ALASKA

● University of Alaska
Anchorage Library
3211 Providence Drive
Anchorage 99508
907-786-1848

Juneau Public Library
292 Marine Way
Juneau 99801
907-586-5249

ARIZONA

● Phoenix Public Library
Business & Sciences Dept.
12 East McDowell Road
Phoenix 85004
602-262-4636

● Tucson Public Library
101 N. Stone Ave.
Tucson 85726-7470
602-791-4393

ARKANSAS

● Westark Community College
Library
5210 Grand Avenue
Fort Smith 72913
501-785-7000

● Central Arkansas Library System
Reference Services
700 Louisiana Street
Little Rock 72201
501-370-5950

CALIFORNIA

Ventura County Community
Foundation
Community Resource Center
1357 Del Norte Road
Camarillo 93010
805-988-0196

● Orange County Community
Developmental Council
1695 W. MacArthur Blvd.
Costa Mesa 92626
714-540-9293

● California Community Foundation
Funding Information Center
606 S. Olive St., Suite 2400
Los Angeles 90014
213-413-4042

● Community Foundation for
Monterey County
177 Van Buren
Monterey 93942
408-375-9712

Riverside Public Library
3581 7th Street
Riverside 92501
714-782-5201

California State Library
Reference Services, Rm. 301
914 Capitol Mall
Sacramento 95814
916-322-4570

Nonprofit Resource Center
Sacramento Central Library
Downtown Plaza South Mall
Sacramento 95812-2131
916-449-2131

● San Diego Community
Foundation
525 "B" Street, Suite 410
San Diego 92101
619-239-8815

● Nonprofit Development Center
1762 Technology Dr., Suite 225
San Jose 95110
408-452-8181

● Peninsula Community
Foundation
1700 S. El Camino Real
San Mateo 94402-3049
415-358-9392

Volunteer Center of Orange
County
1000 E. Santa Ana Blvd.
Santa Ana 92701
714-953-1655

● Santa Barbara Public Library
40 East Anapamu
Santa Barbara 93101-1603
805-962-7653

Santa Monica Public Library
1343 Sixth Street
Santa Monica 90401-1603
213-458-8859

COLORADO

Pikes Peak Library District
20 North Cascade Avenue
Colorado Springs 80901
719-473-2080

● Denver Public Library
Sociology Division
1357 Broadway
Denver 80203
303-640-8870

CONNECTICUT

Danbury Public Library
170 Main Street
Danbury 06810
203-797-4527

● Hartford Public Library
Reference Department
500 Main Street
Hartford 06103
203-293-6000

D.A.T.A.
70 Audubon St.
New Haven 06510
203-772-1345

DELAWARE

● University of Delaware
Hugh Morris Library
Newark 19717-5267
302-451-2965

FLORIDA

Volusia County Library Center
City Island
Daytona Beach 32014-4484
904-255-3765

● Nova University
Einstein Library—Foundation
Resource Collection
3301 College Avenue
Fort Lauderdale 33314
305-475-7497

Indian River Community College
Learning Resources Center
3209 Virginia Avenue
Fort Pierce 33454-9003
407-468-4757

● Jacksonville Public Libraries
Business, Science & Documents
122 North Ocean Street
Jacksonville 32206
904-630-2665

● Miami–Dade Public Library
Humanities Department
101 W. Flagler St.
Miami 33130
305-375-2665

● Orlando Public Library
Orange County Library System
101 E. Central Blvd.
Orlando 32801
407-425-4694

Selby Public Library
1001 Boulevard of the Arts
Sarasota 34236
813-951-5501

● Leon County Public Library
Funding Resource Center
1940 North Monroe Street
Tallahassee 32303
904-487-2665

Palm Beach County Community
Foundation
324 Datura Street, Suite 340
West Palm Beach 33401
407-659-6800

GEORGIA

● Atlanta-Fulton Public Library
Foundation Collection—Ivan
Allen Department
1 Margaret Mitchell Square
Atlanta 30303-1089
404-730-1900

HAWAII

● Hawaii Community Foundation
Hawaii Resource Room
222 Merchant Street
Honolulu 96813
808-537-6333

University of Hawaii
Thomas Hale Hamilton Library
2550 The Mall
Honolulu 96822
808-956-7214

IDAHO

● Boise Public Library
715 S. Capitol Blvd.
Boise 83702
208-384-4024

● Caldwell Public Library
1010 Dearborn Street
Caldwell 83605
208-459-3242

ILLINOIS

Belleville Public Library
121 East Washington Street
Belleville 62220
618-234-0441

● Donors Forum of Chicago
53 W. Jackson Blvd., Rm. 430
Chicago 60604
312-431-0265

● Evanston Public Library
1703 Orrington Avenue
Evanston 60201
708-866-0305

● Sangamon State University
Library
Shepherd Road
Springfield 62794-9243
217-786-6633

INDIANA

● Allen County Public Library
900 Webster Street
Fort Wayne 46802
219-424-7241

Indiana University Northwest
Library
3400 Broadway
Gary 46408
219-980-6582

● Indianapolis-Marion County
Public Library
40 East St. Clair Street
Indianapolis 46206
317-269-1733

IOWA

● Cedar Rapids Public Library
Funding Information Center
500 First Street, SE
Cedar Rapids 52401
319-398-5145

● Southwestern Community
College
Learning Resource Center
1501 W. Townline Rd.
Creston 50801
515-782-7081, ext. 262

● Public Library of Des Moines
100 Locust Street
Des Moines 50308
515-283-4152

KANSAS

● Topeka Public Library
1515 West Tenth Street
Topeka 66604
913-233-2040

● Wichita Public Library
223 South Main
Wichita 67202
316-262-0611

KENTUCKY

Western Kentucky University
Helm-Cravens Library
Bowling Green 42101
502-745-6122

- Louisville Free Public Library
Fourth and York Streets
Louisville 40203
502-561-8617

LOUISIANA

- East Baton Rouge Parish Library
Centroplex Branch
120 St. Louis Street
Baton Rouge 70802
504-389-4960

- New Orleans Public Library
Business and Science Division
219 Loyola Avenue
New Orleans 70140
504-596-2580

- Shreve Memorial Library
424 Texas Street
Shreveport 71120-1523
318-226-5894

MAINE

- University of Southern Maine
Office of Sponsored Research
246 Deering Ave., Rm. 628
Portland 04103
207-780-4871

MARYLAND

- Enoch Pratt Free Library
Social Science and History
Department
400 Cathedral Street
Baltimore 21201
301-396-5320

Carroll County Public Library
Government and Funding
Information Center
50 E. Main St.
Westminster 21157
301-848-4250

MASSACHUSETTS

- Associated Grantmakers of
Massachusetts
294 Washington Street
Suite 840
Boston 02108
617-426-2608

- Boston Public Library
666 Boylston St.
Boston 02117
617-536-5400

- Western Massachusetts Funding
Resource Center
Campaign for Human
Development
73 Chestnut Street
Springfield 01103
413-732-3175

- Worcester Public Library
Grants Resource Center
Salem Square
Worcester 01608
508-799-1655

MICHIGAN

- Alpena County Library
211 North First Avenue
Alpena 49707
517-356-6188

University of Michigan–Ann
Arbor
209 Hatcher Graduate Library
Ann Arbor 48109-1205
313-764-1149

- Battle Creek Community
Foundation
One Riverwalk Centre
34 W. Jackson St.
Battle Creek 49017
616-962-2181

- Henry Ford Centennial Library
16301 Michigan Avenue
Dearborn 48126
313-943-2330

- Wayne State University
  Purdy-Kresge Library
  5265 Cass Avenue
  Detroit 48202
  313-577-6424

- Michigan State University
  Libraries
  Reference Library
  East Lansing 48824-1048
  517-353-8818

- Farmington Community Library
  32737 West 12 Mile Road
  Farmington Hills 48018
  313-553-0300

- University of Michigan–Flint
  Library
  Reference Department
  Flint 48502-2186
  313-762-3408

- Grand Rapids Public Library
  Business Dept.
  60 Library Plaza NE
  Grand Rapids 49503-3093
  616-456-3600

- Michigan Technological
  University Library
  Highway U.S. 41
  Houghton 49931
  906-487-2507

- Sault Ste. Marie Area
  Public Schools
  Office of Compensatory
  Education
  460 W. Spruce St.
  Sault Ste. Marie 49783-1874
  906-635-6619

MINNESOTA

- Duluth Public Library
  520 W. Superior Street
  Duluth 55802
  218-723-3802

  Southwest State University
  Library
  Marshall 56258
  507-537-7278

- Minneapolis Public Library
  Sociology Department
  300 Nicollet Mall
  Minneapolis 55401
  612-372-6555

  Rochester Public Library
  11 First Street, SE
  Rochester 55902-3743
  507-285-8002

  St. Paul Public Library
  90 West Fourth Street
  Saint Paul 55102
  612-292-6307

MISSISSIPPI

  Jackson/Hinds Library System
  300 North State Street
  Jackson 39201
  601-968-5803

MISSOURI

- Clearinghouse for Midcontinent
  Foundations
  Univ. of Missouri
  Law School, Suite 1-300
  52nd Street and Oak
  Kansas City 64113-0680
  816-276-1176

- Kansas City Public Library
  311 East 12th Street
  Kansas City 64106
  816-221-9650

- Metropolitan Association for
  Philanthropy, Inc.
  5585 Pershing Avenue
  Suite 150
  St. Louis 63112
  314-361-3900

- Springfield–Greene County
  Library
  397 East Central Street
  Springfield 65801
  417-866-4636

MONTANA

- Eastern Montana College Library
  1500 N. 30th Street
  Billings 59101-0298
  406-657-1662

● Montana State Library
Reference Department
1515 E. 6th Avenue
Helena 59620
406-444-3004

NEBRASKA

● University of Nebraska
106 Love Library
14th & R Streets
Lincoln 68588-0410
402-472-2848

● W. Dale Clark Library
Social Sciences Department
215 South 15th Street
Omaha 68102
402-444-4826

NEVADA

● Las Vegas–Clark County Library
District
1401 East Flamingo Road
Las Vegas 89119-6160
702-733-7810

● Washoe County Library
301 South Center Street
Reno 89501
702-785-4012

NEW HAMPSHIRE

● New Hampshire Charitable Fund
One South Street
Concord 03302-1335
603-225-6641

● Plymouth State College
Herbert H. Lamson Library
Plymouth 03264
603-535-5000

NEW JERSEY

Cumberland County Library
800 E. Commerce Street
Bridgeton 08302-2295
609-453-2210

The Support Center
17 Academy Street, Suite 1101
Newark 07102
201-643-5774

County College of Morris
Masten Learning Resource
Center
Route 10 and Center Grove Rd.
Randolph 07869
201-361-5000 ext. 470

● New Jersey State Library
Governmental Reference
185 West State Street
Trenton 08625-0520
609-292-6220

NEW MEXICO

Albuquerque Community
Foundation
6400 Uptown Boulevard N.E.
Albuquerque 87105
505-883-6240

● New Mexico State Library
325 Don Gaspar Street
Santa Fe 87503
505-827-3824

NEW YORK

● New York State Library
Cultural Education Center
Humanities Section
Empire State Plaza
Albany 12230
518-473-4636

Suffolk Cooperative Library
System
627 North Sunrise Service Road
Bellport 11713
516-286-1600

New York Public Library
Bronx Reference Center
2556 Bainbridge Avenue
Bronx 10458
212-220-6575

Brooklyn in Touch
One Hanson Place
Room 2504
Brooklyn 11243
718-230-3200

● Buffalo and Erie County Public
Library
Lafayette Square
Buffalo 14202
716-858-7103

Huntington Public Library
338 Main Street
Huntington 11743
516-427-5165

Queens Borough Public Library
89-11 Merrick Boulevard
Jamaica 11432
718-990-0700

● Levittown Public Library
One Bluegrass Lane
Levittown 11756
516-731-5728

SUNY/College at Old Westbury
Library
223 Store Hill Road
Old Westbury 11568
516-876-3156

Adriance Memorial Library
93 Market Street
Poughkeepsie 12601
914-485-3445

● Rochester Public Library
Business Division
115 South Avenue
Rochester 14604
716-428-7328

Staten Island Council on the Arts
One Edgewater Plaza, Rm. 311
Staten Island 10305
718-447-4485

● Onondaga County Public Library
at the Galleries
447 S. Salina Street
Syracuse 13202-2494
315-448-4636

● White Plains Public Library
100 Martine Avenue
White Plains 10601
914-682-4480

NORTH CAROLINA

● Asheville-Buncomb Technical
Community College
Learning Resources Center
340 Victoria Rd.
Asheville 28802
704-254-1921 x300

● The Duke Endowment
200 S. Tryon Street, Ste. 1100
Charlotte 28202
704-376-0291

Durham County Library
300 N. Roxboro Street
Durham 27702
919-560-0100

● North Carolina State Library
109 East Jones Street
Raleigh 27611
919-733-3270

● The Winston-Salem Foundation
229 First Union Bank Building
Winston-Salem 27101
919-725-2382

NORTH DAKOTA

● North Dakota State University
The Library
Fargo 58105
701-237-8886

OHIO

Stark County District Library
715 Market Avenue North
Canton 44702-1080
216-452-0665

● Public Library of Cincinnati and
Hamilton County
Education Department
800 Vine Street
Cincinnati 45202-2071
513-369-6940

Columbus Metropolitan Library
96 S. Grant Avenue
Columbus 43215
614-645-2590

● Dayton and Montgomery County
Public Library
Grants Information Center
215 E. Third Street
Dayton 45402-2103
513-227-9500 ext. 211

● Toledo–Lucas County Public
Library
Social Science Department
325 Michigan Street
Toledo 43624-1614
419-259-5245

Ohio University–Zanesville
Community Education and
Development
1425 Newark Road
Zanesville 43701
614-453-0762

OKLAHOMA

● Oklahoma City University Library
2501 North Blackwelder
Oklahoma City 73106
405-521-5072

● Tulsa City–County Library System
400 Civic Center
Tulsa 74103
918-596-7944

OREGON

Oregon Institute of Technology
Learning Resources Center
Klamath Falls 97601-8801
503-885-1772

Pacific Non-Profit Network
Grantsmanship Resource Library
33 N. Central, Ste. 211
Medford 97501
503-779-6044

● Multnomah County Library
Government Documents Room
801 S.W. Tenth Avenue
Portland 97205-2597
503-223-7201

Oregon State Library
State Library Building
Salem 97310
503-378-4274

PENNSYLVANIA

Northampton Community College
Learning Resources Center
3835 Green Pond Road
Bethlehem 18017
215-861-5360

● Erie County Public Library
3 South Perry Square
Erie 16501
814-451-6927

● Dauphin County Library System
101 Walnut Street
Harrisburg 17101
717-234-4961

Lancaster County Public Library
125 North Duke Street
Lancaster 17602
717-394-2651

● The Free Library of Philadelphia
Logan Square
Philadelphia 19103
215-686-5423

● University of Pittsburgh
Hillman Library
Pittsburgh 15260
412-648-7722

Economic Development Council
of Northeastern Pennsylvania
1151 Oak Street
Pittston 18640
717-655-5581

RHODE ISLAND

● Providence Public Library
Reference Department
225 Washington St.
Providence 02903
401-455-8000

SOUTH CAROLINA

● Charleston County Library
404 King Street
Charleston 29403
803-723-1645

● South Carolina State Library
Reference Department
1500 Senate Street
Columbia 29211
803-734-8666

SOUTH DAKOTA

● South Dakota State Library
800 Governors Drive
Pierre 57501-2294
605-773-5070
800-592-1841 (SD residents)

Sioux Falls Area Foundation
141 N. Main Ave., Suite 500
Sioux Falls 57102-1134
605-336-7055

TENNESSEE

- Knoxville–Knox County Public Library
  500 West Church Avenue
  Knoxville 37902
  615-544-5750

- Memphis & Shelby County Public Library
  1850 Peabody Avenue
  Memphis 38104
  901-725-8877

- Public Library of Nashville and Davidson County
  8th Ave. N. and Union St.
  Nashville 37203
  615-259-6256

TEXAS

- Community Foundation of Abilene Funding Information Library
  708 NCNB Bldg.
  402 Cypress
  Abilene 79601
  915-676-3883

  Amarillo Area Foundation
  70 1st National Place One
  800 S. Fillmore
  Amarillo 79101
  806-376-4521

- Hogg Foundation for Mental Health University of Texas
  Austin 78713
  512-471-5041

- Corpus Christi State University Library
  6300 Ocean Drive
  Corpus Christi 78412
  512-994-2608

- Dallas Public Library
  Grants Information Service
  1515 Young Street
  Dallas 75201
  214-670-1487

- Pan American University Learning Resource Center
  1201 W. University Drive
  Edinburg 78539
  512-381-3304

- El Paso Community Foundation
  1616 Texas Commerce Building
  El Paso 79901
  915-533-4020

- Texas Christian University Library
  Funding Information Center
  Ft. Worth 76129
  817-921-7664

- Houston Public Library
  Bibliographic Information Center
  500 McKinney Avenue
  Houston 77002
  713-236-1313

  Lubbock Area Foundation
  502 Texas Commerce Bank Building
  Lubbock 79401
  806-762-8061

- Funding Information Center
  507 Brooklyn
  San Antonio 78215
  512-227-4333

UTAH

- Salt Lake City Public Library
  Business and Science Dept.
  209 East Fifth South
  Salt Lake City 84111
  801-363-5733

VERMONT

- Vermont Dept. of Libraries
  Reference Services
  109 State Street
  Montpelier 05602
  802-828-3268

VIRGINIA

- Hampton Public Library
  Grants Resources Collection
  4207 Victoria Blvd.
  Hampton 23669
  804-727-1154

- Richmond Public Library
  Business, Science, & Technology
  101 East Franklin Street
  Richmond 23219
  804-780-8223

● Roanoke City Public Library
  System
  Central Library
  706 S. Jefferson Street
  Roanoke 24014
  703-981-2477

WASHINGTON

● Seattle Public Library
  1000 Fourth Avenue
  Seattle 98104
  206-386-4620

● Spokane Public Library
  Funding Information Center
  West 906 Main Avenue
  Spokane 99201
  509-838-3364

  Greater Wenatchee Community
  Foundation at the Wenatchee
  Public Library
  310 Douglas St.
  Wenatchee 98807
  509-662-5021

WEST VIRGINIA

● Kanawha County Public Library
  123 Capital Street
  Charleston 25304
  304-343-4646

WISCONSIN

● University of Wisconsin–Madison
  Memorial Library
  728 State Street
  Madison 53706
  608-262-3242

● Marquette University
  Memorial Library
  1415 West Wisconsin Avenue
  Milwaukee 53233
  414-288-1515

WYOMING

● Laramie County Community
  College Library
  1400 East College Drive
  Cheyenne 82007-3299
  307-778-1205

AUSTRALIA

ANZ Executors & Trustees Co.
Ltd.
91 William St., 7th floor
Melbourne VIC 3000
03-648-5764

CANADA

Canadian Centre for Philanthropy
1329 Bay St., Suite 200
Toronto, Ontario M5R 2C4
416-515-0764

ENGLAND

Charities Aid Foundation
18 Doughty Street
London WC1N 2PL
71-831-7798

JAPAN

Foundation Center Library
of Japan
Elements Shinjuku Bldg. 3F
2-1-14 Shinjuku, Shinjuku-ku
Tokyo 160
03-350-1857

MEXICO

Biblioteca Benjamin Franklin
American Embassy, USICA
Londres 16
Mexico City 6, D.F. 06600
905-211-0042

PUERTO RICO

University of Puerto Rico
Ponce Technological College
  Library
Box 7186
Ponce 00732
809-844-4150

Universidad Del Sagrado
  Corazon
M.M.T. Guevarra Library
Correo Calle Loiza
Santurce 00914
809-728-1515 ext. 357

U.S. VIRGIN ISLANDS

University of the Virgin Islands
Paiewonsky Library
Charlotte Amalie
St. Thomas 00802
809-828-3261

THE FOUNDATION CENTER NETWORK

Participants in the Cooperating Collections Network are libraries or nonprofit agencies that provide fundraising information or other funding-related technical assistance in their communities. Cooperating Collections agree to provide free public access to a basic collection of Foundation Center publications during a regular schedule of hours, offering free funding research guidance to all visitors. Many also provide a variety of special services for local nonprofit organizations, using staff or volunteers to prepare special materials, organize workshops, or conduct library orientations.

The Foundation Center welcomes inquiries from agencies interested in providing this type of public information service. If you are interested in establishing a funding information library for the use of nonprofit agencies in your area or in learning more about the program, please write to: Anne J. Borland, The Foundation Center, 79 Fifth Avenue, New York, NY 10003.

"I think of life as a good book. The
further you get into it, the more it
begins to make sense."
—*Rabbi Harold S. Kushner*

Chapter 14

Recommended Reading

This book grew out of many answers to many questions posed
by clients, fundraisers, and reporters asking the best ways to
raise more money more quickly. Unfortunately, these questions
often seemed to be posed something like, "Well, we have a
minute left, so let me ask you this: What about direct mail?"

Not even I can talk fast enough to explain direct mail in
one minute, so I began looking for books that would be helpful
to both volunteers and professionals. Fortunately many excellent
authors have shared their expertise on topics introduced in this
book. If your fundraisers have an interest in a particular fundraising strategy, get the books listed here for more detailed
information and always ask your librarian to recommend new
titles.

This chapter describes the best fundraising publications.
All prices are for single copies as of 1991. Contact publishers for
bulk rate, Canadian, and foreign prices. Prices are subject to
change without notice.

Start your fundraising office with these:

Flanagan, Joan. *The Grass Roots Fundraising Book: How to Raise Money in Your Community.* Contemporary Books, Dept. SF, 180 N. Michigan Ave., Chicago, IL 60601. Updated 1988. $14.95. The most popular fundraising book in the United States, this bestseller shares foolproof advice on raising renewable, dependable, internally controlled money. It is ideal if your group is new (or new to grass roots fundraising), small (or a small fundraising component of a larger agency, such as a hospital's fundraising auxiliary), or all volunteers. Tested tips will work for any nonprofit organization in any community.

————. *Successful Fundraising: A Complete Handbook for Volunteers and Professionals.* Contemporary Books, Dept. SF, 180 N. Michigan Ave., Chicago, IL 60601. 1991. $19.95. Everything you need to know to raise big money from individuals, corporations, and foundations. New strategies that are both effective and ethical to raise more money and build a self-sufficient organization at the same time.

————. *The Successful Volunteer Organization: Getting Started and Getting Results.* Contemporary Books, Dept. SF, 180 N. Michigan Ave., Chicago, IL 60601. Updated 1984. $14.95. How to build a nonprofit organization with clear goals and great leaders so the fundraising is easy. Step-by-step advice for creating a new 501(c)(3) tax-exempt nonprofit organization, developing committees, building a board of directors, hiring staff, and managing for success.

To order Joan Flanagan's books, use the easy order form at the end of this book.

OTHER RESOURCES

First, check with your national association or network. Most publish how-to materials tailored specifically for your kind of organization. Send your best fundraisers to the national and international conventions with an agenda to interview the most creative fundraising talent. Seek opportunities to cross-train with other chapters in similar communities. Some national organizations also wholesale products for resale.

Second, check your public library, the best free resource for any fundraiser. Get to know the reference room, government publications, and the business section for the most current data on local needs, people with wealth, and for-profit companies. If salespeople can make millions using this data, so can you.

Third, check with your local United Way. Many sell fundraising booklets and research data on local human services needs. Some also offer technical assistance and workshops.

Fourth, join the local professional associations listed at the end of Chapter 3. Ask a successful veteran for the best publications and training in your field.

Finally, visit a Cooperating Collection of the Foundation Center. Addresses are listed in Chapter 13.

FUNDRAISING PERIODICALS

The Chronicle of Philanthropy, P.O. Box 1989, Marion, OH 43306-4089. $47.50 for one year (twenty-four issues). Tabloid-style paper offers the latest on issues, good examples, and foundation grants.

Fund Raising Management, 224 Seventh St., Garden City, NY 11530. $45 for one year (twelve issues). Magazine offers case studies and expert advice, especially good for professionals at larger institutions.

The Grantsmanship Center Whole Nonprofit Catalog, P.O. Box 6210, Los Angeles, CA 90014. Free quarterly tabloid is one-half catalog of the Grantsmanship Center's workshops and reprints, and one-half useful how-to articles.

The Grassroots Fundraising Journal, P.O. Box 11607, Berkeley, CA 94701. $25.00 for one year (six issues). Best nuts-and-bolts advice for fundraisers working with membership organizations. Every issue has good ideas you can apply immediately.

The Nonprofit Times, P.O. Box 408, Hopewell, NJ 08525-0408. Free to full-time nonprofit executives. Monthly tabloid full of current trends and case studies.

SPECIAL TOPICS

The following sources of information are arranged alphabetically by topic. They provide more details about topics introduced in this book. Also, beginning on page 284 are resources especially for fundraising in Canada and the United Kingdom.

ATTITUDE

Hill, Napoleon, and W. Clement Stone. *Success Through a Positive Mental Attitude.* Pocket Books, 1230 Avenue of the Americas, New York, NY 10020. 1960. $5.50. Your attitude determines the success or failure of every fundraising campaign. This classic text is still the best book to learn how to motivate yourself and others to achieve your goals.

BOARD OF DIRECTORS

Klein, Kimberly. *Board of Directors.* Grassroots Fundraising Journal reprint, P.O. Box 11607, Berkeley, CA 94701. 1985. $6.00. Tested advice to motivate your board of directors to ask for money; especially good for new and smaller organizations.

O'Connell, Brian. *The Board Members Book: Making a Difference in Voluntary Organizations.* The Foundation Center, 79 Fifth Ave., New York, NY 10003; 800/424-9836. 1985. $24.95. The best book to give your board. Especially good on accountability, board-staff relations, and keeping good board members.

CONGREGATIONS

Bobo, Kimberly. *Lives Matter: A Handbook for Christian Organizing.* Sheed & Ward, P.O. Box 414292, Kansas City, MO 64141-0281. 1986. 286 pp. $8.95. How to organize a church group to work on any issue; most examples are about hunger. The principles will work for any organization working on an urgent issue. Chapter 19, "Inner Strengths and Outer Witness," alone is worth the price.

Paul, Eileen, ed. *The 1990 Church Funding Resource Guide.* 7th edition. Women's Technical Assistance Project, 733 15th St. NW, Suite 510, Washington, DC 20005. 1991. $50.00. Best information on thirty-five religious funding sources, including application guidelines, deadlines, and how-to advice.

Zehring, John Williams. *You Can Run A Capital Campaign.* Abingdon Press, 201 Eighth Ave. S., Nashville, TN 37202. 1990. $5.95. A clear step-by-step guide, from setting the stage spiritually to concluding the campaign. This is the best inexpensive guide to capital campaigns for any volunteer group. If your organization is not a church, simply skip the part on spiritual preparation, or use it as a model to write your own philosophy for giving.

CORPORATIONS

Contact your chamber of commerce for data on local businesses. Even better, join the chamber and serve on committees to get to know the businesspeople.

For national data, contact the Conference Board, 845 Third Ave., New York, NY 10022 and ask for its *Publication Price List.* Every year the Conference Board publishes a *Survey of Corporate Contributions,* with the most complete analysis of corporate giving trends.

"Double Your Dollars" leaflets name the corporations that match employees, directors, retirees, and/or spouses' donations. There are four versions, tailored for higher education, secondary and elementary schools, cultural organizations, and community organizations. Published annually. Leaflets and more publications on corporate matching gifts programs are available from CASE Publications Order Department, 80 S. Early St., Alexandria, VA 22304; 800/336-4776.

Breiteneicher, Joe. *The Quest For Funds: Insider's Guide to Corporate and Foundation Funding.* Lincoln Filene Center, Tufts University, Medford, MA 02155. 1989. $6. The most readable and realistic guide to raising money from corporations by a man who has been both foundation staff member and CEO of a major corporation.

Clark, Sylvia. *Discover Total Resources.* Community Affairs Division, Mellon Bank, One Mellon Bank Center, Pittsburgh, PA 15258. 1985. Free. Award-winning booklet on how to get money, people, goods, and services from corporations and other funders. Best booklet at the best price to encourage your people to ask for more than just money from local businesses.

Haile, Suzanne W., ed. *National Directory of Corporate Giving: A Guide to Corporate Giving Programs and Corporate Foundations.* The Foundation Center, 79 Fifth Ave., New York, NY 10003. 1989. $175. Complete information on 1,551 corporations giving money through foundations, direct giving programs, or both.

Jankowski, Katherine E., ed. *Directory of International Corporate Giving in America.* The Taft Group, 12300 Twinbrook Pkwy., Suite 450, Rockville, MD 20852; 800/877-TAFT. 1991. $139. Lists 250 foreign-owned (defined as a minimum of 10 percent investment by a non-U.S.-headquartered company) firms that give to American charities, indexed in ten different ways. Includes a listing of international directories and identifies key businesses in Canada, Europe, Japan, and the United Kingdom.

Jones, Francine, managing ed. *Corporate Foundation Profiles.* The Foundation Center, 79 Fifth Ave., New York, NY 10003. 1990. $125. In-depth information on the 250 largest corporate foundations that give more than $100,000 per year, featuring background on foundation officers and board members.

Marcus, Sharon J., ed. *Corporate Giving Directory: Comprehensive Profiles of America's Major Corporate Foundations and Corporate Charitable Giving Programs.* The Taft Group, 12300

Twinbrook Pkwy., Suite 450, Rockville, MD 20852; 800/877-TAFT. 1991. $347. Lists companies that give more than $500,000 per year, indexed seven different ways, including "who runs the company" and "who runs the foundation"; officers and directors indexed by name, place of birth, and alma mater. Each entry includes helpful data on how they decide.

Plinio, Alex J., and Joanne B. Scanlan. *Resource Raising: The Role of Non-Cash Assistance in Corporate Philanthropy.* Independent Sector, 1828 L Street NW, Washington, DC 20036. $12.50. Most comprehensive guide to getting (or giving) corporate facilities, people, services, products, supplies, and equipment. Includes a list of national and international brokers.

Schmertz, Herbert, and William Novak. *Goodbye to the Low Profile.* Boston: Little, Brown and Company. 1986. Mobil's vice president for public affairs devotes a chapter to "Affinity-of-Purpose Marketing: The Case of *Masterpiece Theatre.*" Schmertz is crystal clear on what his company gets from paying for projects from imported television for the upper classes to double-dutch jump-rope competitions for inner-city girls. His book gives you a chance to see the deal from the corporation's point of view.

Simons, Robin, Lisa Farber Miller, and Peter Lengsfelder. *Nonprofit Piggy Goes to Market,* Children's Museum of Denver, 2121 Crescent Dr., Denver, CO 80211. 1984. $9.95. How the museum raised 95 percent of its $600,000 budget by marketing its products, publications, traveling exhibits, and services to corporations.

Steckel, Richard, Robin Simons, and Peter Lengsfelder. *Filthy Rich & Other Nonprofit Fantasies: Changing the Way Nonprofits Do Business in the 90s.* Ten Speed Press, P.O. Box 7123, Berkeley, CA 94707. 1989. $8.95. Myriad examples of fun, creative, effective ways to form profitable partnerships with for-profit businesses and to run your own business.

Zuver, Debbie, managing ed. *Corporate 500: The Directory of Corporate Philanthropy.* Public Management Institute, 358 Brannan St., San Francisco, CA 94107. 1990–91. $355.00. Profiles on 590 corporate donors, indexed in thirteen different ways. Includes a glossary of common corporate philanthropy terms useful for beginners, and highlights names of new decision makers.

EARNED INCOME

Skloot, Edward, ed. *The Nonprofit Entrepreneur: Creating Ventures to Earn Income.* The Foundation Center, 79 Fifth Avenue, New York, NY 10003; 800/424-9836. 1988. $22.95. How-to advice with case studies by seven experts on launching for-profit ventures.

Call the Internal Revenue Service (IRS) at 800/424-FORM to order free publications:

Pub. 552—Record-keeping Requirements and a List of Tax
　　Publications
Pub. 583—Record-keeping for a Small Business
Pub. 598—Tax on Unrelated Business Income of Exempt
　　Organizations

FOUNDATIONS

The Foundation Center operates national collections in Cleveland, New York, San Francisco, and Washington, D.C., and Cooperating Collections in more than one hundred other cities in every state, Puerto Rico, and the Virgin Islands. See the list in Chapter 13 or call 800/424-9836 for the collection nearest you. It will have directories, tax records, and reports on grant makers. Take advantage of other opportunities offered by the collections. Some offer associate memberships; others offer the best training, such as the seventy-five workshops presented every year by the Funding Information Center in San Antonio; others publish the most complete coverage of local grant makers and nonprofits, such as the Donors Forum of Chicago's newsletter *Forum.*

Order the current *Publications Catalog* from the Foundation Center, 79 Fifth Ave., New York, NY 10003; or 800/424-9836. This lists all the best current directories and how-to books on foundations and proposal writing, especially *The Foundation Directory* ("the Bible"), *as well as Source Book Profiles, Foundation Grants to Individuals,* and *The Foundation Grants Index.* See Chapter 13 for more information about the Foundation Center publications and data bases.

Hall, Mary. *Getting Funded: A Complete Guide to Proposal Writing.* Portland State University, Continuing Education Publications, P.O. Box 1394, Portland, OR 97207. 1988. $23.70. Thorough discussion of writing successful proposals for foundations, corporations, and state and federal funding agencies. Packed with real samples from grant makers.

Kiritz, Norton. *Program Planning & Proposal Writing.* The Grantsmanship Center, P.O. Box 6210, Los Angeles, CA 90014. $6. The most popular guide to proposal writing, in an easy-to-read and easy-to-use format.

Margolin, Judith B., ed. *The Foundation Center's User-Friendly Guide.* The Foundation Center, 79 Fifth Avenue, New York, NY 10003; 800/424-9836. 1990. $10.50. Perfect for beginners and a great review tool for veterans, this is the best information in the easiest format. Order one for every fundraiser.

Olson, Stan, ed. *The Foundation Directory.* The Foundation Center, 79 Fifth Ave., New York, NY 10003; 800/424-9836. 1991. $140. The best source of information on America's largest foundations that each give more than $100,000 per year, organized through five indexes, thirty-three types of support, and 187 subject fields.

Foundation News. Council on Foundations, 1828 L St. NW, Washington, DC 20036. $29.50 for six issues a year. Articles, essays, and gossip on foundations and what they fund.

See also *The Chronicle of Philanthropy*, listed previously in this chapter under "Fundraising Periodicals," for reviews of current foundation giving and upcoming deadlines.

International

For information on international foundations, call the Foundation Center at 800/424-9836 for the Cooperating Collections in Australia, Canada, England, Japan, and Mexico. Also ask for the current publications on international grant making. Foundation Center data is accessible via computer from sixteen countries via Dialog or a gateway service. See Chapter 13 for more information.

LEGAL

Hopkins, Bruce R. *The Law of Fund-Raising*. John Wiley & Sons, Inc., 605 Third Ave., New York, NY 10157-0228. 1991. $95.00. Thorough coverage of state and federal laws plus sample forms, IRS cases, and Hopkins's commentaries on common areas of litigation for fundraisers.

MAIL AND MEMBERSHIP

Lautman, Kay Partney, and Henry Goldstein. *Dear Friend: Mastering the Art of Direct Mail Fund Raising*. The Taft Group, 12300 Twinbrook Parkway, Suite 450, Rockville, MD 20852; 800/877-8238. 1984. $59.95. The best advice on direct mail for novices or veteran mailers who want to improve their campaigns. Packed with examples that worked, including the Vietnam Veterans Memorial Fund.

Trenbeth, Richard P. *The Membership Mystique*. The Taft Group, 12300 Twinbrook Parkway, Suite 450, Rockville, MD 20852; 800/877-8238. 1986. $34.95. Proven methods to market memberships with samples from $20 to $15,000 per person, plus tested advice on renewals, record keeping, and doing the arithmetic. These pioneering techniques enabled The Art Institute of Chicago to build the largest membership base of any art museum in the world.

MAJOR GIFTS

Klein, Kimberly. *Getting Major Gifts*. Grassroots Fundraising Journal reprint, P.O. Box 11607, Berkeley, CA 94701. 1991. $10.00 Reprint of the best articles on major gifts; especially good for social-change groups or any fundraiser doing its first campaign for big gifts.

Panas, Jerold. *Megagifts: Who Gives Them, Who Gets Them*. Pluribus Press, 160 E. Illinois, Chicago, IL 60611. 1984. $28.95. Great stories of the people who give gifts of $1 million or more, what motivates them to give (mission—not guilt or taxes), and sixty-four tested tenets for getting the biggest gifts.

Seymour, Si. *Designs for Fundraising*. The Taft Group, 12300 Twinbrook Pkwy., Suite 450, Rockville, MD 20852; 800/877-8238. 1966. $29.95. The classic book on organizing a major-gift campaign, what motivates people to give, and how to get them to ask. The dollar amounts are dated, but the advice is timeless.

Sills, Beverly, and Lawrence Linderman. *Beverly: An Autobiography*. Bantam Books, Inc., 666 Fifth Ave., New York, NY 10103. 1987. $19.95. In 1980, at the age of fifty-one, Beverly Sills retired as a prima donna and began her second career as the CEO/fundraiser of the New York City Opera. She used her drive, humor, chutzpah, and connections to take the company from the brink of bankruptcy to raising $20 million a year. Great examples of asking wealthy donors.

MANAGEMENT

Drucker, Peter F. *Managing the Nonprofit Organization: Principles and Practices*. Harper/Collins Publishers, 10 E. 53rd St., New York, NY 10022. 1990. $22.95. Great lessons from the guru of management and nine nonprofit experts. Drucker stresses leadership development, accountability, and teamwork. Any fundraiser will work better if he or she applies these lessons.

Nonprofit Management & Leadership. Jossey-Bass Inc., P.O. Box 44305, San Francisco, CA 94144-4305. $45 a year for four issues. Sponsored by the Mandel Center for Nonprofit Organizations at Case Western Reserve University in Cleveland and the Centre for Voluntary Organisation at the London School of Economics and Political Science, this journal presents current academic articles on nonprofit management.

Nonprofit Management Strategies. The Taft Group, 12300 Twinbrook Parkway, Suite 450, Rockville, MD 20852. $150 a year for 12 issues. Current management advice on developing your human and financial resources and an "executive digest" of germane articles from the nonprofit trade press and business journals.

MARKETING

Kotler, Philip, and Alan R. Andreasen. *Strategic Marketing for Nonprofit Organizations.* 4th edition. Prentice-Hall, Inc., Englewood Cliffs, NJ 07632. 1991. $47.00. Kotler pioneered in the analysis and application of for-profit marketing techniques to nonprofit campaigns fifteen years ago. This book can help fundraisers reach more people more effectively.

Stern, Gary J. *Marketing Workbook for Nonprofit Organizations.* The Amherst H. Wilder Foundation, 919 Lafond Ave., St. Paul, MN 55104. 1990. $26. Working through the exercises in this exceptionally well written, sensitive, and jargon-free book will give any fundraising team the answers to why their organization is unique, why its programs will get results, and why the public should give money.

MINORITIES

"Pluralism in Philanthropy—How American Indians, Asians, Blacks and Hispanics Are Enriching Our Culture of Giving." *Foundation News* special issue, May/June 1990. $5. Council on Foundations, 1828 L Street NW, Washington, DC 20036. See especially the excellent suggestions for further reading.

PAYROLL DEDUCTION

Bothwell, Bob. *Charity Begins at Work.* National Committee for Responsive Philanthropy, 2001 S St. NW, Suite 620, Washington, DC 20009. 1990. $5. An introduction to United Way, Combined Federal Campaign, and alternative workplace fundraising.

Also contact your local United Way. Ask for its guidelines for application for membership or grants and its catalog of publications and audiovisual materials.

PERFORMING ARTS—SUBSCRIPTIONS

Newman, Danny. *Subscribe Now! Building Arts Audiences Through Dynamic Subscription Promotion.* Theatre Communications Group, Inc., 355 Lexington Ave., New York, NY 10017. 1977. $14.45. Unabashed razzmatazz and scores of ideas to sell subscriptions or pledges by the man who revolutionized nonprofit box offices in the United States and Canada.

PLANNED GIVING

Ashton, Debra. *The Complete Guide to Planned Giving.* J.L.A. Publications, 50 Follen St., Suite 507, Cambridge, MA 02138. 1991. $48.50. Everything you need to know to compete successfully for major gifts, including 1990 Tax Act information. This is the favorite book of the pros.

PLANNING

Barry, Bryan W. *Strategic Planning Workbook for Nonprofit Organizations.* Management Support Services, Amherst H. Wilder Foundation, 919 Lafond Ave., St. Paul, MN 55104. 1986. $25.00. Best introduction to strategic planning as a positive group process for your leadership. How and why to plan with clear worksheets make this the most user-friendly planning guide.

Seltzer, Michael. *Securing Your Organization's Future.* The Foundation Center, 79 Fifth Ave., New York, NY 10003. 1987. $26.95. Everything you need to know to define your mission, design programs, and choose ways to raise money. Numerous worksheets make it easy for any group to use this book.

PROFESSIONALS

Watkins, Clyde P., et al. *Getting Started: A Guide to Fundraising Fundamentals.* Chicago Chapter of the National Society of Fund Raising Executives, 414 Plaza Dr., Suite 209, Westmont, IL 60559. 1988. $12.95. Great advice from seven top professionals for any professional new to development.

See the end of Chapter 3 for information about professional associations.

SMALL TOWNS

Stark, Nancy T., Hamilton Brown, and G. Lawrence Merrill. *Innovative Grassroots Financing. A Small Town Guide to Raising Funds and Cutting Costs.* National Association of Towns and Townships, 1522 K St. NW, Suite 730, Washington, DC 20005. 1990. $11.50. Terrific resource for any small community—covers grass roots fundraising as well as federal and state grants and loans; user fees, fines, and tax options; creative borrowing techniques such as minibonds and economic development loans; and many ways to save money.

SOCIAL CHANGE ORGANIZATIONS

Bobo, Kim A., Jackie Kendall, and Steve Max. *Organizing for Social Change: A Manual for Activists in the 1990s.* Seven Locks Press, P.O. Box 27, Cabin John, MD 20818. 1991. $21.95. The most comprehensive and useful manual on building a permanent, powerful organization. Not just for community organizers; fundraisers also can develop stronger leaders and design better strategies with this book. Features an excellent chapter on fundraising.

Klein, Kimberly. *Fundraising for Social Change.* Chardon Press, P.O. Box 101, Inverness, CA 94937. 1985. $22.00. Fundraising advice tailored to the special challenges of social-change organizations, this book is especially good on direct-mail, telephone, and major-donor campaigns.

Shellow, Jill, and Nancy Stella, eds. *The Grant Seekers Guide.* 3rd revised edition. Moyer Bell Ltd., Colonial Hill, RFD 1, Mt. Kisco, NY 10549. 1989. $27.70. Highlights 212 foundations and 18 religious funders that make grants to a wide range of social-change groups plus how-to advice from ten of the best fundraisers in the field.

SPECIAL EVENTS

Berger, Sally. "Ten Steps to a Million Dollar Fund Raiser," in *Special Events Fundraising*, Grantsmanship Center reprint.

Grantsmanship Center, P.O. Box 6210, Los Angeles, CA 90014. 1975. $5. Berger tells how she netted $1.4 million for the Michael Reese Medical Center in Chicago, primarily through corporate gifts connected to the Crystal Ball of 1973. Proven tactics for pledges, advertising programs, corporate underwriting (Ray Kroc of McDonald's gave $75,000), and a gala ball. The second half of this reprint is a 1977 Timothy Saasta interview of Joan Flanagan on producing profitable grass roots events.

Eley, Mary, ed. *Chase's Annual Events*. Contemporary Books, Dept. JF, 180 N. Michigan Ave., Chicago, IL 60601. $37.50 (for 1992 edition). Many ideas for every month (Black History), week (Smile Week), and day. Find a special theme for any day of the year!

Flanagan, Joan. *The Grass Roots Fundraising Book*. Contemporary Books, Dept. GR, 180 N. Michigan Ave., Chicago, IL 60601. $14.95. Updated 1988. The best advice on organizing small, medium, and large special events, including foolproof tips on choosing the right event, selling the tickets, and getting the best publicity.

Geldof, Bob, and Paul Vallely. *Is That It?*. Ballantine Books, 201 E. 50th St., New York, NY 10022. 1988. $5.95. The man who raised $117 million in one day through the Band Aid concerts and global telethon tells how he did it with great insight, anger, and humor. Plus stories of every 80s rock star on the globe, Prince Charles, and Mother Teresa.

Levey, Jane Freundel. *If You Want Air Time: A Publicity Handbook*. National Association of Broadcasters, 1771 N St. NW, Washington, DC 20036. 1983. $3. How to prepare radio and TV press releases and public service announcements.

Shoemaker, Joanie, ed. *Note by Note: A Guide to Concert Production*. Redwood Cultural Work, P.O. Box 10408, Oakland, CA 94610. 1989. $15.95. The best book to clarify the immense number of details and dangers on any concert or major production. Terrific checklists, budgets, contracts, releases, and forms.

Also order IRS Publication 1391. For details, see the section in this chapter titled "U.S. Taxes."

STATISTICS

Hodgkinson, Virginia A., Murray S. Weitzman, et al. *Giving and Volunteering in the United States: Findings from a National Survey.* 1990 ed. Published every other year. Independent Sector, 1828 L St., NW, Washington, DC 20036. 1990. $30. Survey conducted by the Gallup Organization for the Independent Sector presents useful data on motivations of donors and volunteers.

Weber, Nathan, ed. *Giving U.S.A.: The Annual Report on Philanthropy for the Year.* AAFRC Trust for Philanthropy, 25 W. 43rd St., New York, NY 10036. Published annually. $45.00. Published since 1955, these are the best estimates of American giving and an insightful analysis of trends.

Ask your local library, United Way, and national network for current statistics on your community and constituency. Look for data from the 1990 census as it comes out.

TIME MANAGEMENT

Lakein, Alan. *How to Get Control of Your Time and Your Life.* Signet Paperback, 1633 Broadway, New York, NY 10019. 1973. $4.50. Ever notice how the best achievers always have time to do what *they* want to do? Lakein's book can help you do the most important things (fundraising) first and stop feeling guilty about not doing unimportant things.

TRAINING

Draves, William A. *How to Teach Adults in One Hour.* The Learning Resources Network (LERN), 1554 Hayes Drive, Manhattan, KS 66502; or 800/678-LERN (also ask for the LERN catalog.) 1989. $5.95. Use this booklet to improve your briefings for your leadership and staff. Also recommended: Draves's *How to Teach Adults,* the recognized classic in the field. $8.95; video $105.00.

UNIVERSITIES, COLLEGES, AND SCHOOLS

CASE Publications Catalog, 80 S. Early St., Alexandria, VA 22304; 800/336-4776. Published annually. Free. Books, videos, and reprints tailored for school fundraising, including alumni programs, special events (homecoming), recruiting students, gift clubs, and capital campaigns.

Hodgkinson, Virginia A. *Academic Centers and Research Institutes Focusing on the Study of Philanthropy, Voluntarism, and Not-for-Profit Activity: A Progress Report.* Independent Sector, 1828 L St. NW, Washington, DC 20036. 1988. $10.00. The report comes with a list of current programs with contact names, addresses, and phone numbers. There are now more than thirty university-level programs in the United States devoted exclusively to the study of nonprofits, including a few that offer degrees in the field. Contact the program nearest you for more information on classes and publications.

U.S. TAXES

Order free publications by calling the Internal Revenue Service (IRS) at 800/424-FORM.

To calculate how much is tax-deductible:

Pub. 526—Charitable Contributions

Pub. 561—Determining the Value of Donated Property
(how to estimate fair market value)

Form 8282—Donee Information Return (for the charity)

Form 8283—Non-Cash Charitable Contributions (for the donor)

To calculate how much is tax-deductible at special events:

Pub. 1391—Deductibility of Payments Made to Charities
Conducting Fund Raising Events

For advice, call the IRS Hotline on Fundraising: 202/343-8900.

To lobby as a charity:

Pub. 557—*Tax-Exempt Status for Your Organization* (See
the section titled "Lobbying Expenditures")

Form 5768—Election/Revocation of Election by an Eligible Section 501(c)(3) Organization to Make Expenditures to Influence Legislation

Also check with your national organization or network for their publications on lobbying, such as:
Gray, Sandra Trice. *Lobby? You? Of Course You Can . . . and You Should.* Independent Sector, 1828 L St. NW, Washington, DC 20036. 1987. $3. Best introduction to legal lobbying by tax-exempt nonprofit organizations.

VOLUNTEERS

Gentry, Mary Taylor. *How to Develop a Volunteer Program for Single Adults.* Volunteer Jacksonville, Inc., 1600 Prudential Dr., Jacksonville, FL 32207. 1988. $11.25. How Volunteer Jacksonville recruited five hundred single volunteers, including sample budget, forms, and press releases.

Contact the Foundation Center, 79 Fifth Ave., New York, NY 10003 and Independent Sector, 1828 L St. NW, Washington, DC 20036. Ask for their publications catalogs. Published annually. Free. Both organizations publish useful books for volunteers and professionals who work with volunteers.

Contact the National Retiree Volunteer Center (NRVC), 607 Marquette Ave. S., Suite 10, Minneapolis, MN 55402; 800/833-NRVC. Since 1986, NRVC has mobilized retired corporate volunteers for leadership roles with nonprofits.

Contact the National Volunteer Center, 1111 N. 19th St., Suite 500, Arlington, VA 22209. Associate member dues are $50. Ask for its catalogs: *Readership* featuring how-to manuals for a variety of volunteer programs and *Recognition and Recruitment Items* for inexpensive premiums. Catalogs are published annually. Free.

Also ask your own national organization or network for publications and customized products you can use for volunteer rewards. Your local Volunteer Action Center (VAC), or the office of volunteers for your city, state, or province also may offer training, publications, and premiums.

WRITING
To write better letters and proposals, get these publications:

- A dictionary and a thesaurus. No, the ones on your computer software are *not* enough.
- William Strunk, Jr., and E. B. White's, *Elements of Style* (New York: Macmillan Publishing Co.)—still my favorite book on writing.
- *The Chicago Manual of Style*, 13th ed., (Chicago: The University of Chicago Press)—the most complete and helpful style guide for writers and editors.

CANADA
Corporations
Contact the Institute of Donations and Public Affairs Research (IDPAR), 666 Sherbrooke West, Suite 504, Montreal, Quebec H3A 1E7, and ask for their current publications list and services. The institute publishes *Corporate Giving in Canada* every year and a twice-yearly *Fund Programs Planned* listing of major charitable campaigns.

Other offices of the IDPAR are at 141 Adelaide St. West, Suite 1506, Toronto, Ontario M4W 3M5, and 300 5th Ave. SW, Suite 2050, Calgary, Alberta T2P 3C4.

Foundations
McClintock, Norah, ed. *The Canadian Directory to Foundations*. The Canadian Centre for Philanthropy, 1329 Bay St., Suite 200, Toronto, Ontario M5R 2C4. 1990–91. Can $250.00. Complete information on Canadian foundations and American foundations that make grants in Canada.

The Canadian Center for Philanthropy cosponsors provincial and national fundraising conferences, and also publishes *Canada Gives* with statistics on Canadian philanthropy. Contact the Toronto office at 416/515-0764.

Fundraising in Canada
Young, Joyce. *Fundraising for Non-Profit Groups*. Self-Counsel Press, 1481 Charlotte Rd., North Vancouver, BC V7J 1H1. 1989.

Can$7.95. An updated edition of Young's 1978 classic; especially good for social change organizations.

UNITED KINGDOM

Write the Charities Aid Foundation, 48 Pembury Road, Tonbridge, Kent TN9 2JD England, and ask for their catalog *Publications*. This is not a grant making foundation, so do not send a proposal. It does collect and publish the best current data on philanthropy in England, Northern Ireland, Scotland, and Wales, including publications on investments, payroll deduction, taxes, and charity trends featuring the top four hundred grant making trusts and the top four hundred fundraising charities. Monarchists will enjoy *Royal Patrons*, which lists twenty-one members of the royal family and the charities where they volunteer.

Endnotes

Chapter 1
Opportunities for Fundraising
1. Ross K. Baker, "Frontiers in Tourism," *American Demographics*, June 1990, 68.
2. "NPT Interview/Christopher F. Edley," *NonProfit Times*, November 1990, 10-12.
3. Anne Matthews, "The Thoughts That Count," *Forbes*, February 20, 1990, 126-128.
4. Elma G. Heidemann, "Palliative Care in Canada: 1986," *Journal of Palliative Care*, May 3, 1989, 37.
5. "Project Profile: Turkey," *PolioPlus World Update* (Evanston, IL: Rotary International), October 1989, 2.

Chapter 2
Strategies for Success
1. Lech Walesa, "Solidarity and Freedom," *Vital Speeches*, December 15, 1989. (Speech delivered before the U.S. Congress, November 15, 1989.)

2. Virginia A. Hodgkinson and Murray S. Weitzman, *Dimensions of the Independent Sector* (Washington, D.C.: Independent Sector, 1989), 37.

3. Nathan Weber, *Giving USA: The Annual Report on Philanthropy for the Year 1989* (New York: The AAFRC Trust for Philanthropy, 1990), 7.

4. Virginia A. Hodgkinson and Murray S. Weitzman. *Giving and Volunteering in the United States* (Washington, D.C.: Independent Sector, 1990), 45.

Chapter 3
The Fundraising Team

1. Hodgkinson and Weitzman, *Giving and Volunteering in the United States*, 149.

2. Alfred Borcover, "Time, money, and health put the 65-plus clientele in high demand," *Chicago Tribune*, March 29, 1987, sec. 12, 2.

3. Letty Cottin Pogrebin, "Contributing to the Cause," *New York Times Magazine*, April 22, 1990, 22-23.

4. Sandford D. Horwitt, *Saul Alinsky* (New York: Alfred A. Knopf, 1989), 401-402.

5. Robert Lee, "The Confucian Spirit," *Foundation News*, May/June 1990, 31.

6. Bob Geldof and Paul Vallely, *Is That It?* (New York: Ballantine, 1988), 345.

7. Hodgkinson and Weitzman, *Giving and Volunteering in the United States*, 41.

8. Emmett D. Carson, "Valuing Black Benevolence," *Foundation News*, May/June 1990, 39.

9. Cesar Chavez, "The Organizer's Tale," *Ramparts*, July 1966, 45.

10. Barbara Bush, *Millie's Book*, (New York: William Morrow and Company, 1990), p. 7.

11. Millard Fuller with Diane Scott, *No More Shacks! The daring vision of Habitat for Humanity.* (Waco, Texas: World Books, 1986), p. 95.

12. Geldof, *Is That It?*, 543.

13. Nick Kotz and Mary Lynn Kotz, *A Passion for Equality: George Wiley and the Movement* (New York: Norton, 1977), 238-247. This

chapter "Shaking the Money Tree" is a candid analysis of using charm and guilt to raise money from the rich.

Chapter 4
Special Events

1. Mark Seal, "Imagination, Inc.," *American Way*, December 1990, 90.
2. Peter Jacobi, *The Messiah Book* (New York: St. Martin's, 1982), 37.
3. "UNCF Sports a New Image," *Foundation News*, July/August 1990, 17.
4. Stephanie Mansfield, "Fashion Statement: Nina Hyde's Courageous Campaign," *Lear's*, February 1990, 52-53.
5. Jacobi, *The Messiah Book*, 89.
6. Promotional letter for *American Demographics* (Boulder, Colo.), 1991, 2.
7. Robert Whereat, "Pro-lottery doesn't end debate," *Minneapolis Star-Tribune*, November 10, 1988, 20A.

Chapter 5
The Smaller Gift: Building Your Base

1. "United Ways Raise $2.98 Billion, Up $200 Million in a Year," *The Chronicle of Philanthropy*, May 1, 1990, 6.

Chapter 6
Memberships and Pledges: Do It Yourself

1. "SOCM Adds 236 New Families to Membership Rolls in 1989," *SOCM Sentinel* (Jacksboro, Tenn.: Save Our Cumberland Mountains), Spring 1990, 13.
2. "Organizers Talk About What They Do and How They Do It—Mary Gonzales, Associate Director, United Neighborhood Organization," *Forum*, (Chicago: The Donors Forum), Spring 1986, 5.
3. "Seasonality Study Released," *Fund Raising Management*, June 1989, 12. Most profitable months for mailers were (1) November, (2) August, and (3) February.

Chapter 7
Memberships by the Professionals: Mail, Phone, Door to Door

1. Jill Smolowe, "Read This," *Time*, November 26, 1990, 65.

2. Ibid., 62.

3. Mal Warwick, "Reaching Donors the Second Time Around Is Key to Successful Program," *NonProfit Times,* May 1990, 33.

4. "Ninth Annual Conference Ties Attendance Record," *Fund Raising Management,* August 1988, 54.

Chapter 8
How to Find the Big Givers

1. Thomas J. Stanley, "Feeding on the Rich: Find the Investors with Real Money," *Success,* July/August 1988, 54.

2. Beth Brophy and Gordon Witkin, "Ordinary Millionaires," *U.S. News & World Report,* January 13, 1986, 43-49.

Chapter 9
The Big Gift—Now

1. Elaine Steiner, "Continuing Gifts—Lila Acheson Wallace's Floral Legacy," *Elle Decor,* April 1990, 34-36.

2. Beverly Sills and Lawrence Linderman, *Beverly: An Autobiography* (New York: Bantam, 1987), 328.

3. Anne Matthews, "The Thoughts That Count," *Forbes,* February 10, 1989, 126-128.

4. Calvin Tomkins, "For The Nation" (Profile of J. Carter Brown, director of the National Gallery of Art, Washington, D.C.), *The New Yorker,* September 3, 1990, 48-90.

5. Jordan Bonfante, "Lady Power in the Sunbelt," *Time,* March 19, 1990, 21-24.

6. Geldof, *Is That It?,* 332.

Chapter 10
The Big Gift—Later

1. *Historical Products* catalog, (Cambridge, Mass.: Historical Products), Spring 1990, 4.

2. "Miscellany," *Historic Preservation,* May/June 1990, 11.

3. Kimberly Klein, "Early History of Women in U.S. Philanthropy," *Grassroots Fundraising Journal,* August 1990, 3-7.

4. Beth Austin, "Gloria Steinem," *Chicago Tribune,* January 11, 1987, Sec. 6, p. 3.

5. Elizabeth Brown Pryor, *Clara Barton, Professional Angel* (Philadelphia: University of Pennsylvania Press, 1987), 184.

Chapter 11
Corporate Contributions

1. "With $135 Million Total, IBM Still Top Donor," (Public Management Institute's list), *Chronicle of Philanthropy*, December 11, 1990, 14.

2. Dun and Bradstreet, Interview with author, July 25, 1990.

3. Corporate figures from "IBM Still Top Donor," 14; foundation figures from Stan Olson, ed., *The Foundation Directory*, 1991 ed. (New York: The Foundation Center, 1990), ix.

4. "1988 Corporate Giving Estimate at $4.8 Billion, Up 3.2 Pct. in Year," *The Chronicle of Philanthropy*, January 23, 1990, 4.

5. Sales letter for "John Naisbett's Trend Letter," July 1990.

6. Herbert Schmertz, *Goodbye to the Low Profile*, (Boston: Little, Brown & Company, 1986), p. 222.

7. Based on percent of net earning before taxes. "Rankings of most and least generous corporate givers," *NonProfit Times*, January 1991, 4. From the Public Management Institute data. Soft Sheen data from Teresa Y. Wiltz, "Philanthropy: Soft Sheen makes big strides with small victories," *Chicago Enterprise*, January 1991, 13-14.

Chapter 12
Business Partners and Business Ventures

1. "Cause-Related Marketing Summary," (New York: Worldwide Marketing Development & Communications, American Express TRS Co., Dec. 13, 1990), 1-11.

2. Jim Andrews, ed., "Special Events Report" (speech delivered at the Association of Performing Arts Presenters convention, New York, December 1988).

3. "Pro Tours," *Chicago Tribune*, July 25, 1990, sec. 4.8.

4. David H. Pill, *The English Reformation, 1529-58* (London: University of London Press, 1973), 22.

5. Barbara Mahany, "Making a mint from a sweet idea," *Chicago Tribune*, March 10, 1991, Sec. 5, page 9.

6. "Fall/Winter 1990 Greeting Cards and Gifts" catalog, (New York: U.S. Committee for UNICEF), 1990.

7. Lester Salamon, director, Institute for Policy Studies, Johns Hopkins University, Interview with author, December 21, 1990.

Chapter 13
Grant Makers: Foundations, United Ways, Religious
Denominations, and Civic Organizations.

1. Rose Van Rotterdam, manager of information services, the Canadian Centre for Philanthropy, Interview with author, December 14, 1990.
2. Stan Olson, ed., *The Foundation Directory*, 12th Edition, (New York: The Foundation Center, 1989), v.
3. Ruth Kovacs, ed., *Foundation Grants Index 1990–1991* (New York: The Foundation Center, 1990), xii.
4. Nathan Weber, ed., *Giving USA 1989*, 70–73.
5. Ibid., 48–50.
6. "Publication 557: Tax-Exempt Status for Your Organization," (Washington, D.C.: Internal Revenue Service, 1988), 39.
7. "Community Foundations Raise $615 million in 1989, Assets Near $6 Billion," *The Chronicle of Philanthropy*, September 18, 1990, 10.
8. Francine Jones, managing ed., *Corporate Foundation Profiles* (New York: The Foundation Center, 1990), xi.
9. *Pre-Application for 1990 Funding Cycle, Campaign for Human Development* (Washington, D.C.: United States Catholic Conference, 1990), 2.
10. Cathy Jenkins, "Basic Facts About United Way," *Fact Sheet*, (Alexandria, Va: United Way of America, 1989), 2.

Index

293

If you enjoyed *Successful Fundraising*, try Joan Flanagan's previous books that are available in your local bookstore or by mail. To order directly, return the coupon below with payment to: Contemporary Books, Department SF, 180 North Michigan Avenue, Chicago, Illinois 60601. Or call (312) 782-9181 to order with your credit card.

Qty.	Title	Price	Total
____	*The Grass Roots Fundraising Book:* *How to Raise Money in Your Community* (5746-7)	$14.95 ea.	$_____
____	*The Successful Volunteer Organization* (5837-4)	$14.95 ea.	$_____
		Subtotal	$_____
Add $2.50 postage for the first book ordered.			$__2.50__
Add $1.00 postage for each additional book ordered.			$_____
Illinois residents add 7% sales tax; California residents add 6% sales tax.			$_____
		Total Price	$_____

Name _____

Address _____

City/State/Zip _____

☐ Enclosed is my check/money order payable to Contemporary Books.

Bill my

☐ VISA ＼ Account No. _____

☐ MasterCard ／ Expiration Date _____

Signature _____

For quantity discount information, please call the sales department at (312) 782-9181. Allow four to six weeks for delivery.

Offer expires May 31, 1992.   SF0692